REMARKABLE SERVICE

REMARKABLE
SERVICE

THIRD EDITION

THE WORLD'S PREMIER
CULINARY COLLEGE

WILEY

THE CULINARY INSTITUTE OF AMERICA

President: Dr. Tim Ryan '77, CMC, AAC
Provost: Mark Erickson '77, CMC
Director of Publishing: Nathalie Fischer
Editorial Project Manager: Lisa Lahey '00
Editorial Assistant: Laura Monroe '12

Published by John Wiley & Sons, Inc., Hoboken, New Jersey
Published simultaneously in Canada

Library of Congress Cataloging-in-Publication Data

Remarkable service -- Third edition.
 Includes index.
 ISBN 978-1-118-11687-6 (pbk. : acid-free paper). Food service management. I. Culinary Institute of America.
 TX911.3.M27
 647.95068--dc23
                                        2013037931

Printed in the United States of America
V10014873_102419

We dedicate this book to the students and graduates who have learned the meaning of remarkable service. By applying its principles on a daily basis, they endow our chosen career with the unmistakable hallmarks of a true profession.

Contents

Preface

A GUEST DECIDES TO COME to your to a restaurant for a number of reasons. Maybe the menu looked intriguing, the location seemed perfect, and the hours were convenient. Perhaps friends and family made recommendations, or published reviews caught his or her eye. While these positive factors are all important to guests, what stays in their minds after they leave, and what may determine whether they decide to both come back again and recommend the restaurant to their friends, is the quality of service.

Excellent service may call for different activities, depending on the style of the restaurant. We do not expect the same type of service at a casual restaurant as we might at a four-star, fine-dining establishment. Nonetheless, we expect excellent service in both venues. As customers, we recognize and respond to excellent service to such a degree that we may even overlook any minor shortfalls in the food. Studies in this country and elsewhere have shown time after time that the ability to provide guests with excellent service is good for the guest, good for the server, and good for the entire operation. *Remarkable Service, Third Edition* includes the basic steps of performing service as well as the fundamental principles of remarkable service that will lead to ever higher levels of service for your guests.

Our goals for *Remarkable Service, Third Edition* include:

- Making *Remarkable Service* the go-to book for service professionals.
- Clarifying the essence of *Remarkable Service* by distinguishing between hard skills and soft skills and then demonstrating how to bring soft and hard skills together for top-notch professional service.
- Defining and describing contemporary service practices that complement and enhance modern menus and restaurant concepts.
- Introducing appropriate management information for the operation of a restaurant dining room.
- Teaching the skills necessary to work effectively with the dining room's partners in the kitchen.
- Developing a book that supports learning objectives in introductory and advanced table service/dining room management courses.

The new edition echoes our best efforts to achieve those goals. We begin with an introduction to the profession, including its history and traditions and an overview of various traditional and contemporary service styles. From these fundamental lessons, readers build to more advanced service concepts and then on to dining room operations and dining room management topics.

Book Organization

The book is divided into ten chapters to address key concepts, techniques, and practices critical to the delivery of excellent service. The chapters build from and relate to one another.

Chapter 1, The Principles of Remarkable Service, presents the principles of remarkable service and the basic concepts that underlie great service at all levels of an organization, beginning with the importance of creating a positive environment for the guest and concluding with the notion of providing service that exceeds the guests' expectations.

Chapter 2, Styles of Service, considers the various service styles including French (à la française), Russian (à la russe), English, American, and family styles, by examining the history of these styles, including the how, when, where, and why behind these emerging or evolving styles. More than an interesting story of days gone by, this chapter presents a backdrop that gives context and meaning to much of the etiquette we rely on in our daily operations. As service organizations have evolved, a hierarchy has developed to spell out functions and responsibilities. This chapter includes a look at how your service style and the size of your operation influence the structure of your service team.

Chapter 3 covers the importance of maintaining **A Clean and Safe Dining Room**. Topics introduced here include basic hygiene and safety in the dining room, handling serviceware, avoiding cross contamination, handling perishable foods safely, and dealing with emergencies such as injuries, fires, allergies, and choking.

Chapter 4, Preparing and Maintaining the Dining Room for Remarkable Service, is devoted to preparing and maintaining the dining room. This chapter presents the steps that go into preparing for guests in a logical and coherent manner. The various areas of guest contact from the front door and reception desk to the table are managed to maximize guest comfort and worker efficiency. Techniques discussed here include arranging tables and chairs, clothing with linen, setting covers, and completing mise en place or side work tasks such as setting up the pantry, side stands, and host stand.

Chapter 5, Reservations and Waiting Lists, concentrates on reservations and waiting lists. This newly organized chapter places a special emphasis on providing excellent service to the guest from the first moment of contact, whether they are on the phone, contacting you via a website, or walking in the door. Special situations such as working with a no reservation policy, handling special guests without a reservation, walk-ins, and waiting lists are considered. Seating guests so that the room is filled evenly and appropriately is addressed in this chapter, as are the procedures for managing special table or server requests.

Chapter 6, Serving Guests, presents the soft and hard skills that go into serving guests. Soft skills such as suggesting, recommending, and upselling involve effective communication skills. The ability to read the table is critical throughout the sequence of serving guests as well as whenever it is necessary to engage in "guest recovery". Hard skills in this chapter include plate-handling techniques to serve and clear, table maintenance, check presentation, and payment.

Chapter 7, Beverage Service, presents the basic and advanced skills of serving a variety of beverages, from basic water service to cocktails. Beginning with water, the ins and outs of tap vs. bottled, still vs. sparkling, are explored as they relate to the professional server. Information about cocktails and their ingredients enhance the server's ability to provide the guest with a great experience and to communicate effectively with other members of the service team, including the bartender.

Chapter 8 covers **Wine Service,** beginning with the basics of wine styles so that servers understand how wines and foods are paired. The skills of opening still and sparkling wines as well as the steps in properly decanting a wine are presented and considered as part of the overall sequence of serving wine, from presenting the wine list to presenting wines at the table to the appropriate pouring standards from a bottle of wine.

Chapter 9, Banquet Service in the Restaurant, is dedicated to service for a banquet in a restaurant. This common practice calls for different service skills and techniques than à la carte service. The advantages and disadvantages of catering in a restaurant are presented, as well as approaches to advance planning, dining room arrangement, preparing buffets, and bars for banquets. The various styles of service used at banquets are introduced and the ways in which the menu selection and the type of event can be enhanced by choosing the appropriate service style are considered.

Chapter 10, Remarkable Service Interactions, a completely new chapter, is devoted to understanding and improving service interactions. It begins by presenting the steps to creating a service-oriented culture by hiring guest-focused employees and using training as a key component in providing remarkable service. Various approaches to motivating and empowering remarkable service are evaluated.

For the Student

Remarkable Service, Third Edition, teaches both the specific steps that go into delivering food and beverage to a guest and the general principles of fine service. Learning about the traditions of restaurant dining gives you an insight into how and why we perform certain techniques in a certain way. Those insights give a context for the basic principles in the book. An awareness of how service structures and hierarchies function in different situations prepares you to grow in this career.

For the Instructor

Remarkable Service, Third Edition, has been reorganized and enhanced with additional material for a more thorough and logical approach. The elements in the book include a variety of lists, checklists, and numbered procedures, often paired with either photo sequences to illustrate techniques or display photos that illustrate concepts. This makes it easy for you to pinpoint the material you want students to learn and gives them a model against which to compare their efforts.

New to This Edition

Every chapter in *Remarkable Service, Third Edition* was reviewed and updated to reflect contemporary standards and expectations for restaurant service. To that end, we have introduced the following changes:

- A new chapter, Chapter 3, A Clean and Safe Dining Room, in order to address issues of cleanliness and hygiene for workers, sanitary procedures for handling tabletop items, and safety concerns in the event of accidents or injury in the dining room.
- A new chapter, Chapter 5, Reservations and Waiting Lists, to better coordinate information and procedures to provide the best possible service whether you are taking reservations, timing seating, using waiting lists, managing special requests, or taking group reservations.

- All-new photographs provide clear details and instruction. They make it simple for students to identify the tools of the trade and to master specific service skills, from holding a plate to decanting wine.
- Clear chapter objectives enable student progress to be observed and evaluated.
- The history and traditions of professional table service and styles of table service are combined into a single chapter, Chapter 2, Styles of Service, to give these service styles context for today's restaurant.
- Reorganized materials related to dining room setup into a revised Chapter 4, Preparing and Maintaining the Dining Room for Remarkable Service.
- Chapter 6, Serving Guests, includes a new section on the soft skills of remarkable service, including empathy, communication, table reading, and techniques for suggesting, recommending, and upselling.
- Chapter 7, Beverage Service, now includes all beverage service skills, from water service to cocktails to espresso and tea. New to this chapter are basic drink recipes and updated information about base alcohols used in cocktails. The section on Responsible Beverage Service is included in this chapter.
- Chapter 8, Wine Service, features new tables to make wine information easier to use, including grape styles and updated basic wine and food pairings based on flavor profiles.
- Chapter 9, Banquet Service in the Restaurant, includes a new section on planning that introduces the banquet event order (BEO). The text has been clarified to eliminate confusion between banquet service in restaurants as compared to catering operations.
- Chapter 10, Remarkable Service Interactions, is an entirely new chapter devoted to creating and maintaining a guest-focused, service-oriented culture through hiring, training, motivation, and leadership.
- Newly created supplemental materials are now available to qualified adopters to help support your teaching efforts of this material.

Supplemental Materials

Remarkable Service, Third Edition is now accompanied by an **Instructor's Manual** with a **Test Bank** and Answer Key. Each chapter in the book is presented in the **Instructors Manual** with these features:

- Chapter Overview
- Chapter Objectives
- Key Terms

- Chapter Outlines
- Additional learning activities and projects

The **Test Bank** has been specifically formatted for **Respondus**, an easy-to-use software program for creating and managing exams.

A password-protected Wiley Instructor **Book Companion website** devoted entirely to this book includes access to the online **Instructor's Manual**, the **Respondus Test Bank**, and **PowerPoint lecture slides**. Please visit www.wiley.com /college/cia to access these resources.

Acknowledgments

Remarkable Service is a simple concept, one that can be achieved with no more dramatic costs than that of a welcoming smile, knowledge of the menu, and the willingness to pay attention to your guests for the entire time that they are in your dining room.

This book, with its grounding in basic principles of service, demonstrates the underpinnings of a style of professional service that can only enhance the entire industry, both in terms of the respect with which it is held and the revenues it can generate *for* dedicated professionals.

The goal of this book is to turn every comment into a compliment. The delivery of remarkable service is the only way to ensure a steady stream of positive remarks and engender the word-of-mouth promotion that no amount of money can buy.

Reaching this goal has meant calling on a variety of individuals:

Lead writers: Ezra Eichelberger, John W. Fischer
Content reviewers: Jennifer Purcell, Rory Brown, Doug Miller, Courtnay Dittbrenner, Steven Kolpan, Heather Kolakowski
Photography consultation: Phil Papineau, Ezra Eichelberger, Steven Kolpan, Jennifer Purcell, Doug Miller

Finally, we wish to acknowledge the students and MITs who gave their time and talent to make the photos come alive.

REMARKABLE SERVICE

1

The Principles of Remarkable Service

WHEN EVERYTHING COMES TOGETHER, working in a restaurant's dining room feels like you are giving the best dinner party ever. Trained cooks and a great chef send out delicious food; beautiful surroundings and the right music coax guests into an expansive mood; a professional, highly trained staff brings the guests whatever they need, ideally before they even know they need it. In the dining room we have the opportunity to bring complete strangers into our warm, welcoming space and make them feel like they are a part of our family, so that they will want to return over and over again. We are in the hospitality business. And making hospitality a business involves identifying what takes service from acceptable to remarkable and then reliably performing those actions whenever necessary.

This chapter addresses both practical service skills (sometimes referred to as *hard skills*), such as setting the table, serving food, and presenting the check, as well as the less tangible hospitality skills (*soft skills*). Keep in mind that less tangible does not mean "less important." In reality, tangible skills are exactly what separates remarkable service from ordinary service.

CHAPTER OBJECTIVES

- Define hospitality and service.
- Combine hospitality and service skills for remarkable service.
- List and define the personal qualities of a remarkable server.

What Does the Word *Hospitality* Mean to a Professional Server?

IN ORDER TO SUCCEED in the service industry, you must understand the concept of hospitality. It is not easy to arrive at a succinct definition of what *hospitality* means for the professional server. You can study and master the smallest details of fine table service, but hospitality extends beyond such professional skills. Hospitality in the restaurant can be expressed in a number of ways, such as making eye contact with the guest; anticipating a guest's need based on body language or facial expression; adapting easily and unobtrusively to the needs of the guest; and similar actions aimed at creating a relaxing, positive experience. (These skills are often referred to as the *innate* skills that servers should already possess.) Hospitality implies constant concern for the welfare and enjoyment of the guest. Every action you perform needs to come across as genuine. You can say all of the right words, but if you do not convey certain warmth, your guest will feel the lack of sincerity.

> *HOSPITALITY (hospi'tæliti). [a. OF. hospitalité (12–13th c. inHatz-Darm.), ad. L. hospitalitas,f. hospitalis (see HOSPITAL) a.).] 1. a. The act or practice of being hospitable; the reception and entertainment of guests, visitors, or strangers, with liberality and goodwill.* (Oxford English Dictionary)

Hospitality is often the intangible aspect of our industry, and that can be the most challenging concept to create and maintain. A professional server's people skills are critical to creating hospitality, especially since no two guests are the same. Each guest entering your establishment has different expectations, experiences, and desires, all of which you need to keep in mind when interacting with them.

What Does the Word *Service* Mean to a Professional Server?

THE QUALITY OF SERVICE plays a very large part in determining the long-term survival of a restaurant and its market share of the available business. The most common meaning of the word *service* in the foodservice industry refers to the manner of presenting a meal to the guest. There are other meanings of the

> *SERVICE ('sər-vəs).1. a. The occupation or function of serving; b. employment as a servant; 2.a. the work performed by one who serves.* (Oxford English Dictionary)

term *service* when it is used by a professional server. Traditionally, a *service* referred to the group of dishes composing a given part of a meal, such as a tea service. Service can also signify the utensils necessary to serve a particular part of a meal. Service in this sense would encompass the whole ensemble of objects used at the table: linens, plates, glasses, silver, and hollowware. Guests will often use the term *service* to refer to the timeliness in which the food was served, as in "Wasn't that amazingly quick service?"

Specific actions on the server's part can lead to desired feelings and emotions on the guest's part. These actions can be singled out, defined, described, and put into simple, trainable terms:

- Anticipating the pace of a meal and bringing successive courses at just the right time and presetting necessary utensils

- Avoiding bare-handed contact with plates other than thumb knuckle on rim or glass rims

- Suggesting menu items that will complement dishes already ordered

- Presenting the check at the appropriate moment when the meal is done

These actions can be defined in more tangible and concrete methods. The skills needed to deliver remarkable service include all aspects of restaurant service, from greeting to order taking, service to check presentation, as well as reservations, banquets, beverage service, and special challenges in the dining room, are described throughout this book.

Combining Hospitality and Service Skills for Remarkable Service

HOSPITALITY AND SERVICE may seem, at first glance, to represent very different kinds of activities. Hospitality has to do with intangibles such as attitudes and behaviors, while service is demonstrated through the tangible aspects of presenting a meal for a guest. Hospitality depends on feelings and impressions, while the essence of service resides in actions. Service is being able to carry dinner plates without spilling the sauce, or opening a bottle of Champagne without losing some of the contents in a gush of foam. Though service tasks themselves do not involve emotion, they can evoke positive feelings in guests when they are carried out in a professional manner.

A high level of caring for the comfort of guests—remarkable service, in other words—is the distinctive attribute of the best dining establishments. Providing service is at the heart of all businesses, from auto repair shops to hairdressers to restaurants. The more personalized the service, the more the guests will know they are being treated with respect and care. With the challenges of the restaurant industry today, creating a competitive advantage through remarkable service can lead to significant financial success as well.

When you combine the intangibles and the tangibles encompassed by hospitality skills and the service skills, you create a seamless experience for your guests. It is that state of attention and care for the guests that is the essence of remarkable service.

We have identified nine basic principles of remarkable service that are the foundation of the lessons throughout this book. Since the principles represent various aspects of service and share the common objective of making guests feel comfortable, it should not come as a surprise when two or more of the principles overlap. Nor should it come as a surprise that remarkable service draws upon both the hospitality and service skills in the professional server's toolkit.

REMARKABLE SERVICE CREATES A POSITIVE ENVIRONMENT

Working with positive people is a pleasure—they create an environment that is pleasant for everyone, including the guests. A professional server maintains a happy and positive attitude, even amid chaos. This mindset helps you to see solutions to a problem or situation, and even permits you to see problems as opportunities to improve quality.

The dining room can be a fast-paced and challenging environment, physically as well as emotionally. A professional server needs to assess and understand each guest and what their expectations are, while maintaining a positive attitude that reflects the restaurant's standards for service.

One way to create a positive environment is observing some basic etiquette. There are many levels of etiquette and dining room protocol meant to enhance the entire experience; the more formal the dining room, the more elaborate the etiquette. In any situation, however, the basic concept of etiquette can make social situations run more smoothly. At its most basic, *etiquette* refers to the things you do to make others feel comfortable—smoothing uncertain social interactions, subconsciously informing people that they have nothing to fear. Courteous behavior tells the guests that they are in a caring, comforting environment. When the meal is over, a thank-you for the guests—as well as a thoughtful farewell—is essential.

REMARKABLE SERVICE IS CONSISTENT

Guests visit a restaurant the first time for various reasons. They come back for only one: they like the restaurant, including its food and its service. Making good use of all of the principles of hospitality and service can persuade a guest to come back to the restaurant, and the consistent delivery of high-quality food and service will encourage repeat business. The key to achieving long-term success is the consistent delivery of the best possible service to every guest—every day, every week, every month, and every year. Reliability is the foundation needed in order to create repeat guests and build a strong, positive reputation for your establishment.

REMARKABLE SERVICE IS EFFICIENT

Efficiency is obviously important to the servers and the restaurant. More work can be done (and more money made) with less effort when it is done efficiently. The absence of efficiency, while costly in itself, can also seriously affect the comfort level of the guests. Disorganization and frantic movements are contagious— resulting in guests being made to feel just as stressed as their servers.

Inefficient technique wastes the guests' time as well as that of the servers. It interrupts the flow of the meal and erodes the environment of trust that is essential to a relaxed dining experience. However, when guests see the server's work being done quickly, smoothly, and easily, they are put at ease. They do not feel that they have put the server to any "trouble".

Economy of motion is essential to a server's success. Efficiency means getting the same work done, but with less effort and better results. A general rule for a fast-paced restaurant is "never enter or leave the dining area with empty hands". There is almost always something to be taken to or removed from a table or a service station. The ability to prioritize orders and plan trips to the kitchen and service area saves steps. Economy of motion can be spent on better serving the customer.

Careful attention to mise en place (having everything in its place), an intelligent economy of motion, and a cooperative attitude make the server's job easier to perform, and the resulting ease sends a strong signal to the guests that they are in good hands.

REMARKABLE SERVERS ANTICIPATE THE GUESTS' NEEDS

Remarkable servers anticipate the dining needs of the guests. This begins with the first point of contact—the reservation—and continues through the delivery of the check and a final farewell. If a guest has a reservation, it is imperative that the table be ready for the guests at the time of their expected reservation; otherwise, it creates a negative impression and can dramatically influence a guest's overall experience.

Providing the right items or services to the guest just before they are needed means that your guests never have to wait while you find a clean cup or brew more coffee. There are countless opportunities during service to anticipate the guests' needs. Here are a few examples that are expected:

- Have tables ready and set for guests *before* they arrive.
- Refill glasses or cups *before* they are less than half full.
- Set down the proper flatware for each dish *before* the food is served.
- Bring cream and sugar *before* pouring hot coffee.
- Have the check ready to present *before* the guests requests it.

REMARKABLE SERVICE REQUIRES EFFECTIVE COMMUNICATION

The heart of restaurant service comes down to communication. The art of communication consists of transmitting just the right amount of information exactly when it is needed. Remarkable servers know that effective communication is a two-way street and depends as much on listening as it does on speaking. When you listen to your guests and the questions they are asking, you will be able to provide the right answer. For example:

Guest asks: "What is in the spinach and goat cheese quiche?"

Server replies: "Spinach and goat cheese."

The preceding exchange is technically accurate, but hardly helpful, and certainly does not make the customer feel appreciated. The guest is not asking you to read the name of the dish. The guest wants to know something more than what is written on the menu. With that in mind, the exchange might go like this:

Guest asks: "What is in the spinach and goat cheese quiche?"

Server replies: "In addition to locally grown spinach and farmhouse-fresh goat cheese, the chef includes onions with a bit of pancetta baked in an egg-and-cream custard."

Remarkable servers adapt their communication styles to the situation and the guests to whom they are speaking. Some guests respond well to humor, some prefer

What Makes It Extra-Virgin?

This is an example of the kind of question that a server should be prepared for. Although a witty waiter may have several clever retorts for this question, a professional server has the correct answer:

Olives are pressed much like grapes. The best olive oil is extra-virgin olive oil, and then the next grade is virgin olive oil. Cold-pressed oil from the first pressing of the olive (if under 1 percent acid) is considered extra-virgin olive oil. If the oil from the first pressing contains from 1 to 3.3 percent acid, it is labeled "virgin olive oil." The subsequent pressings of the same olives produce "pure olive oil." Usually a good year for grapes is not as good for olives, and vice versa.

more formality. Your tone is as important as the words you speak; you can use it to convey warmth, welcome, and sincerity.

When you are talking to the kitchen staff and fellow servers, you should use the specific jargon that makes communication between professionals quick and effective, whether you need to ask about the timing of a dish, alert the kitchen to an upcoming rush of orders, or let the chef know about a special request from a guest. However, that same jargon is never appropriate or helpful when you communicate with your guests. You and the kitchen know that "86 chicken" means the kitchen has run out of chicken, but your guest probably will not understand.

The type of establishment very often determines the form and style of conversation between servers and guests. Some of your guests may be looking for peace and quiet or a private conversation, while others may prefer to chat a bit. Reading the table (discussed in Chapter 6) can tell the server which guests want to talk and ask questions about the restaurant and which prefer to be left alone.

Communication takes other forms, as well. For example, uniforms make it easy for guests to locate a member of the service staff. Menus, both printed and spoken, tell the guest what is available to eat and drink. Signs on doors indicate restrooms and exits.

Certain words and phrases (please; thank you; you're welcome; and pardon me) are essential to the vocabulary of foodservice personnel. Polite words and considerate actions indicate a sincere regard for others' well-being—fellow employees as well as guests. Avoid referring to guests as "guys and saying "no problem" responding to thank you.

A Perfect Wine by the Glass

"We were halfway through our main course and my wineglass was empty, though everyone else had plenty. I didn't want to order another bottle of wine. The waiter came to me and told me about a wine they had by the glass that was just perfect with my steak."

REMARKABLE SERVICE COMES FROM KNOWLEDGEABLE SERVERS

Servers must be knowledgeable about the menu they are serving to the guest. You should be able to do the following:

- Pronounce the name of each dish and describe it accurately.
- Describe portions sizes.
- Describe special flavors or textures in a dish.
- Identify any potential allergens in foods.
- Identify dishes that can be modified, as well as those that cannot, in case guests wish to make modifications or substitutions.
- Assist guests who are concerned about too much or too little food to make appropriate selections.
- Point out specialties of the house or the region.

Beyond knowing the menus (including tasting, specials, beverage, wine, and cocktail menus), you are also the source for information about the restaurant itself, chef and owner's names including locations of restrooms, PDRs, and designated smoking areas. You should be able to let guests know about special promotions or special events that will be happening at your establishment or in the community. Guests who are new to the area may want to know about special attractions or other points of interest.

REMARKABLE SERVICE IS ADAPTABLE

Each restaurant has its own standards for the specific actions that go into remarkable service. For instance, it is a common standard that you should stand just behind and to the right of the guest and then set down the plate from the guest's right with your right hand. However, you may often find yourself needing to bend that rules in the interest of the guests' dining experience or common sense. You cannot stand behind guests seated at a banquette, and you should not interrupt a conversation, but you can and should make an effort to serve the food in such a way that you do not show the guest the back of your hand, serve open-handed.

There are several other situations that call for flexibility. One guest may want an appetizer for a main course with a salad to follow, while everyone else orders an appetizer followed by a salad and then a main course. Your restaurant may serve bread only after the order has been taken, but your guests might ask for it when they first sit down. There are no specific rules for these situations. Instead, the best practice is to consider what you would like if the roles of server and guest were reversed.

REMARKABLE SERVICE PROMOTES TRUST AND CONFIDENCE

Restaurants, like people, have reputations. A good reputation grows from the trust and confidence that guests feel. If you are known for treating guests honestly and with respect, everyone benefits.

You want your guest to trust that the dishes on the menu are fairly and accurately described, that the kitchen cooked the food properly and safely, that the glassware and china was properly washed, and that the decaffeinated coffee he or she ordered is actually decaffeinated. Since it is very easy to lose the guest's trust, you should make every effort to meet expectations.

One significant area of trust concerns food allergies. Your guests with food allergies depend on you to know what is in each dish, as well as to know what can be changed and what cannot. You, as the server, have to trust that your guest will tell you about any known allergy so that you can offer the appropriate assistance.

Dealing with guests in a straightforward and honest manner puts them at ease. When they are relaxed, they are happy. When they are happy, they order more freely—and they tip more generously. Trust enhances the dining experience for everyone.

The front of the house is not a place for employees to indulge in unrestrained chattiness. Service personnel should only speak concerning business, limiting their conversations with fellow workers to the job at hand. Using a foreign language while speaking with other employees might give the guests the impression you are talking about them. Service staff should always speak in the language normally used in the restaurant's location, although the ability to converse in the language of the guests (or one appropriate to the cuisine of the restaurant) is an asset. Unless the customer initiates a conversation, the only subjects of discussion with guests should be the meal and its service. Speak in a clear voice with pleasant intonation, and never be loud. A good server is unobtrusive.

REMARKABLE SERVICE EXCEEDS EXPECTATIONS

Exceeding expectations does not need to be time consuming and costly. The challenge is determining what the guests are expecting, and going above and beyond that. While repeat customers expect the same level of service each time they visit, they will be less impressed each time. This may seem unfair, but it's a fact of human nature. What is exceptional today will be expected tomorrow, and be barely adequate the day after tomorrow. Remarkable servers are constantly seeking ways to better their performance—finding new ways to delight the guests through the use of the principles already discussed, and incorporating them into this last principle: The best service is constantly improving service.

Personal Qualities of the Professional Server

IF A SINGLE WORD were to describe the sum of personal characteristics that define a professional server, it would be *caring.* Obviously, caring is not, by itself, enough. In addition to possessing the characteristics described, a professional server must master the skills described in the next chapters. In a very real sense, all of the employees of a restaurant are serving their guests. Every task, no matter how small, is carried out for one reason: to make the guest's stay as pleasant as possible. In order to succeed in this pursuit, a professional server must have certain characteristics, both physical (professional appearance and good personal hygiene) and behavioral (appropriate personality traits).

The most important behavioral characteristic a truly professional server can possess is an ability to deal with people. No amount of polish or knowledge can replace sincere concern for the customers' enjoyment of their dining experience. Maintaining a high level of this personal concern is not always easy. Most servers are familiar with cranky, demanding restaurant customers who aggravate service personnel while expecting them to be pleasant and efficient in return. Everyone has bad days occasionally, but professional servers should never let this be observed by the guests. It is important to remember that if you can see the guests, the guests can see you. In addition to being adept with the public, a person in the front of the house must have characteristics possessed by any individual of integrity, particularly as they relate to conducting business.

The following discussion lists desirable traits that professionals working in the service of foods and beverages should possess:

WELCOMING "You only have one chance to make a first impression." This is the rallying cry for every quality-oriented service business. In the food-service business, guests make decisions within their first minute of contact with the restaurant. Thus, a good server never forgets this oft-quoted but still essential maxim. When guests are met by friendly, welcoming hosts, they are assured that they can relax and enjoy their meal. Good servers are attentive to the guests' needs, not only with the dishes served, but also with the dining environment.

ATTENTIVENESS Professional servers do not daydream at work, nor are they absentminded. They must always be alert to the needs of the guests. No guest should ever have to work to attract a service person's attention. The station must never be left unattended. The ability to recognize the current state of the dining room while keeping track of what is about to occur calls for more skill than most realize. At all times the professional server must have an ongoing knowledge of what is happening at each of the tables. This is accomplished by reading the table. It is necessary to keep a discreet watch on the diners' progress throughout their meals. Anticipating when more wine should be poured, when the table needs to be cleared, and how orders should be coordinated requires that one's attention stay on the job at hand. A server's eyes should constantly be surveying the tabletop with the five areas of table maintenance (covered in Chapter 6) in mind and glancing at the guests' eyes, in case they have a request.

POLITENESS The professional server must do more than anticipate the food and beverage needs of the guest. The professional server should be happy to assist in any area that relates to the customer's comfort. This includes such tasks as opening doors; helping guests with chairs, packages, coats, and dropped items; correcting glare from lights or the sun; eliminating drafts; and adjusting the sound level of music, if necessary. When a guest asks for directions (i.e., to the bar, coatroom, or restroom) it is both rude and insufficient to point. A professional server should offer to show the guest the way, personally. The guest may prefer simple directions, but one should never assume that to be the case.

PROFICIENCY In order to advance in one's career, the professional server must be willing to work constantly at the expansion of their technical skills and multitasking abilities. A skill is the development of proficiency in an art or craft and is improved by practice. Examples of serving skills that are acquired with practice are moving through crowds with a tray of beverages; opening sparkling and still wines; properly decanting red wines; and executing elegant tableside preparations.

DEPENDABILITY Dependability is a sign of maturity and is a desirable trait for individuals in any profession. Dependable people can be relied on to accomplish what they promise, to be at work during agreed-upon hours, and to fulfill commitments. Dependability is a major factor that employers consider in hiring, since guests depend on the server to provide knowledgeable and smooth-flowing service.

ECONOMY Professionals in any business are responsible for doing their share to keep costs down. Untold amounts of revenue disappear daily in food-service establishments through waste—the largest and most unnecessary expense in the industry. Common sense is an important key to economy in the food-service industry; a rational person does not deliberately destroy or dispose of someone else's personal or business property. The professional server avoids waste by doing the following:

- Carefully handle and stack china and glassware.

- Use glass racks designed for that specific glass.

- Carry no more than can be handled safely (ask another server to assist you, or make two safe trips, rather than one risky trip).

- Be careful not to discard silverware with refuse or to put them in the dirty linen baskets.

- Avoid unnecessary soiling of linen.

- Place linens that were received in a soiled or damaged condition in a separate area so they can be returned to the linen company for credit.

- Serve standard-size portions (serve appropriate portions of items such as butter and half and half to avoid waste, replenishing only if required).

- Make sure that all items served are included on the bill, especially coffee.

- Use the recommended amount and type of cleansing chemicals (not only is overuse wasteful, but it can damage the item being cleaned or worse, cause illness).

HONESTY Honesty is an important trait for anyone, particularly an individual who is dealing with the public. During the course of a regular business day, each member of the dining room staff has innumerable opportunities to deceive both the restaurant and the guest. By being, and appearing to be, totally honest in all aspects of the day-to-day routine, the professional server permits the guests to let down their guard a little, thereby allowing them to fully enjoy the time spent in the establishment.

KNOWLEDGE The professional server must be prepared to answer any questions asked by guests, and to do so without continually making inquiries of busy fellow employees. A good server is a good salesperson—and good salespeople always know their product line. A good server would never ask a chef to leave something off a plate that was never there in the first place. It is essential for the server to take the time to become familiar with the menu and beverage list, to know their ingredients, their preparation time, their proper service temperature and their garnishes. This information can be helpful in dealing with special requests, such as substitutions for, or allergies to, certain ingredients. Awareness of the physical features of the dining room and kitchen can help the server to speedily solve any problems that arise.

The professional server's knowledge of the establishment's special services, hours of operation, history and background, and special facilities can be a real help to new customers and, consequently, is good for business. Community news, future and current events in the region, and local places of interest are all topics on which the professional server should be informed.

By reading books and periodicals about wines and foods, the professional server becomes more knowledgeable, and thereby reassuring in discussions with guests, and learns to appreciate the complexities of the culinary field. Winning the confidence of guests by being knowledgeable generates goodwill and increases tips. The successful server takes the time, on and off the job, to work at being well informed by attending wine tastings and cooking demonstrations or by taking service classes.

LOYALTY Professional servers make an effort to obey regulations and behave positively toward the firm for which they are working. Loyalty is also demonstrated by maintaining high standards of quality. Part of loyalty is a sense of proprietorship—of belonging to, and ownership of, one's job. Professional servers who see themselves as proprietors of their business work together for the common good, helping their fellow employees to consistently achieve the highest standards of service. Loyalty to the guest is also important to the development of repeat business.

Servers must never blame the kitchen for delays. The servers and the kitchen staff are both working to achieve the same goal: pleasing the guests. The server is the most visible representative of a unified effort to provide good service to the guest. Showing loyalty to, and working together with, all of the restaurant's staff presents the restaurant as a competent and confident entity dedicated to providing remarkable service to the guests.

PREPAREDNESS The food-service hospitality industry is not a business for procrastinators. Always think ahead; it is the only sensible way to work. Have everything ready before service begins. Putting off work that can be done in advance, such as stocking side stands and folding napkins, usually means having to do it later when time should be spent on the customer. Having all required equipment on hand (a corkscrew, matches or a lighter, an extra pencil or pen, or a small flashlight to aid in reading the menu in dim light) helps to make service personnel more useful and more professional in the eyes of the guest.

PRODUCTIVITY While grace and showmanship contribute to the making of a successful front-of-the-house staff member, the ability to get the job done is no less important. The best combination of these traits is a balanced one. One should enjoy a certain amount of performing, particularly if doing tableside cookery. At the same time, a server must be a real worker—one who always remembers that excellent service is the first goal.

Productivity refers not only to an individual's productivity, but the entire team. When one server drops something, another server should pick it up (and then wash their hands). Accuracy in ordering helps the bartender and cooks be more productive and less wasteful. Assisting other service staff whenever possible makes the entire restaurant more productive.

SENSITIVITY The server must be sensitive to the needs of the guest, and adjust the pace of the meal accordingly. For many guests, a meal is a time to linger, engage in conversation, and eat slowly. For others, particularly at breakfast or lunch, a meal is only an interruption in a series of other events, and not an event in itself. Even the devoted gastronome occasionally has a train to catch or a theater engagement scheduled immediately after mealtime. It is important to be sensitive to the guest's desire for

Feelings You Want a Guest to Have and Ways to Evoke Those Feelings

WELCOMED Offer a smile and a warm, genuine welcome at the front door, such as "Good evening. How may I help you?" Make sure the host's desk faces the guests as they enter.

PAMPERED Provide valet parking and someone to hold the door. Make sure guests' coats and umbrellas are taken and stored securely. Pull out chairs for guests as you seat a party.

IMPORTANT Remember and use returning guests' names, and greet them with "Welcome back." Keep track of regular guests' preferences and important dates.

COMFORTABLE Make sure the dining room's heat, lighting levels, and music are appropriate and consistent. Ensure that the dining room is spotlessly clean and that furniture is attractive and in good repair.

ENTERTAINED Offer entertaining tableside preparations or live music, if appropriate. Know about all of the menu and beverage items you offer, especially novel items unique to your restaurant, and describe them in an enticing way.

RELAXED, AT EASE Make sure the reservations process is clear and efficient. Provide waiters with enough knowledge about menu items so that they can answer questions and make suggestions with confidence, and train them in how to read guests' body language so that they can address needs that the guests may not feel comfortable expressing. Offer diners choosing wine the expert assistance of a sommelier, if possible.

SATIATED Know whether your establishment's portion sizes are considered too big or too small, and help guests by offering guidance if they seem to be ordering too much or too little food.

APPRECIATED Ask guests for their opinions, and listen carefully to the responses. The key to all of the elements in the list above is that each specific action can be learned. For example, you can train yourself to say, "May I put you on hold?" and then wait for the caller to answer before doing so, so that the potential guest does not feel as if they have been dismissed or treated rudely. This is the essence of service—doing things that will lead to a guest's satisfaction.

quick, efficient service in these cases. While the customer should never be rushed, the professional server can expedite the meal in pleasant ways, such as suggesting menu items with minimal preparation times that enable speedy service. Waiters should know how long each dish on the menu takes to cook, and use that information when the guest is ordering. This same knowledge can come in handy when a guest sends back a dish that he or she did not like, and the waiter needs to offer a replacement.

TACT The ability to say or do the right thing at the right time without offense to others is important for anyone dealing with the public. The professional server takes care in correcting a misinformed guest and always steers the conversation into safe, agreeable channels.

PERSUASIVENESS Even before the actual service of the meal begins, the professional server must "sell" the guest on what to order. Selling increases the check average. This, in turn, increases the restaurant's profits and the gratuities, as well. Subtly, a good server will steer guests away from choosing certain menu items (if the circumstances are appropriate) and induce them to order others. Incremental sales in areas such as drink specials, shared appetizers, or desserts not only enhance the guest's experience, they can increase the check average, thus increasing gratuities as well. As the guests enter the dining room, the professional server can begin to determine whether to try selling them expensive items or extras, or whether to suggest items that are more of a bargain. It helps to be able to sense whether the guests are likely to want a simply prepared, standard dish or a more elaborate and unusual one. Guests may not be familiar with all of the menu items or how they may be combined for maximum enjoyment. Therefore, the server is uniquely qualified to increase the guests' pleasure throughout their dining experience. If done properly, the guests will actually appreciate this selling.

WILLINGNESS A willing server routinely does more than is expected—helping coworkers, carrying an umbrella for guests as they walk back to their car, volunteering valuable feedback to management—without being asked. Remarkable service exceeds expectations. Good servers cultivate these behavioral traits, recognizing them as the essential tools of their trade. Good servers also know that they do not work alone; they are part of a team, which is an integrated staff of restaurant personnel.

Conclusion

HOSPITALITY WITHOUT SERVICE SKILLS to back it up is nothing more than a series of platitudes and pleasantries. Service without hospitality is impersonal and cold. When you use service skills to deliver on the promise of hospitality and hospitality skills to make service personal, you are practicing remarkable service.

Although most of the details of this book involve developing the skills you must cultivate in order to provide a great dining experience for your guests, we must not lose sight of the importance of a remarkable server's behavior. Think of it in these terms: A musician studies the notes and chords on the page and develops the skills necessary to play them. But the sounds are not truly music until the musician puts some passion into playing notes. It is the same in table service; the skills of serving do not qualify as hospitality without a sincere desire to provide for the guests. While it is often argued that a musician must play for himself or herself in order to become an artist, a server's passion for remarkable service is developed by keeping the guest's satisfaction with the total dining experience as a goal.

And remember, if a guest has to ask for more of something; more water, more butter, bread, wine, another cocktail, or something that should have been provided before the food was served; a soup spoon, the side dish they ordered, it is a sign that you are not doing your job.

2

Styles of Service

THE HOSPITALITY INDUSTRY is a noble profession with a long and varied history. What servers do today is the result of generations of servers who came before them, struggling with the same issues faced today—and coming up with new and creative ways of dealing with them. The kinds of table service in use today evolved along with the foods that are served. Foods and service are always reflective of the societies around them. By looking at the way the ancients dined at their banquets, dining habits in modern bistros and family restaurants can be better understood. Even the sometimes bizarre jargon used in today's kitchens and dining rooms can, by examining the past, begin to make sense.

The History and Traditions of Table Service

THE EARLIEST WRITTEN DESCRIPTIONS of recognizably Western dining scenes are found in the Old Testament of the Bible and in the Iliad and Odyssey of Homer. In reading these texts, it is obvious that the status of the diners was a major concern. Formal dining, as we know it today, was reserved for wealthy men. These banquets were generally held in private homes, as the Greeks had very few public eating places. Their dining rooms contained couches for the guests, rather than the tables and chairs we see in formal Western dining rooms today. A small table with a basket containing a selection of breads made of wheat or barley was placed in front of each couch. The items served, and the manner in which they were to be served, was well established. Servants brought large dishes from the kitchen and each guest chose his favorite portion, tossing scraps, shells, and bones onto his table.

The meal was divided into three sections. The first course might include fruit, poultry, salted seafood, and small savory meat dishes, much like Spanish tapas today. These light dishes were followed by heartier fare—fresh seafood and roasted meats, such as lamb or baby goat. After the second course, the tables were whisked away with all of the scraps and shells and new tables were brought out. Servants circulated with towels and basins of warm water, scented with essential oils so the guests could clean their hands (much like the finger bowls provided when proper finger foods, such as asparagus or artichokes, are served in fine dining rooms today).

Desserts were then served: dried and fresh fruits, cheeses, nuts, and small pastries or other confections. Wine mixed with water, tableside in *kraters* (large clay pots shaped like wide-mouthed, handled vases) was served with the desserts. Diluted wine was considered healthier than water alone, and drunken behavior (during the early stages of the meal, at least) was discouraged. After the dessert course, again, the soiled tables were removed, signaling the end of the meal and the beginning of the symposium (a curious mixture of literary and philosophical discussions, music, acrobats, and female dancers—all accompanied by the drinking of undiluted wine).

The Romans adopted a great deal of Greek culture, including the culinary arts, but took Greek ideas about the meal as mere starting points. A Roman dining room was called a *triclinium* because it contained three couches, each accommodating three diners. The three couches were arranged in a U-shaped pattern. Diners rested on their left sides, their left elbows propped up on cushions. This left their right hands free to choose from the sumptuous foods, each carried from the kitchen on a large platter called a *discus*. Each guest ate individually from a red pottery bowl or dish, such as the famous samian ware.

Unlike the Greeks, Roman families often dined together. However, they still used the dining room as a means of indicating rank and power. There was a strict set of rules governing the positions of each diner, based on status. The head of the household always had the most prestigious position.

Being invited to dine signaled social recognition that was much sought after. Whom one invited, who accepted an invitation, and to whom one appealed to for an invitation, said much about one's power in ancient Rome. Guests had their positions assigned according to status. This behavior is echoed today in the tradition of seating the guest of honor to the right of the host.

A Roman dinner, like its Greek predecessor, consisted of three courses. The first, the *gustum*, *gustatio*, or *promulsis*, was similar to our hors d'oeuvre or first entrée. It was served with *mulsum*, a light wine mixed with honey. Gustum was followed by the *mensae primae*, or "first table." A red wine, mixed with water, accompanied the mensae primae. The next course was the *mensae secundae*. This "second table" included a dessert of fruits and other sweets—and the first unwatered wines of the meal. As in the Greek symposium, this was the time for serious drinking to begin.

THE EVOLUTION OF ETIQUETTE AND TABLE MANNERS IN EUROPE

The hierarchy of power and status continued to be reflected in upper-class medieval meals. In Anglo-Saxon times, these meals were large-scale affairs, taking place in the main hall of a castle; there were no rooms reserved solely for dining. The tables consisted of immense boards laid across heavy trestles (the origin of the modern sense of board, as in "room and board").

The first thing placed on the table was the saltcellar. It determined the status of everyone in attendance (salt was second only to spices as a valued food commodity in the Middle Ages). High-status diners ate "above the salt," the rest were placed below; only those above the salt were seated on chairs. Diners brought along their own flatware. Knives were used to cut foods into pieces small enough to be conveniently eaten with their hands. Spoons were the primary table utensils. Silver was reserved for the wealthy, which in those times tended to mean nobility. Lesser folk owned spoons of tin-plated iron or, if they were truly poor, wood. The material of which one's spoon was made determined where, relative to the saltcellar, one got to sit.

Typically the only implement on the table was a carving knife. Carving was a manly art and was, at first, reserved for the person of highest status—the host. Later, this task was given over to the "officer of the mouth," the highest-ranking servant. A new concern with courtliness and manners, if not sanitation, demanded that the officer of the mouth "set never on fish, beast, or fowl more than two fingers and a thumb." (*The Boke of Keruynge: The Book of Carving* by Wynken De Worde, Peter Brears, 1508, a book of manners and etiquette for young boys at court.)

Food was served from common bowls, called *messes*—an apt term. Food was scooped, or dragged, to large dishes or trenchers (slabs of stale bread used as plates), which were shared by two or three diners. Wealthy European households had a large number and variety of silver bowls, basins, pitchers, and other serving vessels. Ordinary folk might have no more than a pewter mug and a black bread trencher. The display of wealth, through serviceware, was only one of the ways that status could be expressed through meals.

In the late fourteenth century, people began to think of food and its service as art forms, worthy of study and respect. Taillevent, the famous royal cook (real name Guillaume Tirel, 1312–1395), collected and codified the best of medieval cooking in his books *Le Viander* and *Ménagier de Paris*. In 1475, Platina of Cremona's *De Honesta Voluptate* ("On Decent Enjoyment and Good Health") appeared in Europe as the first printed food book. In it, Platina discussed proper manners, table etiquette, table settings, and more. This book altered the way the wealthy, who still ate with their hands, thought about eating and manners.

During the Renaissance in the fifteenth century, dining and service became more elaborate, just as art and music did. As more people gained financial security, the demand for better service and food increased, particularly in Italy.

A new taste for cleanliness throughout Western Europe and England required that the boards used as tables in banquets be covered with a large cloth called the *nappe*. Its top surface was kept scrupulously clean, but the sides, where it hung down, were used for wiping of hands (made especially greasy by the absence of forks). Occasionally hand towels, known as *manuturgia*, would be available. Some historians trace the origins of classic fine dining to a single aristocratic family of the sixteenth century, the Medicis of Florence. It is said that when Caterina de' Medici (1519–1589) married the future King Henri II of France in 1533, she brought, as part of her trousseau, a small army of Italian cooks, chefs, servants, and wine experts.

If Caterina introduced fine dining and its appropriate service to France, her cousin, Marie de' Medici (1573–1642), wife of Henri IV, certainly continued that mission. New table manners, beginning with Platina, were expanded during the reigns of both Medici cousins. Examples include the ritual of washing the hands before sitting down at the table (hand washing before meals seems to have been a forgotten, then restored, practice from classical antiquity). Among the table refinements allegedly brought to France (and later the rest of Europe) by the Medicis were the use of a spoon to eat soups and other liquids and of a fork to select foods from a platter. It was considered correct to pass the best morsels of food to others at the table. Blowing on hot foods and filching extra dessert by hiding it in a napkin were discouraged.

Henry VIII (1491–1547) initiated formal, luxurious dining in England, but it was his daughter Elizabeth I (1533–1603) under whom the practice flourished. Table manners came to be expected of refined folk. Forks were more widely recommended for the serving of meat (which, by the way, was beginning to be carved by women at the table), although their use as eating implements was still not mentioned. Men and women were seated alternately at the table. Husbands and wives shared a plate—but it was more often a plate, not simply a slab of bread. At this point in time, the host and the family would still out-rank the guests in terms of social status, so guests might still have been given a trencher.

Books about table manners and the right way to serve became popular. Braithwaite's *Rules for the Governance of the House of an Earl* (1617) listed spoons and knives as essentials, but did not mention forks. During the reign of Queen Anne (1665–1714), serviettes and the increased use of forks made it possible to use finer napery. Table setting began to be seen as an art in itself. Books on the subject, including the first titles about napkin folding, began to appear.

The dining room began to be a place of pomp and protocol. A brigade system of officers of the household, complete with uniforms (which even included swords for the highest-ranking servants) was created, not to wait in the trenches, but to wait on trenchermen. This brigade is still observed in the hierarchy of the dining room (see page 34). The first service manual of this brigade, *L'Escole Parfaite des Officiers de Bouche* ("The Perfect School of Private Chefs," 1662), explained, "Give the best portions to the most esteemed guests, and if they are of great importance, give them an extra portion." It signaled the beginning of a shift of emphasis from meals for the sake of promoting the status of the host, to one of providing the most pleasurable dining experience possible for the guests.

In 1808, Grimod de la Reynière published his *Manuel des Amphitryons*, a guidebook for table service. The term *amphitryon* is used in place of the old term officer of the mouth or carver (the person in charge of the dining room), and is henceforth known as the "host." The motto for service staff, according to Reynière, is, "The host whose guest is obliged to ask for anything is a dishonored man." This is a far cry from the kind of host-centered service seen in the courts of the past.

Thomas Coryate

Thomas Coryate (1577–1617) was a traveler and one-time court jester in the court of James I of England. He had traveled to Italy, where he became convinced of the usefulness of the fork. Coryate wrote:

> For while with their knife which they hold in one hand they cut the meat out of the dish, they fasten their fork, which they hold in their other hand upon the same dish, so that whatsoever he be that sitting in the company of any others at meal, should unadvisedly touch the dish of meat with his fingers, from which all at the table do cut, he will give occasion of offense unto the company, as having transgressed the

laws of good manners, in so much that for his error he shall be at the least brow-beaten, if not reprehended in words. Hereupon I myself thought good to imitate the Italian fashion not only when I was in Italy but in England since I came home.

His English countrymen remained unconvinced and, for his efforts to win acceptance of the new device, mocked him with the nickname "Furcifer," a newly coined word combining the Latin word for fork with Lucifer. Indeed, as late as 1897, sailors in the British navy were not permitted to use forks, as their use was considered an affectation.

THE RISE OF THE MODERN RESTAURANT AND TABLE SERVICE

The French Revolution (1789–1799), the rise of democracy, new conceptions of the role of the individual in society, and the ascendancy of capitalism in Europe made possible the restaurant as we know it today. Great chefs, no longer the exclusive perquisite of nobility, began to see themselves not only as artists (in the same larger-than-life sense that painters, poets, and composers began to see themselves), but as entrepreneurs. They were participants in, and chroniclers of, societal changes.

The French Revolution was not, of course, the sole cause of the development of restaurants in France. Rather, both were products of the same democratizing spirit; the first real restaurants in France appeared in 1769, about 20 years before the revolution began. It may be that the rise of popular public eating places aided and abetted the rise of democratic and revolutionary zeal.

The term *restaurant* already existed in France, but it previously referred only to small establishments that sold broth or bouillon, that is, "restoratives." Even before that, there was a tradition of food and beverage service in establishments outside the home. The Romans had small restaurant-type businesses called *taberna vinaria*, from which we get the word tavern. These establishments served a lot of wine, as well as food that was kept warm in stone counters. Cooks' shops of medieval Europe were often little more than booths set up in the market and offered a very limited menu for the common classes. Inns and taverns served fixed menus, at a set price, often served at set times.

Marie-Antoine (Antonin) Carême (1784–1833) lived on the crest of the social changes characterized by the French Revolution. He represented the grandest statement of the old, court-based cuisine, but was inspired by the vigor of a new society creating itself. Carême was one of the last holdouts in favor of service à la française. It was a perfect frame for the exhibition of his art. However, Carême's preference for the grandeur of service à la française could not slow the shift to a more guest-centered form of service.

In 1782, A. B. Beauvilliers opened the first modern restaurant, Le Grand Taverne de Londres in Paris. Beauvilliers and other chefs, notably the famous Antonin Carême, had spent time working in England during the French Revolution, when association with the nobility might have endangered their lives. Beauvilliers contributed the à la carte menu (literally, "from the card"). Offering his guests the opportunity to choose from a number of menu items was a marked change from the table d'hôte of the past, signaling a greater interest in the pleasure of the guests.

From this point on, the development of European, especially French, cuisine became a series of small refinements. The evolution of table service slowed to a crawl, as the needs of fine dining, whether in a home or in a restaurant, were met by fine-tuning the formats of service à la française, and service à la russe. The menus in restaurants were almost exclusively table d'hôte or prix fixe.

While European cuisines and dining traditions had developed slowly from ancient historical roots, American dining reflected the growing nation's sudden need to feed vast numbers of people, spread out over an entire continent, as quickly and cheaply as possible, making efficiency an almost religious virtue. North American culture evolved during the time of the Industrial Revolution. In the nineteenth century, technological changes shaped America's rise to power. Agricultural, transportation, and food-processing industries were transformed. Companies were suddenly manufacturing millions of units of food items that would be sent across the continent and to every state, which led to the standardization of foods and flavors. Companies could not afford to make their products according to the specific tastes of just one or two people. By the early twentieth century, marketing science, with tasting panels, focus groups, and surveys of public opinion, began to be used first to understand and then define the "American taste."

Such significant events had an effect on both sides of the Atlantic, of course. In 1900, the first edition of *Le Guide Michelin* in France reflected the changes in modern society—a society now characterized by mobility, a desire for freedom of choice, and the kind of disposable incomes that permitted not only the wealthy but also the rising middle classes to enjoy that freedom. It also reflected the food-service industry's increasing awareness that the guest's satisfaction was paramount. These modern concepts did not originate in France, the world capital of fine dining. They came from the New World, and they were generated by forces that could never have been imagined by the likes of Taillevent, La Varenne, or Carême.

In the past 40 years, fine dining restaurant service has changed as dramatically as has the food served. During the first half of the twentieth century, American fine dining restaurants tried to emulate European custom. French service was considered the most elegant, followed by Russian and English. American service evolved from these European forms of service, employing aspects of all three styles in varying combinations and customizing them to work in the dining rooms of today (a concept known as "house style," further discussed on page 45). Today's dining is less stratified and formal; it exemplifies the democratic shift that has characterized the history of table service. In less than a century, fine food service has gone from being the province of the wealthy and powerful to being much more egalitarian. Remarkable service has evolved with the times, while keeping the guests and the quality of their experience as the most important goal.

MENUS AND SEQUENCE OF COURSES

The basic sequence of courses in most Western menus is based on that of the ancient Greeks, developed to match the sensory requirements of the diners. The Greeks believed that in order for each course to be enjoyed, it must not be overpowered by the preceding course. The meal should build to a climax at the main course, then gradually relax to lighter foods. Even today's simplified sequence of menu items follows the basic pattern established nearly three thousand years ago.

The general sequence of dishes (with certain exceptions) is:

◻ Cold foods before warm

◻ Light foods before heavy

Written menus were often prepared for banquet dinners in France dating from around the 1550s. The written menu listed the dishes to be presented in the second course, giving guests a graceful way to pace their consumption while maintaining their appetites.

The meal for a banquet was divided into three separate parts, or services. As guests entered the dining room, they found the first course, the entrée, already in place. This course may have included anywhere from ten to forty types of food. Hot items were kept warm on *réchauds* or heating units. After the dishes in the first setting were finished, the guests left the table while it was cleaned and reset for the second service.

The relevés, or removes, was the second course; this course replaced the "removed" items of the first course. It, too, included an astounding number of dishes. And the final course of the meal was called the "entremets," which corresponds to our dessert course. It included not just sweets, but also fruits, a savory item, and a cheese selection.

The Classic Menu

A full classic menu includes seventeen courses, described below:

1. **Hors d'oeuvre (appetizer):** Designed to stimulate the appetite. Special utensils such as caviar spoons (of gold, horn, or mother-of-pearl), oyster forks, or snail tongs may be needed.

2. **Potage (soup):** This could be a clear soup, such as bouillon or consommé, served in a two-handled bouillon cup, accompanied by a bouillon spoon (see page 80). The guests may sip from the cup using the handles or use the spoon. Thicker soups should be served in a soup plate with a soupspoon. The larger, oval-shaped spoon better fits the shape of the soup plate (see pg. 80).

3. **Oeufs (eggs):** A small omelet, poached or scrambled eggs.

4. **Farineaux (starches):** Generally a pasta, such as ravioli, gnocchi, spaghetti, or, sometimes, a risotto (if not served as an entrée). In Italy, "string" pastas are served in a bowl with a fork often set on the right. In America, they are usually served on a plate, with a fork on the left and a tablespoon on the right.

5. **Poisson (fish):** Usually soft and easily digestible, meant to prepare the appetite for the following courses. A fish fork and knife may be supplied to assist in boning the fish.

6. **Entrée (light meat):** The first meat dish: a small portion of fowl, beef, pork, or lamb, garnished but served without vegetables when followed by a relevé.

7. **Sorbet (ice):** Sorbets (sometimes fruit- or liquor-based, often with egg whites added after setting to create more volume) are served between main courses to cleanse the palate and to prepare the stomach for the next course. The sorbet course is sometimes used as an intermezzo ("intermission"), during which the first speech could be given. In Normandy, this course is *a trou normande*, traditionally a glass of Calvados (a dry brandy made from apples), which is meant to aid digestion and refresh the appetite before the relevé.

8. **Relevé or remove (light meat):** This larger course follows, or replaces, the entrée. Traditionally, it is a joint of meat that is carved and served with sauce or gravy, potatoes, and vegetables.

9. **Rôti (roast):** Together with the relevé, this course is the main event. Usually roasted game, often served with a small green salad. The salad is served from the left, with the left hand, and set above the fork.

10. **Légumes (vegetables):** The winding down of the meal, these vegetables are usually served with a sauce.

11. **Salat (salad):** Aids in digestion after the heavy meal and cleanses the palate.

12. **Buffet froid (cold buffet):** A small portion of a cold meat (i.e., ham, roast chicken) or fish.

13. **Entremets (sweet):** In America, this is dessert, the service of which might require forks, spoons, parfait spoons, and so forth.

14. **Savoureaux (savories):** This course is usually served hot on toast; items include Welsh rarebit, grilled chicken livers and bacon, or an unsweetened soufflé.

15. **Fromage (cheese):** A cheese cart or a platter, brought from table to table, bearing an assortment from which the guests may choose. It should include at least one cheese in each of the following categories: hard, semisoft, soft/cream, and blue-veined. One ounce of each type of cheese is an appropriate portion size for a selection of three or four cheeses; for selections of more than four cheeses, serve about ½ ounce each.

16. **Fruit:** Fresh, dried, or candied.

17. **Digestif/tabac (beverages/tobacco):** Coffee, tea, cordials, brandies, cigars, and so on.

TYPES OF MENUS

Today, the menu gives guests at a restaurant a list of options. There are distinct types of menus, described as follows, including table d'hôte, prix fixe, à la carte, and dégustation.

TABLE D'HÔTE AND PRIX FIXE MENUS

The table d'hôte menu was common at inns and taverns. The proprietor (or host) served a fixed menu at a set price, often served at set times, to travelers. Today, the table d'hôte menu is still used to offer a complete multicourse meal for a set price and typically offers a few choices for each course. The prix fixe menu, which is essentially the same as a table d'hôte menu, differs in that there are no options on the menu. Coffee or tea is generally included as part of the price. A variant of the traditional prix fixe or table d'hôte menu is one in which, for an additional charge, appropriate wines are paired with each of the courses. For both types of menus, the guest pays the total price for the meal, whether or not they want the entire menu.

For both table d'hôte and the prix fixe menu there may be a supplemental charge for higher cost luxury items, such as lobster or caviar, espresso or cappuccino.

Table d'hôte menu

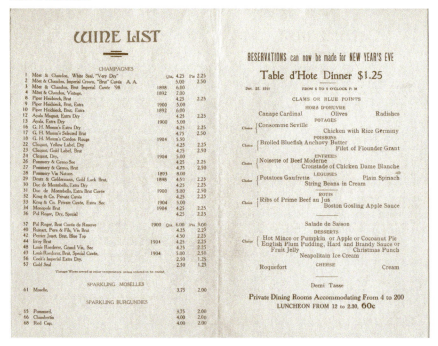

Banquet menu

THE CULINARY INSTITUTE OF AMERICA
warmly welcomes
Pearl Harbor
Commemorative Dinner
with Guest Speakers
Joseph Persico and Captain Glass
to
AMERICAN BOUNTY
Friday, December 7, 2018

~ FIRST COURSE ~
Assorted Hors d'oeurve

Müller-Thurgau, Chateau Benoit, Willamette Valley, Oregon, 2015

~ SECOND COURSE ~
Onion Soup Au Gratin

Müller-Thurgau, Chateau Benoit, Willamette Valley, Oregon, 2015

~ MAIN COURSE ~
**Filet Mignon with Pommes Pont Neuf,
Carrots Vichy, Béarnaise Sauce**

Merlot, Louis M. Martini, North Coast, California, 2014

~ DESSERT ~
Coupe St. Jacques

Gift Certificates are available through our Maître d'Hôtel

Brian O'Rourke
Chef Instructor

Charles Garibaldi '84
Maître d'Hôtel Instructor

A 12 percent service charge has been added to your check. It is used to fund student scholarships, purchase graduation jackets and support student activities. Tips in excess of 12 percent will go directly to the students serving you. The service charge amount reflected on your check is not mandatory. If you are not satisfied with your dining experience, the charge may be adjusted. If you have any questions, please see the Maître d'Hôtel Instructor. Thank you.
NOT-FOR-PROFIT STATEMENT
The Culinary Institute of America is an independent, not-for-profit educational organization pursuing its mission of providing the highest quality culinary education. This not-for-profit status enables us to focus on the quality of education rather than on satisfying the investment expectations of any shareholders.

PREPARATION IS EVERYTHING℠

À LA CARTE MENUS

Beauvilliers contributed the à la carte menu (literally, "from the card"). Offering his guests the opportunity to choose from a number of menu items was a marked change from the table d'hôte of the past, signaling a greater interest in the pleasure of the guests. With an à la carte menu, guests order individually priced items, and have the ability to structure their meal in any way they choose.

À la carte menu

AMERICAN BOUNTY DINNER

STARTERS

Hand Sliced Atlantic Smoked Salmon Warm Potato Knish, Ronny Brook Farm Crème Fraîche	9.
Louisiana Gumbo Beer Steamed Shrimp and Andouille Sausage	9.
✍ **Black Bean Quesadilla** Mango Pico de Gallo and Sour Cream	9.
Rock Shrimp Cake Chayote Slaw and Creole Mustard	9.
Pan Seared Hudson Valley Foie Gras Crispy Potato Cake, Caramelized Onions and Pennsylvania Dutch Black Vinegar Sauce	12.

SOUPS

✍ **Roasted Corn and Tortilla Soup**	5.
✍ **Chilled Gazpacho**	5.
Amish-style Chicken and Corn Soup	5.
A Sampling of all Three Soups	5.

SALADS

Summer Greens Bacon, Cherry Tomatoes and Berry Vinaigrette	7.
Buffalo Chicken Salad House Smoked Bacon, Vegetable Chips, Creamy Blue Cheese Dressing	8.
American Bounty Eggless Caesar Salad Crispy Croutons, Freshly Grated Parmesan and Olives	8.
New York Chopped Steakhouse Salad Summer Vegetables, Pont Reyes Cheese and Red Wine Vinaigrette	7.
Marinated Coach Farms Goat's Cheese Salad Roasted Bell Peppers, Olives and Balsamic Vinaigrette	8.

DEGUSTATION OR TASTING MENUS

Some fine restaurants may offer a menu dégustation ("tasting menu"), consisting of small portions of numerous items to compose a five- to ten-course meal, sometimes accompanied by paired wines, following the basic classical structure. This type of menu may be presented as part of the restaurant's regular offerings, as a special or seasonal offering, or it may be the response to a special request from a guest.

The menu dégustation allows chefs to exhibit their skills creating an extensive and varied meal. This elaborate meal is served to everyone at the table, thereby

Tasting menu

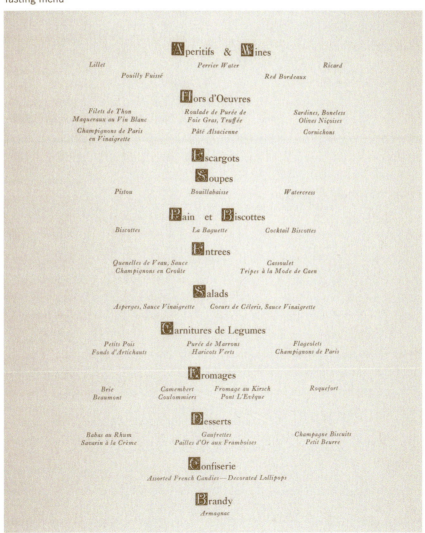

eliminating a situation in which some guests have to wait with no food in front of them while the other guests enjoy the multiple courses. A menu dégustation may be offered at only one seating, as the time required to enjoy such a dinner makes it impossible to turn the tables. It is not unusual for the chef of a fine restaurant to receive a special request in advance for a menu dégustation—often with recommended wines to accompany the dishes.

Dining Room Brigade

EVERY ESTABLISHMENT USES SOME VARIATION on the classic dining room brigade derived from the type and price level of the menu, style of service, and physical structure of the restaurant. In any size organization, it is important that everyone know to whom they report, and to whom their supervisors report. This is the essence of a brigade system, which organizes job functions into a clear hierarchy. To understand some of the hundreds of variations on the classic brigade, it is important to understand the brigade system itself first. Unfortunately, there are various interpretations of the classic brigade titles. So it is most important to understand the job descriptions and responsibilities, regardless of job title.

CLASSICAL/HISTORICAL STRUCTURE

MANAGER (*MAÎTRE D'HÔTEL*)

The maître d'hôtel is traditionally the manager of the house or the entire operation in today's restaurants. This position would be considered the general manager in modern terms. *Hôtel* and *hôte* are both derived from the French word for "host." Fundamentally, that is what the job of maître d'hôtel is about: hosting.

Informally referred to as the "maître d'," today's maître d'hôtel is responsible for the overall management of the dining room: station assignments, public relations, and the physical maintenance of the room itself. In modern bistros or casual restaurants, this position is filled by either the manager or host. The term *chef de sale* is used less frequently today, but it also indicates the manager of the dining room.

RECEPTIONIST (*RÉCEPTIONNISTE*)

The réceptionniste ("receptionist") is the person who greets (and occasionally seats) the guests, takes phone reservations, and looks after the needs of the front desk area. In casual restaurants, this position often replaces all of the previously mentioned positions, and may be called "the host(ess)."

CAPTAIN (*CHEF DE RANG OR CHEF D'ÉTAGE*)

The captain, also known as the *chef de rang* ("chief of the station"), is usually in charge of service in a particular station of tables. The captain must have a profound knowledge of food and wine and be able to translate that knowledge into language that is understandable to each and every guest. The captain takes the order from the guests and assists the front waiter in serving the food. As host of his or her station, the captain should rarely leave it. In some facilities this position was known as "chef d'étage" (literally "chief of the stage" or "floor"), but this term has not been used in many years.

The captain has more interaction with the guests than any other service staff position and may be called on to perform a wide array of dining room and tableside presentations and preparations. For instance, foods served from a voiture are often carved by the captain.

In some very formal establishments with a full hierarchy, these tasks might be performed by a specific individual known as the *trancheur* (which translates from French as "slicer"), who rolls a cart or voiture to the table or prepares and plates foods from specific station. Items served this way might include smoked salmon or sliced joint meats such as hams. In a modern fine dining restaurant, these tableside functions would probably be performed by the captain or the front waiter.

WINE STEWARD (SOMMELIER)

The sommelier (or wine steward) is responsible for the creation of the wine list, the purchasing and storage of wines (maintenance of the wine inventory), the recommendation of wines to guests, and the wine service itself.

HEAD WAITER

Depending on the establishment, the head waiter may have the responsibilities of the maître d'hôtel, or act as the captain of a dining room or of a primary station in the dining room.

FRONT WAITER (*COMMIS DE RANG*)

In some dining rooms the commis de rang is known as the "demi-chef de rang," or "front waiter." Second-in-command of the station, the front waiter takes the order from the captain; relays it to the kitchen through the point-of-sale system or with a hand dupe; and serves the food with assistance from the captain. The front waiter often assists the captain in taking some orders, or assists the commis de suite in bringing the food from the kitchen. The front waiter's position may not be as glamorous as that of the captain, but the captain relies heavily on the front waiter's efficiency.

BACK WAITER OR RUNNER (*COMMIS DE SUITE*)

The back waiter or runner (also known as the commis de suite) brings drinks and food to the front waiter, sets up the guéridon as needed, gets all food and beverage for the assigned station, helps clear, and generally assists the front waiter.

BUS PERSON OR BUSSER (*COMMIS DE DÉBARRASSEUR*)

The bus person is often an apprentice or trainee. This position is typically responsible for stocking side stands and guéridon, setting up the pantry, and cleaning the dining room prior to service. During service, bussers bring bread and water to the table, and assist the front waiter by clearing the tables of soiled items and re-setting tables. A busser may also take on the responsibilities of the back waiter to bring food and drink to the front waiter. A great busser can lighten the burden on the rest of the service team, enabling them to concentrate more on serving the guests.

ORGANIZATION CHARTS

One way to better understand the hierarchy of the restaurant as a total unit is to use an organization chart. Charts on the following pages show examples of the possibilities for each of the restaurant styles discussed in this book. It should be noted that the chef or maître d'hôtel may be a part owner and therefore higher in the organizational chart.

The more casual the restaurant, the fewer staff members are needed to provide good service. If there is no sommelier, either the captain or maître d'hôtel would provide the wine service. In a casual restaurant, the server would do the duties of the captain and front and back waiters, but of course there would be fewer duties to perform and less expectation of services (see Table 2.1).

FINE DINING

Fine dining restaurants have staff to fill most, if not all, of the traditional dining room brigade positions.

TABLE 2.1 Classification of Duties

Classic Hierarchy	Fine Dining	Bistro	Casual
MAÎTRE D'HÔTEL	Owner or general manager	Owner or general manager	Owner or general manager
CHEF DE SALLE	Maître d'hôtel	Floor managers	Floor managers
SOMMELIER	Sommelier		
RÉCEPTIONNISTE	Host	Host	Host
CHEF DE RANG	Captain		
CHEF D'ÉTAGE	Room service waiter		
COMMIS DE RANG	Front waiter	Waiter	Server
COMMIS DE SUITE	Back waiter		
COMMIS DE SUITE	Runner	Runner	
COMMIS DE DÉBARRASSEUR	Bus person	Bus person	Bus person

Organization chart for a fine-dining restaurant

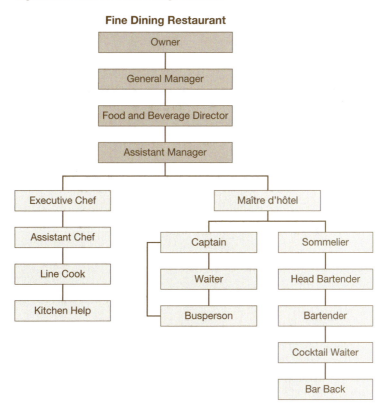

Fine Dining Restaurant

BISTRO

In France, a typical bistro would have no captains. Service positions would include, however, chef de rang, commis de rang, or demi-chef de rang.

Organization chart for a bistro

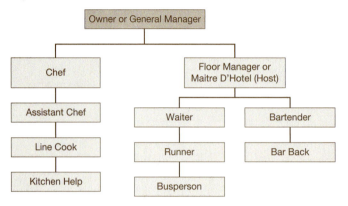

CASUAL (CHAIN)

Chain restaurants may have fewer positions as part of their overall dining room brigade as food service is generally more relaxed than in a fine dining restaurant.

Organization chart for a casual or chain restaurant

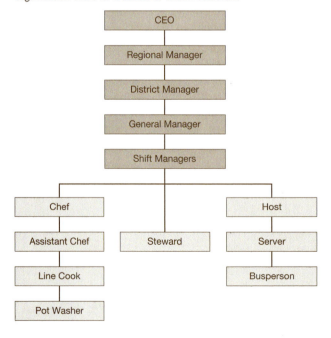

Styles of Service

THERE ARE MANY STYLES OF SERVICE, including French, Russian, and American, as well as English, guéridon, voiture, butler, and buffet. The type of service offered at a restaurant is determined by the menu, the skill and training of personnel, the ambience, and, ultimately, the market the restaurant is trying to reach. No one style of service is better than any other. Each form of service is designed to meet the specific needs and demands of distinct circumstances. Any combination of these styles may be used at different times if consistent with the restaurant's concept.

FRENCH SERVICE

Today's formal service style has its roots in service à la française ("French service"), which reached its full-blown grandeur in the court of Louis XIV, grandson of Marie de' Medici and Henri IV (1638–1715). As guests entered the dining room, the first course was already set up (the origin of the word *entrée* for the first course can be traced to this "entering" other dining room). Hot items were brought to the dining room on silver platters and placed on the guéridon, or covered warmer. After the guests finished a service, they got up and left the table while it was cleaned and reset for the next service. Service was family-style.

Service à la française in the time of Louis XIV had some distinct disadvantages. The tables were overloaded, and not merely with food. Réchauds, centerpieces, flower baskets, and candelabra seemed to fill every available inch. Despite the use of réchauds, the last items served were generally cold or had, at the very least, lost their freshness. Jean-Louis Flandrin provides evidence of family style being the French custom in his book, *Arranging the Meal, A History of Table Service in France*. He quotes a Russian writer, Denis Fonvizin, who describes the frustration with French service as you can only eat from the platters in which you can reach from your seat. It was not the French custom to pass platters down the table.

Today, formal French service generally requires a captain to seat guests and take orders, a sommelier to assist in wine selection and to serve the wine, a front and back waiter to prepare and deliver the food, and a busser to bring water and bread.

Black Ties and White Gloves

The traditional outfit for servers performing formal French service is black tie and white gloves, with the addition of an apron for the front waiter while cooking. Since white gloves must be changed frequently during serving, it is imperative that servers have enough pairs to change them as necessary throughout the service of the meal.

THE GUÉRIDON

In formal service, the guéridon is center stage in the service act. It is often equipped with a réchaud (a heating element) and a large silver dome or cloche for covering food. The guéridon should contain all of the tools and equipment needed for the menu items. It might be used for mixing salads, deboning fish, or carving meat. The fuel is usually alcohol, bottled butane, or Sterno. However, induction burners may be necessary if open flames are not permitted in the dining room.

Guéridons are often used in a formal setting so that some items are fully prepared tableside from the guéridon and immediately plated and served. Some fine dining establishments employ a modified form of formal service in which food is fully or partially cooked in the kitchen, placed on a platter, and carried to the dining room by a waiter. The platter is then placed on a guéridon or heating table and plated. This allows some tableside showmanship with less labor for the server. One example of tableside service you may see in some establishments is the preparation and presentation of a cheese plate. Table 2.2 presents some advantages and disadvantages of tableside service.

TABLE 2.2 Advantages and Disadvantages of Tableside Service

Advantages of Formal Tableside Service	Disadvantages of Formal Tableside Service
Elegant	Requires highly skilled servers
Personalized service	Requires expensive equipment
Showcases the food and preparation	Higher labor cost
Entertaining (flambéing, carving)	Less seating capacity (need guéridon space)
Leisurely dining	Less turnover
Higher check average	Higher labor cost
	Can be too formal for some guests

VOITURE AND TROLLEY SERVICE

The meaning of *voiture* loses something in translation. Literally, "a carriage or car," a voiture is generally a decorative cart, also known as a "trolley," equipped with a heating unit and a hinged cover, to maintain the warmth of prepared hot foods—although cold foods can also be served from a voiture. A voiture differs from a guéridon in that it is large enough to hold an entire roast. In practice, voiture service refers to the plating of a precooked main course, at the guest's table, from a voiture.

RUSSIAN, OR PLATTER, SERVICE

If service à la française expected diners to be impressed by the host's largesse (even if it was served lukewarm), Russian service (service à la russe) assured that each guest's meal was served at its best. The burden of assuring the guest's enjoyment was shifted to the host (or the host's staff), while attracting as little attention as possible.

This change in focus was echoed in 1825, in Anthelme Brillat-Savarin's (1755–1826) *La Physiologie du Gout* ("The Physiology of Taste"). Félix Urbain Dubois's *La Cuisine Classique* (1856) took this approach to service another step forward. It introduced service à la russe ("Russian service") to European dining rooms. Food was served hot from the kitchen, in individual portions, rather than from an immense display where all of the dishes, prepared well ahead of time, had been sitting for maximum visual effect.

In Russian/Fench service, the prongs of the fork should point up when selecting flat items, like sliced bread, meat, or many vegetables.

There are varying opinions on the definitions of French and Russian Service. The common thought is that tableside cooking is the fanciest, and therefore, must be French. However, according to Roy Strong in *Feast, A History of Grand Eating,* French service was actually Family Style service until June 1810 when a Russian diplomat to Clichy, Prince Borosovich Kourakine, hosted a dinner party and introduced tableside carving and pre-plated dishes that was common in Russia. The French were so impressed with the hot food they slowly adopted the style and expanded on the possibilities of tableside preparation.

Russian service is mostly used for banquets today. The main goal of Russian service is to ensure the guest

The prongs of the fork should point down when selecting rounded, more difficult to grasp items, such as rolls.

TABLE 2.3 Advantages and Disadvantages of Russian service

Advantages of Russian Service	Disadvantages of Russian Service
Personalized service	Requires space between chairs for wide platters
Grand style	Requires skilled (and physically capable) servers
Entertaining	Less portion control and may run out of items
Guests may choose portion size	Food can become cold and ragged while serving
Guests may choose quantity of sauces	Dangers of spilling soups or sauces
Server can exhibit skills	

tasteful fashion. It is especially expedient for banquets or wherever it is necessary to serve many people attractively presented food quickly but without sacrificing elegance and a personal touch.

Even though most restaurants do not serve every course in the Russian service style, it remains common for waiters to use Russian service to place bread on guests' plates. Additionally, the same skills required for Russian service can be helpful when splitting menu items into two plates for guests, either on the guéridon, on the side stand, or at the table. Table 2.3 shows the advantages and disadvantages of Russian service.

BUTLER SERVICE

The procedures for butler service are the same as those for Russian service; that is, the food is prepared and arranged in the kitchen and then brought on a tray or platter to the dining room. Butler service indicates that, instead of having the server place the food on the plate, the guests serve themselves while the waiter holds the platter.

This style of service is often used today when passing hors d'oeuvre for guests during a cocktail hour. The filled platter or tray may be held in the left hand, leaving right hand free to offer napkins to the guests from a small plate. Table 2.4 presents the advantages and disadvantages of butler service.

TABLE 2.4 Advantages and Disadvantages of Butler Service

Advantages of Butler Service	Disadvantages of Butler Service
Personalized service	Requires space between chairs for wide platters
Grand style	Less portion control and may run out of items
Guests may choose portion size	Food can become cold while serving
Guests may choose quantity of sauces	Dangers of spilling soups or sauces

ENGLISH AND FAMILY SERVICE

English and family service conjures nostalgic images of families gathered around a steaming roast on Sunday afternoon, with Father carving the meat and passing plates around the table. In restaurants or country clubs, this style of service is usually reserved for private rooms or special group dinners.

As with Russian and butler service, all food is fully cooked in the kitchen for English service. The host, or perhaps the maître d'hôtel, serves the food from platters, bowls, or tureens that are brought to the head of the table or to a sideboard. The host ladles soup into bowls or carves the meat (or whatever the main dish happens to be) and sets it on a plate. Side dishes and sauces may also be plated by the host or they may arrive from the kitchen in large serving platters for guests to pass around the table and help themselves. The host hands the filled bowls or plates to the nearest diner, who then passes them along the table. This carver should be skilled in plating in an attractive and appetizing manner. Alternatively, serving dishes can be placed on a sideboard, from which the server plates all of the food, and then presents it to the guests.

Family style is similar to English style, except that all of the foods are placed on the table in large serving dishes, and guests help themselves. It is quite popular in some value-oriented restaurants, and also in places where the style fits with the theme. It is a remarkably efficient style of service that can make a lot of sense (and money) in the right situation. Customers enjoy the chance to serve themselves, it can lighten the burden in both the dining room and kitchen, and it can lower labor costs. Variations on this less-formal style of serving are becoming popular in the United States, especially at new American restaurants and grills that want to create a more family-like ambience. It is also seen at resorts, on cruise ships, and at banquets. Table 2.5 presents the advantages and disadvantages.

TABLE 2.5 Advantages and Disadvantages of English Service

Advantages of English Service	Disadvantages of English Service
Very casual	Not elegant
Creates a communal atmosphere	Large portions (no portion control)
Guests can have second helpings	No plate presentation
Guests can easily share menu items	
Requires friendly but not necessarily skilled servers	

American style service is informal and allows for a server to carry several plates from the kitchen at once.

AMERICAN SERVICE

Among the least formal styles of service, and by far the most widespread, American service is adaptable to a wide range of restaurant types and cuisine styles, ranging from bistros and trattorias to fine dining establishments. In American service, all cooking and plating of food is completed in the kitchen, which gives the chef greater control over the plating of the dish. A waiter picks up the plated food, carries it to the dining room, and sets-in the plates in front of the guests from the right with the right hand (although some restaurants prefer service to be from the left, with the left hand). This allows two or three plates to be held in the left hand and arm while serving with the right.

American service is usually employed in fast turnover, high-volume operations. It can be used in more stylish types of dining operations with procedures varying depending on the service needs. Some chefs prefer American service because plating the food in the kitchen allows them to showcase their creativity in food presentation. American service is frequently used for banquets because large numbers of guests can be handled quickly by a limited number of service personnel. Table 2.6 lists some advantages and disadvantages of American service.

TABLE 2.6 Advantages and Disadvantages of American Service

Advantages of American Service	Disadvantages of American Service
Portion control and lower food costs	Less personalized service
Plate presentation	Informal
Consistency	Guests cannot choose portion size
Fast service	Servers merely set-in plates
Fewer servers required	
Less formal and more accessible	
Limited skill required	

House Style

THE MAIN POINTS OF GOOD SERVICE, regardless of the style of service, are as follows:

- All foods served at their appropriate temperatures; hot foods served hot on warm plates, cold foods served cold on cool plates.

- All foods and beverages served in a timely, courteous, sanitary manner.

The techniques a restaurant may use in order to achieve the two main goals of good service are based on variations of the classic styles, adjusted and adapted to suit the style of restaurant.

The way any establishment goes about achieving these points can vary dramatically, depending on the type of service that is practiced in that establishment—in other words, the restaurant's house style. The kind of food to be served is an important deciding factor, but it is not the only one. Certainly the price range, ambience of the room, and the demographics of the market one wishes to attract must be considered. Other considerations go into determining a restaurant's house style as we have already seen, including the type of restaurant (fine dining, bistro, or family-style); the restaurant's personality (formal versus casual); and the type of menu. Table 2.7 summarizes the various styles in terms of serving the guests.

TABLE 2.7 Summary of Serving Styles

Style	Activity	From Guest's	With Waiter's	Move Around Table	Begin With
French	Set down empty plates	Right	Right hand	Clockwise	Woman at host's left
Russian Plated	Set down filled plates	Right	Right hand	Clockwise	Woman at host's left
French Plattered	Serve from platter to plate	Left	Right hand	Counterclockwise	Woman at host's right
American	Set down filled plates	Right (or left, according to individual house standard)	Right hand (or left, according to individual house standard)	Clockwise (or counterclockwise if serving from left)	Woman at host's left

Restaurant Types

TO FACILITATE COMPARISON, RESTAURANTS can be divided into three basic styles, as shown in Table 2.8.

TABLE 2.8 Three Styles of Restaurants

Type of Restaurant	Description
Fine Dining	Upscale, luxury, three-, four-, and five-star, "white-tablecloth" restaurants. Examples: An American Place, Jean-Georges, Nobu, Nora's, The French Laundry, The Inn at Little Washington
Bistro/Trattoria	Grills, cafés. All have less ceremonious approaches to food service. Examples: Da Silvano, Lulu, Fog City Diner, Spago, TraVigne, Wild Ginger
Casual/Family	Family-style restaurants Examples: Olive Garden, Applebee's, T.G.I. Friday's, Red Lobster, Ruby Tuesday

FINE DINING

Fine dining establishments offer luxurious and comfortable surroundings, usually including tabletop silver, china, linen, and crystal. A maître d'hôtel directs the dining room and the staff of captains, waiters, and bus persons.

A typical menu usually offers many choices as well as specials, plus a table d'hôte or prix fixe meal. The wine list is appropriately extensive and well paired to the food. A sommelier may be on hand to help guests.

The service staff attends to every detail of the guests' experience in a fine dining restaurant. The pace of service is leisurely, which befits the elegance of a meal that may last three hours or more.

BISTRO/TRATTORIA

The most common type of dining in American cities today, bistros and trattorias range from white-tablecloth establishments, with a range of food styles, to animated and bustling bare-bones places serving simple fare and beverages. The strict definition of a bistro—a family-run establishment, serving foods with a wine theme—has all but been abandoned in the United States. The term *bistro* now refers to any simple, cozy restaurant. Service should be polite, attentive, and efficient in this level of restaurant, though not as grand as in fine dining venues.

CASUAL/FAMILY

This category encompasses family-style restaurants, diners, many theme restaurants, and the like. The principles of good service apply here as well, although servers may be less experienced than in the other classifications of restaurants.

Conclusion

THE STANDARDS OF TABLE SERVICE CONSIST of a set of parallel developments:

- □ There has been a general increase in the sophistication of the food served, and a concomitant rise in sophistication of the manner in which it is served. Although there have been occasional detours, the trend has been toward a more subtle understanding and integration of the parts of the meal.

- □ The importance of sanitation has received increasing emphasis. The development, and gradual acceptance, of the fork and of table manners were indicators of that change. Pristine cleanliness is still regarded as a sign of quality.

There is no single style of service that works for all restaurants or in all situations. Remarkable service occurs when the demands of the menu, the expectations of the management and the guests, and the skills of the dining room's personnel are taken into account. As we will see in Chapter 9, there are some further modifications to service styles for special circumstances such as buffets and receptions.

3

A Clean and Safe Dining Room

SPARKLING GLASSWARE, Gleaming flatware, fresh linens, and perfectly clean uniforms tell your guests a great deal about your restaurant, without saying a word and within just a few seconds. This chapter is devoted to the most fundamental aspect of remarkable service: Wholesome food served in a clean and safe environment.

Although the appearance of the dining room and the servers reflects the restaurant's standards for cleanliness, servers must do more than simply clean the room. They are also responsible for keeping the dining room safe for everyone, guests and workers alike, and protecting them from potential hazards such as food-borne illness and cross contamination, spoiled foods, chipped china, burns, choking, or cuts. Accidents can happen, but with the proper planning, organization, and training in best practices related to safety and sanitation, they will happen less frequently, and when they do, can be managed efficiently and appropriately.

Cleanliness

SURVEYS CONDUCTED BY THE NATIONAL RESTAURANT ASSOCIATION have consistently ranked cleanliness as one of the most important customer considerations when choosing a restaurant. Here are a few of the several areas that need a systematic approach to maintaining a positive public image:

Cleaning the Dining Room

- Clean, level and wipe down tables and chairs, including the bases and rungs.
- Vacuum rugs and carpets.
- Sweep floors.
- Dust window ledges and counters.
- Clean display areas and restock as needed.
- Wash windows.
- Clean tabletops and bases.
- Clean, sanitize and stow booster seats or high chairs.

Preparing the Restroom

- Clean door handles.
- Clean toilets and sinks.
- Mop and dry floors.
- Clean and refill soap dispensers as necessary.
- Clean and refill hand towel and toilet paper dispensers.
- Empty and reline wastebaskets.
- Clean and polish mirrors.

HYGIENE AND SAFETY

We are often told not to judge a book by its cover. However, people base important decisions about any business on their first impressions, especially in the food-service industry. The first (and possibly most lasting) impression you make on the guest is through your appearance. Make it a positive one.

The uniform you wear at work—be it a waitress's dress, a tuxedo, or a stylized costume—is a badge of professionalism. Wear it with pride. Uniforms give each employee a recognizably similar appearance that helps the guests distinguish between servers and other guests. It is a good idea to keep an extra uniform or shirt on hand for emergencies in the front of the house. Well-groomed people always look clean because they *are* clean. Professional servers apply these principles to their everyday grooming habits:

- Hair neatly cut and combed

- Hands and fingernails clean

- Clothing that fits properly, is clean, and is wrinkle free

- Shoes shined and in good condition (including the heels)

Beyond being in the appropriate uniform, every server must have impeccable personal hygiene. Since servers are in close proximity with so many people, daily showers and unscented or subtly scented deodorants are essential. Wash your hands about every half hour, when possible. Keep your fingernails clean and neatly trimmed, but do not use nail polish, since it can peel off and get into the food.

The scent of food encourages food sales. The scent of colognes and perfumes can conflict with the aromas of the foods being served, however, so they should be avoided.

Good hygiene is important for everyone's well-being. However, it represents just the beginning of the care and attention that any professional server gives to guests. Whenever you serve foods, you must practice sound sanitary practices. Since it is easy to pass a food-borne illness or toxin from one surface to another, it is in everyone's best interest to keep everything as clean as possible, as safely as possible. Every establishment should have at least one employee who is knowledgeable about specific local and state health codes. Regardless of local laws, strict observance of the following rules is essential:

Checklist for Personal Hygiene and Health

- Take baths or showers daily.

- Use deodorants.

- Refrain from perfumes and colognes.

- Keep hair clean, neat, and restrained in accordance with food sanitation guidelines.

- Wear clean, suitable clothing at all times.

Service personnel are required to stand for long periods, so take special care to keep your back, feet, and legs comfortable.

- Select sturdy shoes with ample room for toe movement and good arch support. Having more than one pair of work shoes is a good idea.

- Wear absorbent socks or hosiery. For extra comfort, try wearing support hose or purchasing cushioned insoles.

- During long work periods, perform simple stretches (hamstring stretches or calf stretches).

- Stretch only as far as you comfortably can and keep your movement slow and smooth.

- Be aware of your spinal alignment and stand straight.

- Keep your weight evenly distributed between both legs.

- Keep your hips in line with your knees and ankles.

- If you are working more than one shift, changing your shoes and socks will refresh your feet.

- After work, soak your feet in warm water to sooth any muscle tension.

- Wash hands frequently with soap and hot water before starting work and after using the bathroom, clearing dishes, smoking, and preparing food, handling money, or whenever they are soiled.

- Remove dangling jewelry or hair ornaments that might drop into food.

- Keep fingernails clean, trimmed, and unpolished.

- Cover any burns or cuts with clean rubberized finger bandages (finger cots).

- Keep hands away from hair, faces, arms, and eyes.

- Do not spit, whistle, or chew gum in the restaurant or on the premises.

- Smoke only in designated areas, if permitted, and wash your hands before returning to work.

- Cover your mouth and nose when sneezing or coughing and wash your hands immediately.

- Do not come to work if you have a contagious disease.

Preparing Serviceware

SERVICEWARE IS A GENERAL TERM for all utensils and wares used in the dining room to serve the guest, in addition to certain kitchen utensils such as carving knives and forks, ladles, and perforated spoons. The main classifications of serviceware are:

CHINA: plates of all sizes, dishes, cups, saucers, underliners

FLATWARE: knives, forks, and spoons, regardless of style or usage

GLASSWARE: items such as glass decanters, carafes, pitchers, and all drinking vessels used at a table or at the bar for beer, wine, and cocktails

HOLLOWWARE: technically, service items of significant depth or volume; more generally, large service items including platters, coffeepots, silver trays, etc.

One of the first things the patron will notice on entering the dining room is the tabletop design. For this reason, serviceware must be compatible with the overall design and motif of the operation. When service items are selected to work with each other and to complement the dining room, the effect created in the dining room is one of symmetry, simplicity, and good taste. Here are other qualities to consider when selecting serviceware, aside from aesthetic concerns:

WASHABILITY: Is the item cleanable using the sanitation capabilities of the operation, without requiring excessive time, equipment, and effort?

DURABILITY: Will the item selected stand up to the wear and tear of daily use?

ECONOMY: Is the item affordable?

WAREWASHING

Regular, effective cleaning of china, glassware, and flatware will prevent the spread of disease and infection. County, city, and state health regulations vary from place to place. It is best to contact the local health department to assure compliance with local requirements, water properties, and temperature levels.

An automatic dishwashing machine can maintain clean and sterile dishes only if it is operated properly. Follow these basic steps for cleaning dishes:

1. Scrape all dishes thoroughly.

2. Pre-rinse.

3. Stack the dishes ready for racking.

4. Do not overload the racks.

5. Invert cups, glasses, and bowls.

6. Wash flatware in a single layer.

7. Make sure enough detergent is used.

8. Maintain the proper water temperature—a minimum of 120°F (49°C) for washing, and 190°F (88°C) for sterilization. Where equipment or facilities cannot reliably produce or maintain these temperatures, chemical sanitizers can be injected during the rinse cycle.

9. Drain, dry, and stack prior to storing in a clean cabinet.

10. Once clean, handle serviceware as little as possible.

After the completion of all dishwashing, the area around the dish table and the machine must be thoroughly cleaned. Screens, spray arms, and rinse pipes should be removed and cleaned thoroughly. All water should be drained dry and the tank and machine properly cleaned inside and outside.

FLATWARE

Flatware should be impeccably clean and polished to a glow. You must handle flatware properly to be sure it is ready to go on the table. Stainless steel flatware is the most common, since it stands up to warewashing and heavy use. It is easy to polish; all that is required is hot water and a clean, lint-free cloth. Silver (or, more commonly, silver-plated) flatware and service pieces require special care.

The choice of flatware in a given establishment will vary, depending on the consideration of several factors:

BALANCE: Sizes, proportions, and weights should be attractive and comfortable to use and hold.

DESIGN: Flatware design should reflect the establishment's overall theme.

DURABILITY: Flatware should be chosen with regard to the use and to methods of handling and washing.

HANDLES: May be made of nylon, compressed wood, solid steel, or hollow plate. Flatware may be one solid piece or have handles fitted with a bolster or rivets. (*Note:* Some wooden handles do not stand up well to the rigors of commercial dishwashing machines—and may be unsanitary since they must be hand-washed.)

KNIFE EDGE: Knives should retain sharpness of edges and serrations; sharp edges require less force in cutting, and therefore result in less accidental cuts and spills.

LONGEVITY: Make sure the pattern will remain in production for replacement purposes. Beware of a pattern offered at a discount price, as the pattern may have been discontinued.

QUALITY: Composition and finishing plate should be of a quality appropriate to the establishment's overall standards.

RANGE: The style chosen should be available in all pieces needed for the establishment's menu items, such as cocktail forks, serrated knives, lobster picks, etc.

STACKABILITY: Nesting should be possible with a minimum of scratching.

Place flatware in warm water and detergent for presoaking in order to loosen any food particles. After this procedure, run it through the machine on a wire rack, in single layers, for effective cleaning. Flatware can be sorted into sleeves with the handles down to be washed a second time, then inserted into clean sleeves with the handles up for sanitary handling. Air dry flatware and store it with the handles protruding to prevent any contamination.

When you arrive in the dining room and are setting up for service, the flatware has probably already been washed. The way it was handled during washing can have an impact on what kind of preparation it may require before it is ready to go on the tabletop or into the side stand. Some restaurants separate flatware and place it in sleeves (mouth-end up) before washing; others wash the flatware loose in flat rack before it is sorted into sleeves (handles up) and washed a second time.

If the flatware is separated by type and then placed in sleeves up before washing, it is possible that the flatware will stack together so tightly that the hot water cannot reach all surfaces and the flatware may not be completely cleaned. Be sure to check flatware carefully; it may need another washing.

GLASSWARE

Glassware contributes sparkle to the dining room, and tall, stemmed glasses add elegance. Glass is produced by heating sand (silicon dioxide) and other mineral substances to a very high temperature. The molten mass is blown or molded into shape and then allowed to cool and solidify by careful regulation of its temperature. This process is called *annealing*. Handles, stems and other parts are attached by welding during this process. The following considerations affect the selection of glassware:

DESIGN: Coordinate glassware with other dining room equipment.

MANUFACTURE: Examine the clarity of glass. Inspect for cracks, faults, bubbles, and distortions.

MARKETING: Consider the amount of liquid in the capacity size of the glass. Glasses with a very large capacity may cause a standard pour of wine to look skimpy.

RANGE: When possible, order multipurpose stock so that pieces may be interchanged.

REPLACEMENT: Are additional supplies readily available? Will the patterns continue to be produced?

SERVICEABILITY: Durable glasses with smooth, simple shapes are preferable.

For additional information on glassware for the bar, see Chapter 7, and for wine, see Chapter 8.

Glass washing is, no doubt, the most difficult part of the dishwashing operation. For the best results:

- Refill the machine with clean water before washing glasses.

- Wash glasses before the china or flatware.

- Prior to washing, look for (and remove) lipstick or any other foreign material that may be difficult to remove in the wash cycle.

CHINA

In the course of history many types of dishware have been developed, each comprised of different mixtures of clay, feldspar, flint, and sometimes bone, and baked in kilns (fired) at different temperatures. The characteristics of ceramics are determined by their composition and firing temperature. Most restaurant china manufactured today has been vitrified. Fired at very high temperatures, this china becomes more durable, easier to clean, and able to withstand relatively high heat and extreme cold, as long as the temperature changes gradually. China that is fired only enough to harden is porous, with large interstices that permit air or liquids to pass through them.

BISQUE: Unglazed ceramic material that has been fired once, at a low temperature.

PORCELAIN: Glazed and nonporous, with a fine texture that has a ring when tapped. It is a form of stoneware made from special clay that consists almost entirely of kaolin, a soft, white mineral.

POTTERY: Low-fired, hence, it has large pores, but because it is generally glazed, it does not absorb much liquid.

STONEWARE: Usually white, somewhat porous, and frequently with a transparent glaze. Stoneware is bisque that has been glazed and refired at a higher temperature.

TERRA-COTTA: Low-fired (bisque) red clay, usually unglazed, relatively soft, and very porous. A familiar example of terra-cotta is a common flowerpot.

China that has a patterned design should always have a layer of glaze on top of the pattern; the patterns can begin to show wear rather quickly if they are not handled properly. Special china pieces may be used for a specific presentation. There are many shapes, colors, and materials in use in contemporary dining rooms, ranging from wood to metal, glass to acrylic. Treat these pieces carefully, as you would hollowware, to avoid chipping or denting them.

- ◻ Whenever you stack china pieces, make sure the stacks are stable and that all the pieces in a stack are the same size. You might be able to stack twenty underliners for coffee cups, but you can only stack cups with handles that do not touch the rim of the cup below two or three cups high before the stack is in danger of tumbling over.

- ◻ Replace all chipped or cracked china and glassware. Not only are they difficult to clean and sanitize properly, but they may injure patrons as well. Some establishments do not allow employees to take chipped items home as this may lead to an increase in "accidentally" chipped items.

Food Safety

FOODS CAN SERVE AS CARRIERS for many different illnesses. The most common symptoms of food-borne illnesses include abdominal cramps, nausea, vomiting, and diarrhea, possibly accompanied by fever. These symptoms may appear within a few hours after consumption of the affected food, although in some cases several days may elapse before onset. You might think that only the kitchen is responsible for keep foods safe, but as a server, you play an important role as well.

Food-borne illnesses are caused by adulterated foods (foods unfit for human consumption). The severity of the illness depends on the amount of adulterated food ingested and, to a great extent, the individual's susceptibility. Children, the elderly, and anyone whose immune system is already under siege generally will have much more difficulty than a healthy adult in combating a food-borne illness.

The source of the contamination affecting the food supply can be chemical, physical, or biological. Insecticides and cleaning compounds are examples of chemical contaminants that may accidentally find their way into foods. Physical contaminants include bits of glass, rodent hairs, and paint chips. Careless food handling can mean that even an earring or a plastic bandage could fall into the food and result in illness or injury.

Many foods provide the three conditions necessary for bacterial growth and are therefore considered to be potentially hazardous. Meats, poultry, seafood, tofu, and dairy products (with the exception of some hard cheeses) are all categorized as potentially hazardous foods. Foods do not necessarily have to be animal based to contain protein, however; vegetables and grains also contain protein. Cooked rice, beans, pasta, and potatoes are therefore also potentially hazardous foods. There are also other unlikely candidates that are ripe for bacterial growth such as sliced melons, sprouts, and garlic-and-oil mixtures.

Food that contains pathogens in great enough numbers to cause illness may still look and smell normal. Disease-causing microorganisms are too small to be seen with the naked eye, so it is usually impossible to ascertain visually that food is adulterated. Because the microorganisms—particularly the bacteria—that cause food-borne illness are different from the ones that cause food to spoil, food may be adulterated and still have no "off" odor.

Although cooking food will destroy many of the microorganisms present, careless food handling after cooking can reintroduce pathogens that will grow even more quickly without competition for food and space from the microorganisms that cause spoilage. Although shortcuts and carelessness do not always result in food-borne illness, inattention to detail increases the risk of creating an outbreak that may cause serious illness or even death. The various kinds of expenses related to an outbreak of food-borne illness, such as negative publicity and loss of prestige, are blows from which many restaurants can never recover.

With more and more concern about health and sanitation, many restaurants have developed HACCP (Hazard Analysis Critical Control Point) plans for perishable items, designed to reduce the possibilities of food-borne illnesses. While HACCP plans were originally created for use in the kitchen, systems may be set up for dairy products. For example, an inventory list may be developed for the replenishment of pantry items for each day's service. This list could include a place to record the temperature of the refrigerator and next to each item, a column could be available for the expiration date listed on the carton or package. This becomes a constant reinforcement for the servers to check on critical information. Spoiled milk might not make someone ill, but it reflects poorly on the restaurant when it curdles in a guest's coffee.

Snacking during setup and service is not allowed as it involves the placing of fingers in or near the mouth. Those fingers then touch guest plates, bar fruit, glasses, and numerous other items that could spread germs. In fact, those fingers already touched menus, doorknobs, and coffeepot handles (potentially laden with other people's germs) before they went to the server's mouth—possibly exposing the server to disease. These are good reasons for frequent hand washing with soap and hot water.

Eating should take place away from food prep areas and not in pantry or server stations. Most establishments provide an employee dining area for those taking breaks to replenish. Beverage containers should be used and discarded or washed through the dish area. If a beverage is held at the station for hydration breaks, then it must be covered and labeled with the owner's name. Consume the beverage through a closed top or straw to avoid contamination with service foods.

Sanitation is also an issue when serving takeout or *doggie bags.* Since the restaurant has no idea how the guests will handle the food when it leaves, written instructions can be helpful. Even a verbal reminder to guests not to leave the leftover chicken leg in the hot car while shopping can prevent a bout of food poisoning—and will be appreciated.

AVOIDING CROSS-CONTAMINATION

Many food-borne illnesses are a result of unsanitary handling procedures in the kitchen or dining room. Cross-contamination occurs when disease-causing elements or harmful substances are transferred from one contaminated surface to another. Use separate work areas and cutting boards for raw and cooked foods. Clean thoroughly and sanitize equipment and cutting boards between uses.

Excellent personal hygiene is one of the best defenses against cross-contamination. An employee who reports for work with a contagious illness or who fails to properly bandage an infected cut on the hand puts every customer at risk.

Perhaps the single most effective way to avoid cross-contamination is proper hand washing. Any time your hands come in contact with a possible source of contamination (your face, hair, eyes, and mouth; money; door handles; or credit cards) they must be thoroughly washed before continuing any work.

DANGER ZONE

One of the golden rules of food safety is hot food hot and cold food cold. For most pathogens capable of causing food-borne illness, the friendliest environment falls

Safety Procedures for the Dining Room

Ice Handling

- Use an ice scoop or tongs for handling ice cubes, never scoop with a glass.

- Store the ice scoop in a holder outside of the ice bin, when not in use.

- Keep all containers and glassware out of the ice bin.

- Do not serve ice that was used to cool foods.

Tasting Foods

- Use a clean spoon or fork each time you taste a food.

- For sauces, soups, and foods with a similar texture, use the two-spoon technique: Use a clean spoon to dip up a small amount and transfer it onto a second clean spoon.

Broken Glassware or China

- Use a bin or container to hold broken glassware or china.

- Do not throw broken serviceware in with regular trash.

---

within a range of 41° to 135°F (5° to 57°C). This temperature range is referred to as the danger zone. Most pathogens are either destroyed or will not reproduce at temperatures above 135°F (57°C). Storing food at temperatures below 41°F (5°C) will slow or interrupt the cycle of reproduction.

When conditions are favorable, bacteria can reproduce at an astonishing rate. Therefore, controlling the time during which foods remain in the danger zone is critical to the prevention of food-borne illness. Foods left in the danger zone for a period longer than four hours are considered adulterated. Additionally, the four-hour period is cumulative, meaning that the meter continues running every time the food enters the danger zone. Once the four-hour period has been exceeded, heating or cooling cannot recover foods.

Keeping foods at safe temperatures matters to everyone. Soups should always be properly heated in the kitchen before they are placed in a steamtable or in the service area, and the temperature should be monitored to make sure that it stays above 140°F (60°C). Perishable foods like milk, soft cheeses, butter, and salad dressings must be kept below 40°F (4°C).

CONDIMENTS

Condiments include things like salt, pepper, mustard, relish, mayonnaise, conserves, as well as sweeteners and cream for coffee that are meant to add a bit of flavor to foods. These items are not added by cooks in the kitchen; instead, they are brought to the table by the server and added to the dish by the guest. The term covers many different foods, some of which require careful handling in order to keep them fresh, safe, and wholesome throughout service.

Some condiments, such as sugar or salt, can be held safely at room temperature almost indefinitely. Some have a more limited shelf life, even though they do not require refrigeration: olive oil, or vinegar, for instance. Some require refrigeration once they are opened: mustard, ketchup, or jellies, for instance. Still others are stored under refrigeration in the kitchen or in the pantry: butter, milk, grated cheeses, or cream, for example.

Many items needed for service are kept in the walk-in refrigerator along with kitchen items. Raw meat products (such as chicken, beef, pork, and fish) should be stored below other items so they will not drip on, and possibly contaminate, the contents of the refrigerator. Milk, butter, lemons, and other server needs should be stored on higher shelves, above the meat and fish.

CONDIMENTS SERVED IN THE ORIGINAL CONTAINER

Observe the following standards for condiments served in the original container:

- ◻ Remove storeroom prices and stickers from the container.

- ◻ Write the date that the container was opened directly on the label.

- ◻ Replace half-empty containers with fresh containers before service. (*Note:* In some places, there may be a regulation that prohibits adding the contents of one container to another, a practice often referred to as "marrying" the containers.)

- ◻ Clean the lids or covers, rims, and body of the container and wipe them dry.

- ◻ At the end of service, clean the containers and lids again, close the containers tightly, place them on a clean rack or tray, and store under refrigeration.

- ◻ Use the FIFO rule (first in, first out) to keep stocks rotated and fresh, and check expiration dates periodically.

CONDIMENTS SERVED IN RAMEKINS
AND OTHER CONTAINERS

Some fine dining establishments will prefer to offer condiments in a small ramekin with a spoon rather than setting a bottle or jar directly on the table. Some states have sanitation regulations restricting the type of containers in which condiments maybe served. Observe the following guidelines for condiments served in ramekins or similar containers:

- Use only containers specifically designed for serving condiments.

- Clean squirt bottles or similar condiment dispensers meant for more than one use at least once a week.

- Chill containers for perishable condiments, but fill them as they are needed to avoid waste.

- Fill single-use containers for items such as salsa or cream no more than two-thirds full, rather than filling them to the top. This reduces the quantity of unused condiments discarded when a table is cleared.

- Discard unused items such as butter, bread, and half-and-half when the table is cleared—they cannot be given to another guest. The same is true of unused but sealed butter pats or creamers.

Safety

A CONSCIENTIOUS EFFORT must be made to assure the personal safety of everyone in the facility—guests and fellow workers alike.

Accidents rarely just "happen." They are more often the result of neglect, carelessness, thoughtlessness, or ignorance. Avoiding those situations in the first place goes a long way toward maintaining a safe space for workers and guests. This rest of this chapter's focus is on safety practices in the dining room.

FALLS

Falls account for the largest percentage of accidents in food-service operations. People can easily fall over furniture, cords, and equipment. They can slip or fall on wet or greasy floors. Improper shoes might cause you to trip or fall. Handles and straps on handbags can protrude into walkways during service. Fortunately, most falls can be avoided by keeping your eyes open for accidents waiting to happen and observing the following precautions:

- Keep chairs out of dining room traffic aisles.

- Keep stairs and doorways, especially fire exits, clear.

- Keep electrical cords out of walking areas and up off the floor.

- Put all furniture back in place as soon as possible.

- Put all equipment away immediately after its use.

- Report and repair any loose threads or tears in carpets that might trip someone.

- Ask guests to move handbags to a safer place if they are in the path of guests and servers.

When a spill occurs, the first available person should clean it up, regardless of who is actually responsible for the spill. Someone should stand guard by the spill to alert others while another employee gets the tools and materials necessary for cleaning up the spill.

Unsuitable shoes can cause accidents. Shoes that are perfect in the dining room are not necessarily safe in the kitchen. Safe, nonskid rubber soles can be applied to any shoe bottom.

Do not stand on unsafe ladders, chairs, or windowsills (a safe ladder is one that is tall enough to permit working comfortably while standing no higher than one step from the top).

LOADING, LIFTING, AND CARRYING FOOD TRAYS

Many restaurant incidents can be prevented through the correct handling of trays in the dining room. Proper balance, with equal distribution of items, is essential for transporting food and related items. Some servers prefer to rest the tray on their spread fingertips instead of their flattened palm. They feel it gives more balance and maneuverability. Only experience can tell what will work best for a particular person. Try both methods but practice with an empty tray first, then when that feels comfortable, practice with a loaded tray.

If a door is hinged on the right, the tray is carried on the left hand; if hinged on the left, the tray is carried on the right hand. This leaves you with a free hand to open the door and protect or balance the tray as you walk through. However, if either the right or left hand is not strong enough to support a loaded tray, the stronger hand should be used.

The carrying of heavy trays or awkward loads should not be attempted until the server has practiced enough to do so confidently. Use the following guidelines to carry oval trays:

- Adjust the tray so that about six inches of the tray should project over the edge of the tray stand, side table, shelf, or counter on which the tray is resting.

- Place the flattened palm under the edge of the tray, toward the middle of its broad side.

- Grip the edge of the tray with your free hand and slide the tray out and onto the flattened palm or fingertips.

- If the tray is heavy, maintain your grip on the edge of the tray.

- Bend carefully at the knees and lift with the legs and back, not the arms.

To carry a tray at shoulder level (known as a *high carry*), hold the upper arm close to the body and keep the elbow securely against the body. Resting the tray on the shoulder does give some additional support, but should be avoided as the tray can easily become unbalanced, allowing items to slide off and fall. The high carry is particularly effective when a tray must be carried through a crowd.

When carrying a tray at waist level (as you might when carrying a cocktail tray), the shoulders should be kept back. Slouching forward will make the tray unstable. While the tray may touch the forearm, the load should not rest there. Rest the weight of the tray on the hand. If the weight rests on the forearm, the tray can easily tip.

To maneuver through a crowd, guard the tray with the unoccupied hand. Support the tray with both hands when guests lift drinks from a cocktail tray. When a tray is supported by only one hand, the sudden shift in the balance of weight will cause it to tip.

BURNS

Some dining room equipment and utensils can cause severe burns. All serious burn injuries should receive medical treatment immediately.

To avoid burns, always move or position hot plates and platters with the aid of a serviette. Verbally inform guests and other service staff whenever any serviceware is hot. Never carry a coffee pot or bottle on a beverage tray. Hot beverages are another potential hazard. Tea is brewed with boiling water, and coffee is best brewed between 205° and 208°F (96° and 98°C). Remember, service should never be rushed: take care in transporting hot liquids, especially when moving through a crowded dining room.

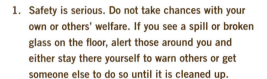

Ten Rules of Restaurant Safety

1. Safety is serious. Do not take chances with your own or others' welfare. If you see a spill or broken glass on the floor, alert those around you and either stay there yourself to warn others or get someone else to do so until it is cleaned up.

2. If a guest has a handbag or some other personal object on the floor by the table ask the owner to move it or offer to move it or place it in the coat check. Members of the floor staff might trip over it and hurt themselves or the guests.

3. Report all injuries to management, no matter how slight, and get immediate first aid.

4. Never run in the restaurant. It is easy to get hurt, or hurt someone else. In addition, if guests see someone running, it can make them nervous, thinking that something might be wrong.

5. Use the correct doors into and out of the kitchen. When using the "in" door, go all of the way in without stopping. There is a good chance that someone is right behind you walking just as fast as you are. By stopping in the doorway, you can both get hurt. The same applies to going through the "out" door.

6. Avoid horseplay and practical jokes. Harmless fun can result in injury.

7. Report all defective equipment. Obey safety rules when you are working with any equipment.

8. Avoid backing up or making sudden, jerky movements.

9. Always wear shoes with nonskid soles.

10. Always store cleaning chemicals far away from any food products or serviceware.

CHOKING

Choking on food is one of the leading causes of accidental death. Very often, other guests do not notice that someone is choking because they tend to pay the most attention to someone who is speaking.

Unless treated, a choking victim will die in four minutes. Choking victims may exhibit some of these symptoms:

- Panic
- Inability to breathe
- Inability to speak
- Clutching their throats
- Blue skin
- Collapse

ALLERGY CHART — EVENING MENU — MARCH 20XX

KEY:

	√	Allergy item free

	Gluten-Free (omit)	Dairy-Free (omit)	Vegetarian	Garlic-Free (omit)	Onion-Free (omit)	Nut-Free (omit)	Shellfish-Free (omit)	Pork-Free (omit)	Alcohol-Free (omit)
Apps.									
Beet									
Pate									
Escargot									
Mixed Greens									
Scalops									
Foie									
Soups									
Pistou									
Carrot									
Entrees									
Lamb									
Bass									
Duck									
Pork									
Halibut									
Beef									
Sides									
Beans									
Gnocchi									
Dessert									
Crème Brulee									
Crepes									
Choc. Cake									
Tarte Tatin									
Ice cream									
Sorbet									

AMERICAN BOUNTY DIETARY NEEDS CHART—PM

	Gluten-Free (omit)	Dairy-Free (omit)	Vegetarian	Garlic Free	Onion Free	Contains Nuts	Contains Shellfish	Additional Pairing
Apps.								
Foie								
Scallops	√						!	
Carpaccio	√	(feta)		√				
Gnocchi		(asiago)			√			
Cakes				(aioli)			!	
Soups								
Mushroom	√		(pancetta)	√	√			
Butternut	√	(cream)	√			(pecans)		
Salads								
Caesar	(crouton)							
Country	√					!		
Goat Cheese	√		√	√	√			
Mesclun	√	√	√	√	√			
Spinach	√			√	√			
Entrees								
Short Ribs	(onion rings)	(puree)		√	(onion rings)			
Lobster	√			√			!	
Monkfish	√	(sauce & puree)		√	√			
NY Steak	√							
Game Hen	√			(sauce)				
Pork	√	√	√	√				
Veg Entrée	√		√	√				
Sides								
Smashed	√				√			
Fries	√	√	√	√	√			
Spinach	√	√	√	√	√			
Fingerling	√	√	√	√	√			
Brussel	√	(butter)	√	√	√	(pecans)		

AMERICAN BOUNTY DIETARY NEEDS CHART—PM

	Gluten-Free (omit)	Dairy-Free (omit)	Vegetarian	Contains Nuts	Additional Pairing
Dessert					
Cobbler	(biscuit)	(ice cream)	√		
Banana			√		
Choc Cake			√	!	
Profiteroles			√	!	
Bread Puddin			√		

Ice Creams: Vanilla, Caramel, Pistachio, Brown Sugar Rum
Sorbets: Ruby Sipper

The Heimlich maneuver is generally considered the best first aid for choking. Caution is recommended, however. Any administrator of first aid must, according to law, exercise "reasonable care and skill" or else be liable for negligence. It is recommended that dining room personnel be certified in the use of the Heimlich maneuver and in CPR. Be sure to know the location of the first aid posters in your establishment for reference.

ALLERGIES

Many guests have severe and deadly allergies to food items. Failing to provide the proper care or being negligent about communicating and documenting the allergy is a serious problem for the restaurant. The guest might suffer severe sickness and even death. When a guest asks you if a menu item contains a specific ingredient, you should immediately be on the alert for an allergy. If you suspect your guest is asking about dishes and ingredients because they have an allergy:

- Ask if he or she has an allergy. Most likely the guest will tell you any and all items to which he or she is allergic.

- Inform the kitchen staff and chef about the guest allergy. Failure to do so can result in death for the guest and a potential lawsuit for the server and restaurant.

- Enter the allergy into your point-of-sale system to create a paper trail and document the allergy.

- Modify each item the guest might eat that includes the allergen. Even if the server thinks that the menu item is safe, it must be modified for proper documentation.

- An epi pen is not a universal treatment for all allergies; in fact, it only provides temporary relief until medical assistance arrives.

- If a guest has ingested an allergen and is having an allergic reaction, call 911 immediately.

Fire Safety

FIRES ARE DANGEROUS FOR TWO MAIN REASONS: First, there are the injuries and destruction caused by the actual fire, and second, there is the panic that overcomes people in a fire that stops them from thinking and acting rationally. Practicing fire safety encompasses both preventing fires and doing the right thing if a fire breaks out.

The best way to fight fire is to prevent its occurrence. As with "incident" prevention, fire prevention depends on the application of common sense by everyone in the operation. Service personnel must be sure to follow these measures:

- See that ashtrays and receptacles are provided and used in all appropriate areas of the dining room.

- If candles or oil lamps are in use, watch to be sure that napkins or menus do not catch fire.

- Take care in cleaning ashtrays. They should never be emptied directly into wastebaskets or other rubbish containers.

- Never use defective electrical outlets. They should be reported to the manager.

- Never use an improper extension cord (too long or rated too low for intended use), or adapters (plugs have three prongs because the ground is important—do not attempt to defeat their purpose by using two-pronged adapters).

- Never overload a circuit.

- Report all frayed cords and loose connections to the manager.

- Take special care when lighting gas jets or alcohol burners on guéridons.

- Extinguish all flames before moving a guéridon in the dining room.

- Exercise extreme caution when flambéing food in the dining room. Always remove the pan from the flame before pouring the alcohol. Keep guéridons at a safe distance from the guests, draperies, sprinklers, and heat sensors.

Every establishment must have a prefire plan in effect. This is an orderly sequence of steps that is coordinated with the local fire department, in compliance with local building codes.

If a fire does break out, the emergency action taken in the first five minutes is extremely important. To be prepared in the event of a fire, the staff should be trained to know the floor plan of the area and the entire building, be familiar with exit routes and alternatives, and know the exact location of fire extinguishers and how to use them. Every member of the staff should be trained in assisting guests to leave the building safely in the event of an emergency.

If a fire breaks out:

- Do not panic.

- Pull the nearest fire alarm box.

- Notify the main switchboard and fire company as to the exact location and nature of the fire. Take the reservation list and logbook from the front desk if still used (it contains information about the number—and locations—of people inside the building).

- Assist guests to safety.

- Send someone to explain any special concerns to the firefighters when they arrive.

EMERGENCY PROCEDURES

In order to be prepared for any kind of accident or emergency, each food-service establishment must have its own specific course of action. As there is seldom time to consult a book when faced with an emergency, be aware beforehand of what to do and how to do it. In a dining room, there can be a variety of emergencies, some of which can be dealt with easily by defusing a situation with a calm, reasoned approach. Others are more serious and require additional action, and perhaps the involvement of others to keep everyone safe.

As soon as the emergency has been handled, write a report covering the details, location, and severity of the accident.

Emergency exits must be kept clear and the doors should open easily. Fire extinguishers should be in working order and easy to locate. Contact phone numbers should be kept current. These procedures and other general emergency strategies should be reviewed periodically.

Here are some general guidelines to follow whenever an emergency occurs:

□ Do not panic.

□ Call or send for help immediately and give explicit details as to the location and nature of the emergency. If calling emergency services, do not hang up until they do. More information may be required, or they may be able to offer some advice over the phone about temporary assistance to be administered until professional help arrives.

□ Do what needs to be done in a logical order.

□ When giving first aid, do not attempt more than you are qualified to do.

□ Do not endanger yourself or anyone else to save an object. Things can be replaced; people cannot.

Conclusion

A CLEAN AND SAFE DINING ROOM is the foundation of good service. Safety matters to everyone, from the owner to the staff to the guest. Maintaining food safety, preventing fires, avoiding accidents like slips, trips and falls, and having a plan in case of fires and other emergencies are all part of your professional training.

4

Preparing and Maintaining the Dining Room for Remarkable Service

THE FIRST STEP Toward Remarkable service is regular, conscientious attention to a full and complete mise en place. This French phrase means, "to put in place" and it includes all the activities that servers perform behind the scenes to ensure the quality of their guests' dining experiences. The tasks that go into preparing the dining room include arranging tables and setting tables as well as those commonly referred to as *sidework* such as cleaning and polishing tableware, restocking condiments, and folding napkins. In this chapter, we consider all aspects of preparing the restaurant for service, from the impression given at the front door through the impression in the fully set and properly organized dining room.

Opening the Dining Room

THE SUCCESS OF ANY RESTAURANT depends on everyone working together to assure that the entire dining room runs smoothly. There is nothing more frustrating for a server than having to wait: for coffee to brew, for more ice, for clean glasses, for folded napkins. This consideration for your colleagues creates a more productive environment and helps everyone do their best, especially when circumstances are most demanding.

A restaurant's workday can be very long, so some restaurants schedule opening and closing waiters. This system puts an emphasis on teamwork. The closing waiters rely on the opening crew, and the opening waiters depend on the closing crew. When everyone completes his or her work in a timely fashion, everyone benefits. Servers will find it easier to be efficient and attentive and guests will enjoy a higher level of service.

OPENING CHECKLISTS

The first step in preparing the dining room is cleaning it completely. Different surfaces require different cleaning techniques. Be sure to use the appropriate cleaning or sanitizing product and follow all safety guidelines and handling procedures. (*See Chapter 3 for more about cleaning the dining room.*)

The mise en place of the opening dining room crew includes setting up the dining room and making sure that everything used for service is clean or polished, readily available, easily accessible, and in ample supply.

Particular tasks to be performed as part of the opening mise en place include the following:

Sidework

- Wipe down menus and replace out-of-date lists.
- Wipe clean or replace table tents and other promotional materials as needed.
- Make sure any guest paging systems are charged and working.
- Check supplies for printing checks and replenish as needed (filled staplers, pens, pencils, etc.).
- Fold enough napkins for tables and resetting.
- Polish any serviceware, hollowware, flatware, china, and glasses.
- Set tables.

- Stock side stands.

- Stock backup paper for printing checks.

- Prep de-crumbing plates.

- Prep STP (silverware transport plates).

Pantry and Bussers

- Set up table-cleaning supplies, including clean towels and proper sanitizing solution in spray bottles.

- Prep coffee/tea area with items for brewing and serving coffee and tea (filters, pots, timers, creamers, sugar caddies, serving pots, etc.).

- Fill butter crocks if used and refrigerate.

- Line breadbaskets.

- Fill salt and pepper shakers, sugar caddies, etc. Wipe tops clean and close tightly.

- Cut lemons for tea.

- Prepare butter curls or pats for bread service.

- Line breadbaskets with napkins and fill baskets with bread.

- Prep any underliners and service plateware.

- Fill wine buckets with ice (just prior to service).

- Ice and fill water pitchers (just prior to service).

- Wipe and polish all coffee cups and saucers.

The pantry should be stocked according to the needs of the service. Items such as coffee, tea, and pitchers are typical pantry items.

KEEPING CHECKLISTS RELEVANT

As you may have surmised, having a list is not enough. You have to use it to keep track of what has been done and what is still needed. In addition, the list itself has to be kept up-to-date. Menu changes, the addition of tableside preparations, and changes to the interior of the restaurant can create new tasks, so the list should be under constant scrutiny.

Once the list is in place, it can become a tool to help even out the day's work. For example, if the pantry is never setup on time for lunch service, no matter who is doing the job, it is likely that there is just too much work for one person to do. The manager can use that insight to make some scheduling changes or to reassign tasks more appropriately. That might mean having some team members sharing tasks or it might mean scheduling a task for closing instead of opening.

Another way that some restaurants manage opening and closing tasks is to assign some servers to come before service to complete opening tasks. Another set of waiters comes in later, after the dining room is prepared, and then stays later to complete the closing tasks. The opening crew finishes their shift as soon as the last check is rung up and their last guest has left the dining room.

THE FRONT DOOR

That old saying about first impressions is true—they are important, and you only have one chance. The initial contact that potential guests have with your place of business must be welcoming and overwhelmingly positive.

Sometimes the restaurant is new to the guests, and sometimes the guests are making a return visit to a favorite place. How guests are treated (i.e., reservation taking, the first greeting, the manner in which they are seated, or the handling of special requests) in large part defines the quality of their dining experience. This is the moment when the restaurant and the dining room staff establish a relationship with the guest.

The actual front door is the very first physical contact guests have with a restaurant. Whether consciously or not, the guest will have a reaction to the condition of your entrance. These first impressions may determine whether or not a guest chooses to come inside the restaurant.

It is important that someone on the staff be responsible for the appearance and upkeep of the restaurant entrance. Make sure you attend to the following:

- Polish all hardware (such as door handles) so that they gleam.

- Keep glass on the door and windows sparkling clean.

- Remove anything that does not belong in the entrance area.

- Check trash from the sidewalk or floor.

- Put down floor mats when it is raining or snowy, and keep them clean.

THE RECEPTION DESK OR HOST STAND

A properly set-up reception desk makes it simple for you to take and review reservations and assign tables, greet, and seat guests (see Chapter 5). It should include the following:

- A hospitality handbook (Chapter 5, *page 123*)
- A reservations log (Chapter 5, *page 118*)
- Clean copies of all menus and menu covers and promotional materials
- Up-to-date listing of names and contact information for staff
- Emergency contact numbers (police, ambulance, fire, poison control, etc.)
- An up-to-date telephone directory
- Public transportation maps and schedules (if applicable)
- Plenty of pens and pencils
- A backup telephone answering machine

Not essential, but thoughtful things to have at (or near) the reception desk are maps of the area and local attractions (which can often be obtained at no cost from local real estate firms or the chamber of commerce); inexpensive umbrellas that can be given to guests in the event of an unexpected downpour; reading glasses; flashlights and extra batteries; umbrella bags and a wheelchair.

Arranging Tables and Chairs

LARGE-SCALE PRECISION STARTS with the placement of dining tables in the room. Each individual dining room will have its own characteristics that may dictate where tables can be placed. The goal is to arrange tables so that they are evenly spaced and in neat lines.

There should be enough room surrounding the table so that guests can get in and out of their seats with ease as well as to allow the waitstaff to walk around and between all of the tables. Spacing tables 4 feet apart generally leaves enough space for the guests with a foot-wide path between the chairs for servers.

Once the tables are in position, check to see that they are level. Some tables have screw glides on their base; these can be adjusted by loosening or tightening the screw. If the tables do not have screw glides, place wedges (also known as "shims") under the legs. If the base of the table is steady, tighten the center bolt that holds the tabletop to the base. If these tactics do not resolve the problem, it may be that the table should be removed from the dining room until it can be repaired.

Set chairs square to the table edge, with the front edge of the seat just touching, or "kissing," the tablecloth, if there is one, or pushed in even with the edge of the table, if there is no tablecloth.

Ensure that tables and chairs are straight and uniform, creating a clean line-of-sight for the guest.

TABLE NUMBERS

The system of numbers for tables and chairs in dining rooms is based on long experience and has been designed with a great deal of thought. It also includes a nod to a long-standing aversion to the number thirteen. Even if a restaurant has thirteen tables, it rarely has a table number thirteen. A common, but confusing practice is to skip from twelve to fourteen.

- Number the first row of tables using single digits and number the second row using the twenties to bypass "table number thirteen."

- Number the first table using a number that ends with a one, not a zero. The system makes it easier to count (i.e., third row, fourth table is thirty-four—not thirty-three as it would be if the tables in that row start at thirty).

SEAT NUMBERS

Seat numbers are usually assigned by the management with reference to one of two spots in the dining room: the front door or the kitchen door. The seat numbers at individual tables run as follows:

- Seat number one is the chair with its back to the door.

- Subsequent seats are counted clockwise from seat number one.

Often, tables are set at different angles, and a chair may not be in a direct line with the door. In such cases, the chair closest to the number one position, moving clockwise, is designated seat one.

Seat numbers remain constant, whether the seats are occupied or not. If three people are seated at a four-top, in seats one, three, and four, those numbers are used in ordering. This way, if a fourth person joins them and sits in seat two, there is no need to inform the entire staff of a new numbering system at that table.

Should a server need assistance in serving, it is more specific (and more courteous) to request of another server, "Please pour some more water at table twenty-three, seat three," than to point and say, "Pour some more water for the dark-haired man at that table over there."

Preparing Wares for Service

SERVICEWARE IS A GENERAL TERM for all utensils and wares used in the dining room to serve the guest, in addition to certain kitchen utensils such as carving knives and forks, ladles, and perforated spoons. The main classifications of serviceware are:

CHINA: plates of all sizes, dishes, cups, saucers, underliners

FLATWARE: knives, forks, and spoons, regardless of style or usage

GLASSWARE: items such as glass decanters, carafes, pitchers, and all drinking vessels used at a table or at the bar for beer, wine, and cocktails

HOLLOWWARE: technically, service items of significant depth or volume; more generally, large service items including platters, coffeepots, silver trays, etc.

FLATWARE

When you arrive in the dining room and are setting up for service, the flatware has probably already been washed. The way it was handled during washing can have an impact on what kind of preparation it may require before it is ready to go on the tabletop or into the side stand (see Chapter 3, *pages 54–55*).

- Work carefully to avoid contaminating or smudging flatware as you work with it.

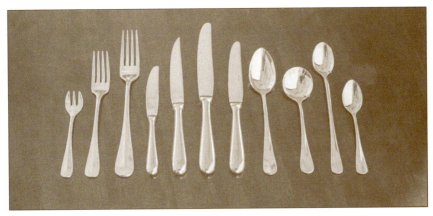

FROM LEFT TO RIGHT: seafood fork, appetizer fork, entrée fork, bread and butter knife, steak knife, entrée knife, appetizer knife, soup bowl spoon/AP (all purpose) spoon/dessert spoon/pasta spoon, bouillon spoon for a cup, iced tea spoon, coffee/tea spoon.

- Wear food-handling gloves or handle pieces with clean polishing clothes instead of bare hands if necessary.

- Handle pieces by the handles and avoid touching blades or bowls.

- If cleaned flatware is sorted into sleeves, handles down, put an empty sleeve over the flatware and flip it so the flatware now has its handles exposed. Or, empty the flatware from the sleeve onto a clean serviette on a flat surface or a tray.

Now you are ready to polish the flatware to remove any water spots or smudges. As you polish, remember to hold flatware by the handle.

1. Have a container of clean, hot water ready. You will dip the clean flatware into this hot water to dampen it.

2. Have clean, lint-free serviettes on hand to wipe the flatware dry and polish it.

3. If flatware is not already separated, separate it by type.

4. Dip a handful of clean flatware into the hot water and then transfer it to a clean serviette, held in the other hand.

5. Hold the flatware in the serviette with one hand. With the other, use the serviette to wipe the flatware dry and rub away any spots.

6. Place the polished flatware into a clean, dry container or separator.

Use a clean serviette to polish flatware as it is placed on the table.

Use a clean serviette to polish flatware as it is placed on the table.

Start with main-course forks and knives, since they are typically placed on the table first.

CARRYING FLATWARE

Once flatware is polished, it is ready to set the table or to be placed into side stands. Always carry or hold flatware by the handle to avoid cross-contamination. While you are preparing the dining room, you may find it more convenient to carry flatware on a tray since it is easier and more sanitary to find what you need rather than having to pick through a bundle of forks, knives, and spoons. During service, carry the flatware on a plate lined with a serviette. This also cuts down on noise in the dining room as well as prevents any smudges on the flatware.

SILVER-PLATED FLATWARE

If your flatware is silver plate, it requires slightly different care and handling than stainless steel. Silver can become tarnished easily, and because it is a soft metal, it develops fine scratches on the surface that can make it look dull.

To remove tarnish from silver, you may use a high quality paste or liquid polish and a soft, clean cloth to polish silver, or a treated silver cloth.

Another option for removing tarnish from silver-plated flatware is to use chemical polishing compounds such as sodium carbonate, sodium hydroxide, and

The electrolytic reaction between the aluminum in the pan and the silver sulfide on flatware removes the tarnish.

1. Partially fill a large aluminum pan with water.
2. Add 1 teaspoon of baking soda for every quart in the pan.
3. Bring the solution to a boil and then turn off the heat.
4. Add the silver and let stand a few minutes.
5. Remove the silver, wash it in hot sudsy water, rinse, and wipe dry.

Once you are finished, scour the aluminum pan with a soapy steel wool pad, or fill it with a solution of vinegar or cream of tartar and water and bring to a boil.

sodium carboxylates. These compounds are mixed into warm water in a container along with a piece of aluminum foil. The silver is dipped into the solution quickly, rinsed in clean water, and then wiped dry with a clean dry polishing cloth or serviette.

Once silver items are cleaned and polished, avoid touching them with bare hands, as oils from skin cause new tarnish spots. To prevent tarnish on silver-plated pieces that you do not use on a daily basis, wrap them in anti-tarnish cloth and then clear film wrap before storage. Be sure to cover the flatware completely with the anti-tarnish cloth before wrapping in plastic. If the plastic wrap stays in contact with the silver, the flatware may be marked by any wrinkles in the film.

Over time, fine scratches on silver-plated pieces will dull the finish. A burnishing machine restores the finish on silver plate by pushing a tiny amount of

Dangers of Using Ammonia

Some establishments add a few drops of ammonia to the soapy water to cut through residue and add to the brightness of flatware. This is *not* a recommended practice because so many of the disinfectants used in a restaurant have a chlorine base. When chlorine and ammonia compounds come in contact, they release toxic gases. The easiest way to prevent this occurrence is to keep ammonia products out of the kitchen.

the flatware's silver around, filling the abrasions with this smoothed bright layer of silver. Unfortunately, the use of burnishing machines can cause a gradual thinning of the flatware's silver plating, making it appropriate for only wares with adequately thick plating, and even then, should be done no more than twice a year.

GLASSWARE

Glassware contributes sparkle to the dining room, and tall, stemmed glasses add elegance.

In most establishments, glassware is washed, double-rinsed, steamed, polished, and dried with a clean, lint-free cloth before it is placed on the table or at the bar. To prepare enough glassware for a service period, you can set up a rack over a chafing dish filled with steaming water. For spot cleaning while you are setting up the tables, you can hold the glasses over a pitcher filled with hot water until they are evenly coated with a mist of steam.

Use lint-free cloths to dry and polish the glassware. Your linen company may rent polishing clothes suitable for this use. While you are polishing glassware, take special care to check the glasses for water spots, lipstick, and other foreign substances, as well as to look for cracks or chips. Dispose of any glasses that have a crack or chip. Always hold the glass up to the light to make sure spots are gone.

FROM LEFT TO RIGHT: carafe, all-purpose wine glass, white wine glass, red wine glass, champagne flute, water goblet, water glass, Collins glass.

Steaming and polishing glassware for service   Steaming and polishing glassware for service

Steaming and Polishing Glassware

1. Set up a glass rack or a perforated pan over steaming water.

2. Place the glasses in the rack or in the pan, stems up and let them steam until the entire glass is fogged. To ensure that the bottoms of the glasses gets steamy, place a napkin or polishing cloth over them.

3. Holding one corner of the polishing cloth in one hand, lift the glass at its base.

4. Gently push the other end of the polishing cloth into the bowl of the glass.

5. Hold the bowl of the glass with one hand, and with the other hand, polish inside and outside of the bowl of the glass with the other hand, keeping the cloth between your fingers and the glass.

6. The polished glasses are ready for setting tables and filling side stands.

STORING GLASSWARE

Cleaned and polished glasses can be placed upright on a side stand or shelf for short-term storage. We do not suggest placing them upside-down, unless you are sure the surface is clean. Glassware may be stacked with separators in the bar or pantry area, or they may be placed into hanging racks if they do not violate health codes in your area.

For longer-term storage, place glassware upside down in a rack of the correct size and keep the racks in a low-traffic area. Always place glassware in the correct-size rack; the stems should not extend above the lip of the rack.

HANDLING GLASSWARE

Whether you are setting tables before service or bringing either a drink or a fresh glass to a guest during dinner, always handle glassware so that your fingers are as far from the rim of the glass as possible, and never place your bare fingers inside a glass, whether you are polishing, serving, or clearing. You do not want to mar the gleam of the glassware with greasy fingerprints, in the case of a glass that is clean. In the case of a glass from which someone has drunk, you do not want to put yourself at risk of person to person cross-contamination.

The way you carry glasses depends on the type of restaurant, as well as whether the glass is full or empty, clean or dirty.

- ▫ Carry clean, empty stemless glasses to the table on a bar tray.
- ▫ Carry clean, empty stemware to the table on a bar tray or by hand (*see photo below*).
- ▫ Always clear dirty glasses on a bar tray.

Carrying Stemware by Hand

Slide the stem of the glassware between the fingers of the left hand.

Continue to slide more stemware into position, catching the base of each glass under those added earlier.

This technique promotes efficiency—at least eight glasses can be carried this way, and there is no tray to dispose of once the glasses have been placed on the table.

1. Hold your hand in front of you, with your palm facing up (use the left hand since you will be setting in the glasses from the right with the right hand Insert the stem of a glass between your index finger and thumb, so the glass is upside down and the base of the glass is resting on the fingers and palm of the hand. Slide the glass as far back as it will go so you can add another row of glasses.

2. Continue adding glasses between your fingers until you are holding four glasses. The second glass goes between the index and middle finger, the third between the middle and ring finger, the fourth between ring and the pinky finger. The base of each glass should go under the previous, locking them together.

3. For the fifth glass, insert the stem between the thumb and index finger and secure it in place by sliding the base of the fifth glass under the bases of the first and second glasses. Add the sixth glass in the same way, between the index and middle finger. Place the seventh glass between the ring and pinky finger. The eighth glass is placed between the ring and middle fingers. Flex your hand slightly and curl the tips of your fingers upward for a secure grip on the glasses.

CHINA

In an à la carte restaurant, much of the china is kept in the kitchen. Many shapes, colors, and materials are used in contemporary dining rooms, ranging from wood to metal, glass to acrylic. Treat these pieces carefully to avoid chipping or denting them. Some specific pieces are the responsibility of the servers. Observe the following standards and guidelines for handling china:

- As you place china on the table or in the side stand, check it carefully. Discard and replace any chipped or cracked china.

- Handle china so that you do not place the flat of your thumb or your fingertips on the rim or the interior of the plate.

- Wear gloves during setup to keep china clean and unsmudged.

- Stack china of the same size carefully so that the stack is stable.

CLOCKWISE FROM TOP LEFT: soup or pasta bowl on salad plate; bread and butter plate on appetizer plate; soup cup with handles on underliner; entrée bowl on entrée plate; espresso cup and saucer; coffee or tea cup and saucer

HOLLOWWARE

Hollowware pieces used in the dining room are usually specialty items: tea and coffee sets, covered serving dishes, tureens and bowls, ice buckets, oval platters and trays, café diablo sets, chafing dishes, punch bowls, suprême sets, and the like.

Often hollowware is made from some form of metal. Metal items are stronger and better able than ceramic items to withstand the impact and stress arising from frequent handling. In addition, the weight of a large metalware dish can be appreciably lighter than ceramic. The metal should be noncorrosive (i.e., does not react with acidic foods) and nontoxic (i.e., does not release any poisonous substances into foods) and should not transfer any odors to the food (e.g., stainless steel).

Some pieces may become very hot when filled with a hot food or beverage; handles should be wrapped with a serviette to protect the unwary from getting burned.

□ Clean and polish all hollowware. Some hollowware requires the use of specific serving pieces; a soup tureen calls for a ladle for instance; those pieces

FROM BACK LEFT: pepper grinder, hot water/coffee pitcher with lid, ice water pitcher, salt cellar, creamer, condiment bowl, sugar caddy

should be cleaned and ready to use. Store them with or near the hollowware they accompany.

◻ Clean and polish plate covers and stow them in the kitchen or pantry. Check the fit of plate cover. The bottom of the plate should fit securely into the top of the plate cover, if it is necessary to stack plates during service. Keep covers of different sizes separated.

◻ Component pieces may be sold separately or in sets; for example, soup tureens are available with or without covers. In using hollowware, make provisions for the appropriate accompanying serving utensils, such as spoons and ladles.

Setting the Table

LIKE FIRST IMPRESSIONS OF PEOPLE, the guest's first impression of the dining room—both the individual tables and the effect they create together—will dramatically influence the guest's dining experience.

When a guest walks into the room and everything is lined up perfectly, it provides a comfort level and confidence that their experience will be nothing short of remarkable. If there is an even number of guests at a table, one guest's forks should line up directly across from the opposite guest's knives and vice versa. If wine glasses are preset, they should almost make an X on the tabletop.

At one time, the presence of a gleaming white tablecloth was a sign that you were in a fine-dining establishment. Today, table surfaces may be left bare or be set very simply with a placemat even in the most luxurious restaurant setting. No matter what your establishment's style, the surface of the table is the first step in setting the table.

Proper table setting involves a number of elements: the linens, the flatware or silverware, the glassware, and the china. All require the careful attention of the professional server. Whatever the place setting consists of, there should be standards. Perhaps in your establishment, water glasses are placed one inch above the dinner knife, for example. With the tables lined up and all set in the same fashion, the room has a satisfying appearance. When the glasses or linens are placed in a haphazard manner, the table setting looks unfinished, even if all of the right pieces are on the table.

Preparing the Table

Before laying a tablecloth or setting the table, certain preparations should be made:

- Clean the tabletops.

- Level the tables by turning screw glides on the bases of adjustable tables, or by inserting pieces of cork or plastic wedges under legs of nonadjustable tables. Tighten the center bolt of pedestal tables. Never use matchbooks or wadded napkins—they offer only temporary relief, they are unsightly, and give the dining room an unprofessional appearance.

- Make sure there are no loose nails or splinters that might catch or snag the tablecloth.

- If two tables must be pushed together to accommodate a larger party, it must be level where the two tables meet. Cloth tables separately in case they need to be moved.

TABLE LINENS

Until modern times, tablecloths and napkins were traditionally made of linen, a natural fiber produced from flax. Today, man-made fibers are often substituted for, or combined, with natural ones. For example, many tablecloths are made of a blend of polyester and cotton. The term *linen* still applies in a general sense to all fabrics used at or on the table. Visa (polyester) leaves no lint, but is not absorbent.

Linen can be a significant expense in the restaurant, so it is important to handle linens properly. When linen is delivered to the restaurant, it has been pressed and folded by the linen company and wrapped in plastic. Observe the following guidelines:

◻ Inspect all tablecloths before using them in the dining room. Most linen companies will give a credit for linens that were received soiled, stained, shredded, or torn.

◻ Store linens on covered shelves, organized by size with the size tag facing out and label the shelves so that it is easy for everyone to find the right size quickly.

◻ Never store liquids above linens.

TABLECLOTHS

It is important to choose the proper tablecloth size. Table 4.1 provides standard tablecloth sizes to fit various dimensions of tables.

TABLE 4.1 Standard Table and Tablecloth (All Sizes in Inches)

Table Sizes	Tablecloth Sizes
30 × 26, 30 × 30, 30 round	42 × 42 minimum, 54 maximum
36 × 36, 36 round	48 × 48 minimum, 60 maximum
42 × 42, 42 round	52 × 52 minimum, 64 maximum
44 × 44	56 × 56 minimum, 66 maximum
48 round	60 × 60 minimum, 66 maximum
54 round	66 × 66 minimum, 72 maximum
60 round	72 × 72 minimum, 76 maximum
66 round	78 × 78 minimum, 84 maximum
72 round	84 × 84 minimum, 90 maximum
72 × 30 wide (6-foot banquet table)	52 minimum × 96
72 × 36 wide (6-foot banquet table)	60 minimum × 114
96 × 30 wide (8-foot banquet table)	52 minimum, × 96
96 × 36 wide (8-foot banquet table)	60 minimum, × 114

Statler tables (square four-tops that can be opened to a round six- to eight-top) should be clothed with this conversion in mind (the table should always remain covered, even when opened during service). Select a tablecloth that is appropriate for the fully opened size of the table (the drop—the distance the cloth should hang over the edge of the table—should extend to a point just even with the seat of the chair). The tablecloth should be aligned so that the table can be converted back to a four-top if needed, without having to relay the tablecloth.

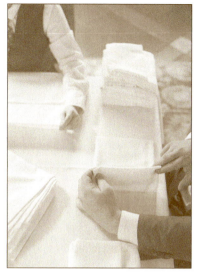

Folding napkins before service

NAPKINS (SERVIETTES)

Cloth napkins are usually folded in the style of the house. There are countless napkin folds. Generally speaking, the trend is toward simple table settings that are not compatible with the involved and elaborate folds of the past. Uncomplicated folds take less time and create a mood of simple elegance. Complicated folds involve extra handling by the waiter and may be perceived as being less sanitary. The final choice depends on the ambience and décor of the dining room, the skill of the staff, labor costs, the time available to actually do the folding, and compatibility with the other tabletop items. Cotton serviettes leave lint on guests' clothing whereas VISA will not, but are less absorbent.

Napkins are usually delivered to the restaurant already folded in halves or quarters, so the existing creases should be incorporated into the chosen fold design. This will save time and eliminate the need of having to work around the existing crease. After repeated use, the edges of cloth napkins tend to become uneven and the stitching around the edges can become loose or frayed. If possible, choose a fold that avoids exposing the edges of the napkin.

Folded napkins are also used in the dining room for ornamentation. For example, napkins can be folded to create a pocket for dinner rolls or bread presented "a la serviette." They can be folded to use for wine service or to wrap around service ware that might be too hot to hold, such as coffee pots, or that might drip, such as water pitchers.

DRESSING THE TABLE

The tabletop is the "canvas" for the meal. The way that the tabletop is prepared depends on your house style. Some tables are left bare intentionally; the service is set directly on an impeccably clean tabletop. Placemats can be set at individual places. For many restaurant patrons, however, a table that has been clothed in linen remains a symbol of a fine dining establishment.

SILENCE CLOTH

A silence cloth (*molleton*) makes the table feel plush, soft, and luxurious. This smaller cloth is placed on the table first and is then covered with a second larger tablecloth. Silence cloths cushion the noise of plates and cutlery placed on the table during service. Besides preventing noise, a silence cloth protects the table-top, soaks up spills, and prevents the top cloth from sliding. In addition, the silence cloth keeps the bare tabletop from being exposed when you must change the tablecloth during service.

If there are no spills, the silence cloth can be used for several seatings. However, any linen used in the dining room carries some cost, so its use is more common in fine dining restaurants. As an alternative to a silence cloth, some tables have permanent cushioning on the tabletop to serve as silencer.

LAYING A TABLECLOTH

Place tablecloths on the table according to your house standards. Some restaurants call for the peak of the center crease to be pointing up, toward the ceiling, regardless of whether the hem is facing in or out, while others call for the hems to be facing in, no matter which direction the peak of the crease is facing. Some establishments pay a premium to have linens pressed according to their specific requirements while others iron the creases out of the cloths after they are on the table rather than risk wrinkling the cloth while transferring it to the table after ironing.

When you put two tables together for a large party, cloth the individual tables separately instead of using a single large cloth. That gives you more flexibility in the event that tables need to be moved or separated for smaller parties during service.

No matter which standard your establishment observes, it is important that all of the tables be clothed consistently for the most elegant look in the dining room.

| Unfold the tablecloth across the width of the table. | Hold one edge of the cloth, and then release the other side to catch the far end of the table. | Pull one side of the cloth toward you, stopping when the crease reaches the center of the table. | Smooth and straighten the cloth, ensuring that the crease is at seat number one. |

1. Stand at the table with seat number one directly to your right hand or left hand.

2. Unfold the tablecloth to its widest point.

3. Hold one edge of the cloth with the hem down (this side will lay along the side on which you are standing).

4. Reach across the table releasing the other folds of the cloth to catch onto the far side of the table.

5. Pull the one edge of the cloth toward you as the cloth opens up, stopping when the center crease reaches the center of the table and the crease will be at seat number one.

THE COVER

The French term *couvert* or "cover" has a few distinct applications in the dining room. A place setting intended for use with a specific type of meal and service is called a *cover* and refers to the flatware, glassware, and china that are set for the guest. The term can also refer to the number of guests at a table or the total number of guests for a service period, or it may refer to a minimum amount charged to a guest who does not order a full meal as in "cover charge".

Throughout this chapter, the word *cover* refers to a place setting. The cover determines what goes on the table, as well as the pieces you should stock in your side stand or prepare as setups in the pantry to ensure smooth, efficient service.

SPACING AND ALIGNING COVERS

When you set the tables during opening mise en place, observe the following standards:

- Allow a minimum of eighteen inches for each setting.

- Settings on two-tops (or deuces) may be positioned banquette-style (side-by-side) to allow the guests to face the dining room or at right angles or across from the table so the guests can face each other.

- The napkins for seat number one and the seat directly across from seat number one should be on the center crease of the tablecloth.

- At tables with an even number of guests with the guests are seated directly across from one another, the flatware should be aligned so one guest's fork is directly across from the opposite guest's knife, whether the table is round or square.

- On rectangular or square tables, arrange the bottom edge of all flatware, napkins, and cover plates in a straight line, about one half inch or a decrumber's width from the edge of the table.

Set the appetizer knife to the right of the dinner knife.

Place the water goblet to the right of the cover, above the dinner knife.

Use the thumb as a guide to align the bottom of flatware.

- On round tables, arrange the bottom edge of flatware, napkin, and show plates in a straight line, rather than following the curve of the table; the outer-most pieces of flatware will be closer to the edge of the table than the plate, which is in the center of the setting.

- If the cover includes preset wine glasses, they should almost make an X on the tabletop.

Many restaurants opt for a streamlined cover that includes only a main course fork and knife, a napkin, and a water glass. In fine dining establishments, the server is expected to bring additional flatware and glassware to the table in response to the guest's order. Some restaurants prefer to include flatware for appetizers or wine-glasses for a more elaborate cover. Show plates, also known as *chargers*, may also be part of the setting. The meal period affects the cover as well; breakfast service might call for a cup and saucer to be included, for example.

Each establishment has its own guidelines for the exact placement of napkins and flatware, depending on the style of service and complexity of settings. Some may have settings placed as close as one finger's width from the edge of the table; others require more space. To ensure adequate space for the china, make certain that the innermost flatware leaves enough space for the largest plate to be served, which typically has a 12-inch diameter.

- Place show plates first, if you are using them, in the center of the place setting and about 1 inch from the edge of the table. Position the show plates so that logos or designs are correctly displayed.

- Place the folded napkin according to house standards. The most common placement is in the middle of the place setting directly in front of the guest, between the fork and knife, one inch from the edge of the table, or in the center of the show plate, if you use one.

PLACING FLATWARE

Flatware should be positioned in the opposite order in which it is to be used; for example, utensils to be used first are placed on the inside, 12'" apart, with flatware for the succeeding courses placed on the outside.

In the United States, it is traditional to place forks with the tines facing up, but in Europe, the tines sometimes face down to display the silversmith's water-mark. Knives are placed on the right with the cutting edge facing to the left. When a guest picks up the knife with the right hand, it is already in the natural position for proper use.

- Place the main-course fork six inches to the left of the center of each place setting (or ¾ inch away from the show plate) followed by the main course knife, placed six inches to the right of the center (or ¾ inch away from the show plate).

- Set the appetizer fork to the left of the main-course fork and the appetizer knife to the right of the main-course knife, if your cover includes appetizer flatware. Note, however, that oyster or cocktail forks are placed on the right side of the setting, since most guests pick up seafood shells in their left hands.

- Some restaurants align the tines of the forks and the tips of the knives; others align the bottom of the handles.

- Place spoons to the right side of the knives, with the bowl of the spoon face up.

PLACING BREAD-AND-BUTTER PLATES

Place the bread-and-butter plate (B&B plate) to the left of the place setting. Some establishments call for the top of the B&B plate to be in line with the tines of the main course fork; others may position it so that the bottom of the B&B plate is aligned with the base of the tines. There are several acceptable positions for the butter knife: parallel to the forks with the blade facing away from the center of the plate, or perpendicular to the forks across the top of the B&B plate with the blade toward the center of the B&B plate.

PLACING GLASSWARE

Position glassware to the right of the cover, above the tip of the dinner knife. When you are setting more than one glass for the cover, arrange the glasses in a line that angles from the tip of the knife toward the center of the table. The glasses should be arranged in order of service from right to left in a line that extends up from the point of the dinner knife. If the red wine is to be served after the white wine, place it to the left and slightly above the white wineglass.

If a water glass is to accompany the wineglasses, it is generally placed just above the dinner knife with the wineglasses angled slightly above from the right to the left. In Europe, it is common to place the water glass to the left and slightly above the wineglasses with champagne, tulip, or port glasses positioned to the left of the water glass. (For additional information on glassware, see Chapters 7 and 8.)

COVERS AND SETUPS

A cover, for our purposes in the chapter, refers to the flatware, china, and glassware that is already on the table when the guest is seated. A setup refers to the flatware, china, or glassware required for a special dish or presentation. If your restaurant serves specialty items that call for specific setups, you should prepare them in advance so that there is no delay while you find the correct fork. This may be part of the work done in the waiter's station or pantry, or you may prepare setups and store them in side stands or on the guéridon.

Simple à la carte cover

Standard Covers

The following list describes and illustrates some standard covers used in restaurant service:

A simple cover for à la carte service includes main course fork and knife, water glass, bread-and-butter plate, butter knife, and napkin. Additional flatware and glassware is placed according to house standards. For example, some restaurants preset both appetizer and main course forks and knives and also include a wineglass as well as a water glass. Some include a show plate.

Full dinner (banquet) cover for American service includes all flatware, and glassware for the entire menu, with the exception of coffee cups.

Full dinner (banquet) cover for French/Russian, platter, or family service includes all flatware and glassware as well as the china for the entire menu. The china is stacked at the place setting. A "full stack" might include an entrée plate on the bottom, salad, or appetizer plate on top of entrée plate, and soup cup with an underliner on top of the appetizer plate.

Breakfast cover includes main course fork and knife, coffee spoon, coffee cup and saucer (or mug), napkin and sugar caddie. Creamers should be filled and placed as guests are being seated.

Standard Setups

Here are some setups for special presentations or foods:

Bouillabaisse is served on large soup plate on a large underliner. The setup includes a soupspoon (set on the right side of the cover), and smallplate or bowl for discarded shells (set on the left side or just above the cover).

Breakfast cover

Caviar is served in a small bowl that is either chilled or set in ice accompanied by toast points in a basket and a plate of butter. The setup includes a small plate and a knife made of mother of pearl, gold, or horn, placed on the right side of the cover.

Finger bowls are set up as follows: small bowl on an underliner (with a doily if necessary). To prepare finger bowls for the guest, fill the bowl one third with warm water and add slice of lemon in water. Set this to the left of the cover.

Half grapefruit is served in a bowl on an underliner. The setup calls for a citrus spoon set to the right of the cover and a teaspoon, set to the right of the citrus spoon, with a sugar bowl or sugar caddy.

Lobster is served in a large, deep plate. The setup includes a lobster fork and lobster cracker set to the right of the cover and a finger bowl set to the left of the cover.

SALT AND PEPPER

In the 1800s, guests at banquets were provided with their own salt cellar at the top right of their place setting. At that time, no ground pepper would have been served. Later, when salt and pepper shakers began appearing on the table top, the pepper was placed to the left of the salt, leaving the salt in its traditional spot on the right. Most restaurants still observe this tradition and place the salt and pepper shakers so that the salt is to the right of the pepper in terms of the guest seated at seat number one.

Like most condiments, one set for every four guests is customary. If more than two sets are placed on the table, salt should always be on the right side as the guest faces the table. For large round tables such as a 72-inch round for six to ten guests, place the condiments within reach of the guests rather than in the center of the table. For a table this large, place three or four sets of salt and pepper (and other condiments) on the table so that guests will not have to interrupt the other guests to "pass the salt, please."

Stocking Side Stands, Waiter Stations, and Guéridons

A PROPERLY STOCKED SIDE STAND HOLDS all the tabletop and service items that a server might need during service for his or her station right in the dining room, so that servers can stay in the dining room with the guests, rather than dashing to the dishroom for glassware or flatware.

There is typically a side stand for every station in the dining room, and it may be the location for the POS system. A waiter's station or pantry, on the other hand, is used by all the waiters; there is typically someone assigned to the pantry station throughout service. It is often used to store service items, as well as to brew and dispense coffee and tea, fill water pitchers, hold backups of salt, sugar, pepper, and even cleaning supplies. There may be some refrigeration in the pantry to hold butter, cream, milk, bottled water, and condiments including mustard, ketchup, or mayonnaise. In some operations, you will find the POS system located in the waiter station, instead of in the dining room itself.

Side stands should be set for the specific needs of a dining room and might include flatware, glassware, and condiments.

A guéridon or cart is generally used for tableside service of foods as well as for opening and decanting wine (see Chapter 8 for more about wine service). Depending on how it is used in the dining room, it may include cooking units, flatware and china for serving foods, a cutting board and knife, or other items as required.

Each dining room will have its own specific needs when it comes to stocking and setting up a side stand, guéridons, or the pantry, so a standard checklist and even a photo or diagram of the proper set up is helpful for everyone. It should note the items and quantities for each item as well as information concerning where it should be stored in or on the stand. Setting up all of the side stands so that they are all the same way makes it easier for you and for everyone else in the dining room.

At the start of the shift, you should check to be certain that the side stand or the pantry is clean, including all shelves and drawers. Take an inventory and then gather any additional items that you may need and put them into their proper positions.

TABLETOP ITEMS

The side stand should have backups for all items that are on the tabletop. At the very least, you will need the following:

- Salt and pepper shakers
- Cleaned and polished glassware (water and all-purpose glasses are most common)
- Clean and polished flatware
- Napkins, folded in the house style

Other tabletop items you might store in a side stand include lined baskets for bread, water pitchers, peppermills, doilies, candles, and matches.

SERVICE ITEMS

The list of service items you might need at a side stand depends on the style of service in your establishment, as well as the requirements of the individual menu items. Among the basic requirements are the following:

- Plates, including a plate for de-crumbing and silver transport plates (STP)
- Serviettes, folded into pockets for STP and stacked to use for wine service or as needed

- Tongs or serving spoons and forks for serving bread or rolls

- Folders for check presentation

- Dupe pads or replacement paper for point-of-service (POS) system

Many restaurants fold a napkin or serviette to form a pocket that is placed on a large plate and used to transport flatware to the table during service, known as a silverware transport plate, or STP. Insert the blades of the knives into the pocket; place the utensils on top of the pocket. The pocket fold also serves to differentiate the flatware plate from the de-crumbing plate.

You may also need a knife for cutting items tableside; peppermills; coasters for wine bottles; graters for cheese or chocolate; a candle and candlestick holder and decanters for wine; small dishes or plates to hold dipping oil; and so on.

Condiments include things like salt, pepper, mustard, relish, mayonnaise, conserves that are meant to add a different flavor to the foods, as well as sweeteners and cream for coffee. These items are not added by cooks in the kitchen; instead, they are brought to the table by the server and added to the dish by the guest. The term covers many different foods, many of which require careful handling in order to keep them fresh, safe, and wholesome throughout service.

Some condiments, such as sugar or salt, can be held safely at room temperature and can be stocked in side stands in the dining room. Those that require refrigeration should be stored in a pantry area. For more about condiments and food safety concerns, see pages 60–62.

TRAY STANDS

Tray stands, or jack stands, may be part of the dining room's mise en place. In some establishments, there are defined spots for tray stands to be set up. In others, servers store the tray stands in the waiter's station and carry them to the table just before or at the same time that the tray of dishes arrives at the table.

They may be made of either wood or metal, but neither is especially elegant to look at. Clean them well before each shift. Fine dining establishments and bistros often cover tray stands with a 60-inch tablecloth for a neater appearance.

Some tray stands are equipped with a small shelf midway between the floor and the top, but avoid placing any items on that shelf because whatever you put there will invariably fall off if you move the tray stand.

Ambience

THE AMBIENCE OF A DINING ROOM is the way the dining room "feels" to the guests. It is the result of bringing together several elements—lighting, décor, flowers, temperature of the room, china and glassware patterns, uniforms, linens, or music—in order to enhance the guest's experience. Once the tables and chairs are arranged and the covers set, it is time to review the entire dining room to make sure it is as inviting and comfortable as possible.

FLOWER ARRANGEMENTS

Freshly cut flowers can enliven a dining room, but—if not maintained—the effect will be exactly the opposite. A few large arrangements in the room may look better than a vase on every table. In many cases, deuces cannot spare the room for flowers—except for a very small vase, possibly containing a single flower.

In selecting flowers for the dining room, consider fragrance as well as appearance. Some fragrances do not blend well with foods, and some are so overwhelming that they could disturb your guests or make them sneeze. Consider the height of any flower arrangements or centerpieces on the table. Your guests should be able to see each other without having to crane their necks or peer around the arrangement.

A great variety of materials may be used in flower arranging, including branches, berries, leaves, colorful fruit, and even decorative products from the vegetable garden. Properly dried materials can also be used. The charm of an arrangement is a result not only of its composition, but also of the variety of shapes, sizes, colors, and textures of its assorted materials. Avoid potted plants at the table, as they contain soil that sometimes attracts small mites or bugs.

The following list features flower varieties that are long lasting, relatively inexpensive, appropriately sized, and nearly fragrance-free:

- Alstroemeria (Peruvian lilies)
- Smaller chrysanthemums (home-grown varieties can have strong scents, but commercial varieties generally do not)
- Miniature carnations
- Dwarf anthurium
- Smaller haliconias (such as parakeet)

EDIBLE FLOWERS

Edible flowers are very popular both on the plates and as part of the tabletop, but it is important to note that not all flowers are safe to eat. Some flowers are inherently toxic (i.e., lily of the valley and foxglove). Some are sprayed with poisonous compounds or have been treated with systemic poisons, which cannot be washed off. Some are fertilized with untreated waste. For all these reasons, only flowers grown specifically for consumption should be used as garnishes.

CARING FOR CUT FLOWERS

Proper care of cut flowers will extend their beauty and life.

- ◻ Upon delivery, place cut flowers in tepid water in a cool room or refrigerator.
- ◻ Check arrangements daily and change the water every day or two to keep them smelling fresh.
- ◻ Nightly refrigeration will also help extend the life of most floral arrangements.
- ◻ Store flowers away from food, especially apples—they give off ethylene gas, a natural ripening agent that causes flowers to fade prematurely.
- ◻ Crush hardwood stems slightly with a hammer so they can absorb more water.
- ◻ Split soft stems about one-half inch with a knife or scissors.

Soft-leafed flowers (such as poppies), wild flowers, flowers that have wilted may be revived if you dip the tips of their stems into boiling water for a few seconds. Be careful to shield the heads and blossoms with paper or cloth.

The stamens of some lilies can stain linens; clip them out of the flower before placing on the tables. Peruvian lilies (alstroemeria) look good and last a long time—but they contain a sap that can cause severe skin irritation. Everlastings (*limoneas*) such as statice and heather can be used dry in combination with silk flowers, or simply be allowed to dry in an arrangement—in which case they will last up to three weeks.

LIGHTING

Light has a great effect on our moods. Each of the various forms of light (fluorescent or incandescent lights, gas lamps, candles, or natural sunlight) has its own quality that can be featured effectively in the dining room. Lighting can be used to attract attention to a display or other areas, make a space feel larger or smaller, and indicate

5

Reservations and Waiting Lists

RESERVATIONS, GREETING, AND SEATING the guest are the first opportunity you have to deliver remarkable service. Reservations are often a part of a truly outstanding experience in a restaurant; however, not all restaurants require them. Even restaurants that do ask for reservations can occasionally handle guests who arrive without them. Deciding how to handle reservations is a management decision, but if it is the policy of the restaurant, it is important that the reservation experience be on par with the rest of the dining experience. From the moment guests arrive at the door, the professional server strives to maintain the caliber of the experience. The way you greet a guest, the table you seat them at, even the direction their chairs face can be a matter of concern to the guest, and, therefore, to you.

Reservations

IN AN IDEAL WORLD, all restaurants would be so busy every day that they could operate on a first-come, first-served basis and do away with reservations altogether. In that same ideal world, considerate customers would happily call restaurants in advance to ask what time would be convenient to arrive so as not to overburden the chef and service staff.

We do not, alas, work in an ideal world. It often seems that everyone on the planet wants to dine between 8:00 and 8:30 on Saturday evening. Consequently, the vast majority of fine dining and bistro establishments must grapple with the issues of taking reservations. The question of whether or not to accept reservations is not a simple one to answer, but it is likely you will have to deal with it eventually. Consider the following factors when making this decision.

STYLE OF RESTAURANT

Is the style of your place formal or casual? The fancier the restaurant, the more likely it is that you will need to accept reservations. A couple planning an anniversary dinner will often choose a more formal restaurant, and almost certainly will not be interested in waiting an hour for a table to open up. Conversely, when you and your friends are going out for Mexican food as a group, it is usually fine if you wind up waiting in the bar of the cantina, drinking margaritas and eating chips and salsa.

NUMBER OF SEATS AND PROJECTED COVERS

The number of seats in the dining room is usually decided early in the planning stages of a restaurant and is integral to the type of service offered. A casual restaurant tends to have more seats with tables closer together; the opposite is true for restaurants that are more formal. A large, casual restaurant tends to turn tables faster, and usually has a table coming available soon; thus, reservations might not be necessary. However, in a formal restaurant where people usually take more time to eat and the number of seats is limited, tables don't free up as quickly—this might be the right place to take reservations.

Like the number of seats, the number of reservations (or covers) you are anticipating for the shift is important. A high volume of tables that turn over quickly might not require a reservation policy.

POPULARITY

The more famous or visible a restaurant or restaurateur, the higher the demand for tables. For instance, if Tom Collichio opens a restaurant in your neighborhood, you would want to know the reservations policy before getting your hopes up for a table. Meanwhile, a restaurant with a talented but as-yet-unknown chef might open on a first-come, first-served basis, then start taking reservations as the place gets more popular and the host finds it necessary to spread the diners across the period of service rather than taking them whenever they want to come in.

OTHER CONSIDERATIONS

If you're next door to a theater, there might be an entire seating of the restaurant that leaves before 8 P.M. and one that comes after the show. Handled correctly, the restaurant can have the pre-theater, dinner, and post-theater crowds arranged into three seatings. Being near a convention center can make a difference as well, so you should know when a show or group is coming into town and be ready for more business than usual.

Most restaurants want to have a reasonable estimate of how many diners to expect on a given day. A reservations system can help with staffing, purchasing provisions, planning the menu, and general estimation of costs. Of course, it is often impossible to be exact—some customers, inexplicably and without notice, fail to appear (or show up late), while spur-of-the moment arrivals can increase numbers at unexpected times.

Different establishments have different reservation systems. Many restaurants continue to use a physical reservation book either exclusively or as a supplement and backup for computerized systems in case of crashes.

One step up from the pencil-and-paper method is to input the information into a spreadsheet program. You could also link a spreadsheet to your database in order to keep track of regular customers' birthdays, anniversaries, likes, dislikes, and dietary restrictions. The more information you have at your fingertips, the higher the level of hospitality that you can provide for your guests.

There are computer programs that are specifically designed to accept and keep track of restaurant and hotel reservations. Your own staff can maintain some of them. In addition, there are web-based companies that can manage your reservations while maintaining a database of your guests' pertinent information, such as mailing addresses, birthdays, allergies, personal preferences, and so on. The downside of such systems is lack of complete control and privacy.

TABLE 5.1 Advantages and Disadvantages of Accepting Reservations

Advantages of Accepting Reservations	Disadvantages of Accepting Reservations
Helps an establishment estimate customer flow. Better for kitchen and dining room staffs, as well as guests.	Extra staff needed to work the reservation desk and make reconfirmation calls.
Some guests feel more comfortable when they have a "guaranteed" table.	No-show problem skews customer estimates.
Allows more efficient table assignments.	Requires effort on part of customers who might rather just drop into an establishment at the last minute.
Allows restaurant to become familiar with customers' names and eating preferences.	
Easier to deal with special requests (birthdays, special menus, allergies) at the time of reservation rather than after the customer walks in.	
Phone numbers and e-mail addresses available for future promotions, in case guests leave something, etc.	

It is not necessary to make a firm commitment to the taking either of reservations or of not taking reservations. Some restaurants use both methods. Reservations may only be required for large groups—for example, Carmine's in New York City only takes reservations for parties of six or more. Table 5.1 lists the advantages and disadvantages of accepting reservations.

When Reservations Might Be Necessary

FINE DINING AND BISTRO RESTAURANTS need to weigh the advantages and disadvantages of taking reservations. Some fine dining "destination restaurants" are 30 minutes or more by car or public transportation from residential areas, for example. Their managers cannot expect guests to travel such distances on the off chance they may find a table. Reservations are necessary in such cases. In addition, the exigencies of a fine dining restaurant require knowing in advance roughly how many guests to expect. Table 5.2 lists the advantages and disadvantages of not accepting reservations.

TABLE 5.2 Advantages and Disadvantages of a No-Reservations Policy

Advantages of a No-Reservations Policy	Disadvantages of a No-Reservations Policy
Reduces personnel needed to staff the phones.	Susceptibility to the Yogi Berra syndrome: "Nobody goes there anymore because it's too crowded." That is, crowds can scare away newcomers.
Maximizes table use through constant turnover. Tables do not sit empty between seatings.	An establishment can reach the decibel level of a sheet metal plant with all of the voracious cocktail-sipping folks waiting at the bar.
Eliminates dreaded and costly no-show problem.	Customers might get tired of waiting and leave—or worse, tell friends not to bother.
May increase bar sales. Even if guests waiting for tables do not buy an extra drink, a busy bar creates a lively ambience and attracts more bar business.	Some customers will not patronize a restaurant if they are not guaranteed a table.
In some cases, it lends a more casual and spontaneous aura to an establishment.	The service staff may feel compelled to rush diners to free up tables.
It is a more democratic system; fewer complaints about favoritism.	Additional space is needed for people to wait, especially in cold weather.
Hordes of people anxiously standing outside of your establishment gives passersby the impression that you must be "a find."	

WHEN RESERVATIONS ARE UNNECESSARY

If a restaurant is so successful that it cannot be bothered with such trivialities, its staff may not have to think about reservations. Some restaurants take customers in the order in which they arrive at the front door. These restaurants are so busy that reservations are unnecessary. This works for bistro/trattoria places like P.F. Chang's, The Cheesecake Factory, and Carnegie Deli in New York City and Le Bar Lyonnais in Philadelphia. Most of us are not in that situation.

In addition, many casual and ethnic restaurants dispense with the formality of a reservations system. This approach sometimes forces guests to wait for an available table (see Waiting Lists on page 132).

TAKING RESERVATIONS

The reservations procedure should be standardized to eliminate confusion and overlooked items. Use of a reservation checklist guarantees that all essential information is secured.

In many restaurants, reservations are handled just inside the front door (at the reception desk, the maître d's podium, or the front desk), either in person or over the phone. In some places, reservations are made by phone to a reservations department that is not even a part of the dining room. Indeed, it might not even be in the same building—they may be made over the Internet. No matter how the reservation process is managed physically, one must never forget that it is the first opportunity to impress the guest with first-class service. It is management's responsibility to make sure that everyone who might be called upon to take a reservation is trained, not only in the use of the reservations system and all of the policies and procedures involved but also in proper telephone technique and etiquette (see Table 5.3).

PHONE ETIQUETTE

The reservationist's demeanor on the telephone is every bit as important as that of the maître d' in the dining room. If the receptionist has poor reservation-taking skills, the caller is likely to be left with negative feelings about the establishment. On the other hand, if the receptionist sounds welcoming, helpful, and intelligent, the guest will look forward to a pleasant experience.

The first way a reservationist can make a guest feel welcome is by answering within the first three rings of the phone.

To minimize the chances of an error, every restaurant should have a written, standardized greeting for anyone who may answer the phone, acknowledging the time of the day and stating the name of the establishment and the first name of the person speaking. For example:

"Good morning, Restaurant Z—Adam speaking."

Repeat information back to the guest when you are taking a reservation:

"So, that's five people for dinner at seven-thirty on Friday, December fifth, for Marian Evans; is that correct?"

In addition, whenever a credit card number is involved, the entire number should be confirmed, including expiration date and security code.

It is essential that reservationists be familiar with the names of important or repeat customers. If a name is not familiar, try to write it down and then use it while speaking with the guest.

TABLE 5.3 Reservation Checklist

NUMBER OF GUESTS	How many in the party? This allows you to consider tables that are available before taking the caller's name, permitting the most efficient use of available seating and making maximum use of the dining room's capacity.
DATE AND TIME	Note the date and time. If the caller's request is not available, discuss alternatives. If your restaurant has a waiting list, offer that to the client. Explain the procedure to the caller, saying that if a cancellation arises during the reconfirmation process the person will be called.
SPECIAL REQUESTS	Some guests prefer certain tables or servers, or may wish to order a special dessert (such as a birthday cake) or wine. When such requests can be honored, they should be noted here.
GUEST NAME	Last name, first initial.
GUEST TELEPHONE	Ask for a daytime number when you can call to confirm. Some restaurants ask guests to call to confirm (see pages 123–124).
RESERVATION NUMBER	If using a computerized system, make sure that the guest notes this number in case any changes are needed later on. These numbers can help in finding solutions when seating errors have been made.
DATE RESERVATION TAKEN	This can be useful in reconstructing details that the guest or restaurant may have confused. It can also be useful when you have to decide which of two reservations should get the window table that both requested. The guests who called first should get it.
YOUR NAME	The reservationist should leave his or her initials next to the party's name in case questions arise.

Putting people on hold can be annoying, but if it is unavoidable, always ask politely,

"May I put you on hold?"

It is extremely rude to cut guests off before they have a chance to reply to that question. If it looks as if it might be a long wait, ask callers if it is all right to call them back. When picking up a line on hold, say,

"Thank you for holding; how may I help you?"

RESERVATIONS FOR EFFICIENCY

The primary goal of the reservationist is to fill the dining room to capacity, while staggering the timing of the seatings to ensure the best service from the kitchen

TABLE 5.4 Reservation Log

Time	Number	Name	Phone	Table
5:30	2–3			
5:30	2			
5:30	4			
5:30	4			
6:00	2–3			
6:00	2			
6:00	4			
6:00	4			
6:00	6			
6:30	2–3			

and dining room staff. In many restaurants, several people may take reservations, but they may not all understand the intricacies involved in attaining this goal. It is as important to count chairs as it is to count tables. On a busy night, you do not want to book all deuces at four-tops (except on nights like Valentine's Day, when it becomes necessary).

The reservationist has a responsibility to accommodate as much business as the staff can efficiently serve. To assist the reservationists in understanding the maximum seating capacity, it can be helpful to print the times and number of covers in the reservation book in advance (see Table 5.4). It also may be helpful to indicate whether tables can be moved to accommodate different-size groups. If this information is written in advance, then all reservationists know that if they take a reservation for three people at a table for four, they have lost revenue for the restaurant. If, however, they know they can comfortably seat three people at a deuce, and take the reservation in a slot for two to three guests, they have increased revenue. Computer systems can be programmed in a similar manner. Nevertheless, the reservationists need to be aware of the room's flexibility.

If there are no available tables, always mention that guests sometimes cancel their reservations and ask for a number where the caller may be reached if a table becomes open.

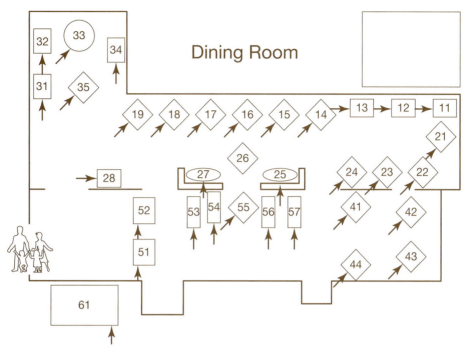

Dining room floor plan, showing sections and stations

TRAFFIC CHART

deuce	3	4	5	6	7-10	TOTAL
6.00	IIII	I	II	IIII		34
6:30	IIII	IIII	I	IIII	IIII I II 1-10, 1-7 91	
7:00	0					
7:30	II	I	8			
8:00	II	I	I	14		
8:30	III	I	II	I	22	
9:00	I	4				
9:30	I	2				
10:00	IIII	I	12			
10:30	III	II	14			
11:00	III	IIII	26			
11:30	II	II	I 1-8	26		
TOTAL	253					

Dining room traffic chart

Combining the covers list with a floor plan of the room, and writing in the times the tables are reserved or seated, will help in keeping track of which tables are available (and at what times) for a second or third seating. Informing the chef of the total number of guests expected does not provide enough information to prepare for the evening's business. For example: A restaurant seats 130, and has 253 reservations. The chef might think that means two seatings—and send part of the staff home early. However, if the restaurant has a theater crowd, there might be 125 guests between 6:00 and 6:30, 50 between 8:00 and 9:30, and 78 between 10:00 and 11:30. A traffic chart like the example shown in Table 5.4 tells the kitchen to allow for some prep time before the late-night rush.

TIMING RESERVATIONS

How do reservationists stagger seatings to achieve a smooth flow in the dining room and kitchen? They take into consideration many factors: the menu, the number of courses offered, the style of service, the type of client attracted (at lunch and at dinner, pre-theater or pre-movie crowd), the ambience of the restaurant, and so on.

Your guests may know exactly what time they want a reservation, but you need to take into account the entire dining room, not just one table. Determining the timing and number of reservations you can accept for a specific evening calls for a thorough understanding of your menu, your service style, and about how long it takes parties of different sizes to dine.

How long does it take for a couple to dine compared to a larger group? One and a half hours? Two hours? Three hours? Dining time varies with the type of restaurant. For example, at casual grills, bistros, and establishments catering to a business lunch crowd, guests could easily be in and out in 45 to 90 minutes. However, at some renowned fine dining shrines around the country, dinner could last all evening.

When planning the reservations for an evening, the reservationist takes into account that larger tables usually take longer to dine than smaller groups. Large parties that take up an entire room in the restaurant will often be in for the night. Therefore, she might choose to book the large table for eight for two seatings while deuces right next to that big table will be turned four or five times.

As a rule, restaurants want to seat to full capacity. However, doing so can be inefficient. You might end up seating two people at a table meant for four and then end up having to turn away a party of four, while the two empty seats at the four-top go unused. A full dining room looks impressive, but service may suffer if all the tables order at once. Some food will come out earlier than guests want, some later, making the diners unhappy. Moreover, there is a downside financially, as well—those guests who get their food late will therefore be leaving later; longer stay times mean fewer table turns, which, in turn, means lower sales.

If the number of new tables is managed so that they are introduced every fifteen minutes (instead of all at once), the waiters have time to get each table started, the bartender is working at a steady if busy rate, and the dinner orders are going into the kitchen in a nice, steady flow. The restaurant machine works more efficiently. Menu and staffing changes (including training) can increase the dining room's efficiency, so it is important to remain flexible. After adding additional touches such as tablecloths and candles, the management may watch for signs of service slowing down. They may not necessarily find the slightly slower service a bad thing, though, because they may be able to raise prices a little to counter the loss of revenue from reduced covers.

FIXED SEATINGS

This system is generally used by restaurants that have relatively long seatings of one and a half to two hours or more. Fixed seatings at this type of establishment, for example, could be at 6 P.M., 8 P.M., and 10 P.M. This is ideal for prix fixe menus because the kitchen is able to calculate the serving time with more precision. This kind of slower-paced meal has fewer turnovers in the dining room but often yields higher check averages. Fixed seatings also allow the kitchen to pace itself better, especially if the menu is extensive or complex.

CONTINUOUS SEATING

This system tends to work best for fluid, high-volume establishments, such as bistros, where meals are shorter. Reservations might be taken for one table in each station every fifteen minutes—which prevents orders from crashing down on any one server (or the kitchen) all at once. Of course, this assumes that customers respect reservation times and orders are taken promptly and accurately. Lower check averages can be compensated for by higher volume.

The continuous seating system allows restaurants to accept walk-ins, provided there are empty tables.

MAKING NOTATIONS IN THE RESERVATION BOOK OR SYSTEM

Since situations change so quickly, it is best to use pencil in the actual reservation book. The types of notations made in the book can help make service more efficient. For example, since some parties do not always arrive together, a common practice is to draw a half circle around the number in the party when some arrive, and complete the circle when the full party is seated.

Things to Do At The Reception Desk

- Make a good first and last impression.
- Recognize regular guests.
- Thank the guests for coming.
- Help check guests' coats.
- Look happy.
- Answer the phone within the third ring.
- Greet the guests within fifteen seconds of their arrival.
- Make eye contact with the guests.
- Repeat the guests' names.
- Scan the room for problems and alert appropriate staff.
- Continually review the reservation plan and status of tables for the next seating.
- Make every attempt to maximize seating while maintaining even service.
- Become familiar with guests' names, especially repeat customers.
- Pay attention to guests who are waiting for a table. Explain why they are waiting and keep them updated as to the status.

Cancellations in the reservation book should be noted distinctly so any staff member could quickly determine which tables are available. The reservationist simply makes a pencil line through the name (so it is still legible) and writes "cxl" or "cncl" in the table number column. It is best to avoid erasing the names, unless that is the only available method to maximize seating.

Keep a clock at the host stand and write the time next to the name on the reservation sheet or the floor plan. This way you will know which section got the most recent party of guests, and which should be next.

LOGBOOK

A valuable tool for comparing business from season to season or from year to year is a written logbook that records number of covers, seating times, and any special problems. This way you can look at your holiday experiences from the year before to determine volume, peak seating times, and other considerations to plan better the coming year.

The maître d' should make daily entries in the reservation log detailing the manager on duty, expected number of covers, final number of covers, number of waiters and kitchen crew, lost-and-found items, sundry incidents and names of people involved, and even weather conditions. Weather is one of the biggest reasons guests are late or fail to show up.

The previous year's data—number of covers, weather, and any other extenuating circumstances—can be noted in the new logbook for quick comparison. Recaps

Hospitality Handbook

The hospitality handbook is the resource book that the reservationist can use to answer guests' questions. It should be accessible at the reception desk and placed near any phones used to take reservations. The handbook should be updated on a monthly basis. Information might include:

- A description of the cuisine
- Chef's name
- Maître d'hôtel's name
- A price range of the menu
- Wine and beverage information
- Hours of operation
- Guest dress code
- Accepted methods of payment
- Directions to the restaurant from various areas
- Area hotel accommodations

- Area restaurants
- Parking facilities
- Public transportation
- Emergency phone numbers (police, fire department, EMT)
- Taxi phone numbers
- Special events in the area
- Facilities for people with disabilities
- Children's menu
- Cake order forms
- Incident report forms
- A log of problems encountered, including complaints, accidents, food-borne illness reports, and maintenance problems

should be formulated and recommendations made to the following year or similar event.

IF THE SYSTEM CRASHES

In the event that your computerized reservation system crashes, emergency backup system should be kept at the reservations desk. This might include a printed copy of the reservations list, a flashlight, sequentially numbered guest checks, a sales tax chart, a battery-powered calculator, backup batteries for flashlight and calculator, extra candles, and a manual credit card machine with a supply of manual forms.

RECONFIRMING RESERVATIONS

Many establishments try to minimize no-shows and latecomers by reconfirming reservations on the appointed day. A staff member might begin working the phones in the afternoon, calling reserved customers to ask if they still intend to come. This might help somewhat, although even reconfirmed reservations have been known to result in no-shows.

Jean-Jacques Rachou, chef and owner of La Cote Basque in Manhattan, says that on a Saturday night his restaurant could have had a no-show rate of more than 30 percent. "And these are people we had called at home just hours before," he said. Maître d's contend that many no-shows are caused by inept reservation taking. For example, if a guest wants to come at 8:00 P.M. and you offer only 9:00 P.M. or 9:30 P.M., the chances of a no-show rise dramatically. Some professionals note that a reservationist should feel out the customer to determine if there might be another solution—even dining in the cocktail lounge (if there are tables) or at the bar itself. If a customer reluctantly accepts an unsatisfactory reservation, you can be sure the person will start calling other establishments to see if something better is available—and might not call back to cancel the reservation.

Sometimes, guests become no-shows without realizing it, through no fault of their own (their reservation might have been written on the wrong day, for instance). If reservations have not been confirmed a day ahead of time, it is good practice to call the no-shows the next day. By asking if the restaurant has made a mistake, the guests are not made to feel guilty, but gain an appreciation for the importance of reservations. Such guests will probably be more considerate about cancellations in the future. It is not advisable, however, to give away a customer's table if the party is only a few minutes late. It is a good idea to establish a minimum time after which you give away a reserved table, taking into account weather conditions, traffic, difficulty of finding the restaurant, and how well you know the guest. The time might range from 20 minutes to a half hour or more. However, it might be preferable to lose a table for a night rather than risk losing a valuable customer.

DEPOSITS

The best insurance against no-shows is a deposit. Many restaurants now require deposits for major holidays, special events, and large groups. However, aside from the ill will that required deposits might create, they can result in bookkeeping headaches for restaurant operators. Consequently, many managers prefer to persuade diners to cancel reservations at least an hour in advance so restaurants have a chance to fill the vacancy. That takes some finesse.

Another recent approach used by some restaurants is a reservation contract. The guest receives, then fills out and returns (by fax or email) a contract that includes the date, time, number in party, and all credit card information. Some restaurants even require scanned copies of both sides of the guest's credit card.

Other restaurateurs find these practices too confrontational and decline to try them. Gordon Sinclair, of Gordon's in Chicago, used a simpler, less alienating

Securing Reservations

Gordon Sinclair suggested that when one asks guests for their credit card numbers to secure a table, precise language is important. *"You can't pause when you are asking because the client might start thinking about it. For example, you say, 'We need a credit card to guarantee your table. What credit card would you like to use?' If you pause in the middle of that, the client might start asking questions about the policy. Don't give them a chance to demur."*

When a restaurant has a no-show rate of about 15 percent, you need to do your best to confirm reservations. You cannot really do much about people who have not put down any kind of deposit. There is something about getting a credit card number from the guest—even if you are not going to use it—that makes people more inclined to call and cancel.

Here is a small, country-restaurant perspective: Priscilla

Martel, who for thirteen years owned and ran the dining room at Restaurant du Village, in Chester, Connecticut, says that her type of establishment had a more personal relationship with customers, and no-shows were far less frequent.

"It can happen, but it is not usual with the local people who are the bulk of our clients. On the other hand, a small restaurant (forty-five seats) does not have the flexibility to protect itself by overbooking even slightly."

method. He had his reservationists ask, "Will you agree to call us if you change your plans?" when taking reservations. This phrasing involved the guest in the process, rather than threatening some form of retaliation. It still managed the situation, but the guest felt respected, not suspected.

While asking guests to secure their reservation with a credit card or to confirm a reservation on the day of their visit may seem a simple matter, the guests often perceive it as an inconvenience. A friendlier method is for the restaurant to call on the day of (or the day before) the visit to confirm the reservation. This may not be necessary for regular customers, as they are more likely to call in the event of a cancellation. No single method for preventing no-shows is ideal for all restaurants or all guests. Each manager must use judgment and tact, and consider the record of no-shows in the particular situation, when deciding on the best approach.

VIP GUESTS

The best guests deserve special treatment, and there is no excuse for greeting a regular guest with, "And how do you spell your name, sir?" The maître d' should meet periodically with the receptionists to go over the names of important clients so they can be welcomed on the phone. Caller ID can help identify guests before they identify themselves. This allows the reservationist to search through a computerized customer database for preferences and be prepared for the guest's requests (this process does not absolutely require a computerized database; a simple card file system can also be used to keep track of birthdays, anniversaries, special preferences, allergies, and so on). With a customer database, the reservationist can see all relevant information about the caller.

For these reasons it is advisable that as few people as possible take reservations. If someone else books a table, the regular reservationist should be informed so nothing (or no one) falls through the cracks.

HONORING RESERVATIONS

Just as restaurants expect customers to show up on time for a reserved table, diners expect restaurants to have their table ready at the appointed hour. This, unfortunately, is not always the case. The unpredictability of customer flow inevitably leads to occasional logjams, but they should be the exception, not the norm. In general, customers are very understanding about delays if they are treated with respect and straightforwardness. The worst thing a restaurant can do is to manipulate customers with half-truths and obfuscations ("It will just be a minute" when it will be a half hour). It is always better to tell the guests that some of the guests have stayed longer than anticipated, apologize for the situation, and try to offer drinks (where legal) or some sort of snack if they are willing to wait. While a lack of information is annoying, candor can do wonders.

If diners arrive, say, half an hour late for their reservation and you have given away their table, it is best to inform them of the situation and make every effort to seat them as soon as possible. Some guests are content to dine at the bar, especially if that helps them catch a movie or theater curtain. Other situations might call for offering a free cocktail, snacks at the bar, or a bottle of wine with dinner.

What do you do for people who have to stand in line because their tables are not yet ready? The philosophy at Disney attractions (e.g., Disney World) is that people do not mind waiting on lines if they are entertained and kept informed while they are waiting. Some guests will want to see menus, so they can reduce the time in making decisions once they are seated.

How long can a restaurant expect customers to wait for a reserved table before making some sort of amends? Ten minutes? Fifteen minutes? We asked a cross-section of owners, managers, and maîtres d'hôtel the following question: Customers arrive on time for a reserved table at, say, 8 P.M. The table is not ready. How long do you think a customer can wait before management should intervene with a free drink, a bite to eat, or some other tactic to keep the customer happy? Their answers are given in Table 5.5.

TABLE 5.5 Remarkable Service Strategies When the Table Is Not Ready

Policy	Restaurant
10 minutes, buy drink	Chez Josephine, New York City
15 minutes, buy Champagne	Lespinasse, New York City
20 minutes, buy drink	Restaurant du Village, Chester, CT
15 minutes, apology; 20 minutes, buy drink	Sign of the Dove, New York City
20 minutes, bring tidbits; intervene every 5 minutes	Gordon's, Chicago
15 minutes, apology; 20 minutes, complimentary food	Lon's at the Hermosa Inn, Phoenix, AZ
15 minutes, apology and tidbit	Patina, Los Angeles

NO-SHOWS AND LATE ARRIVALS

Restaurants can make reservations for guests, but they cannot force them show up at the restaurant, nor can they guarantee that the guests will arrive on time. No-shows and late arrivals are frustrating and can be very costly to a restaurant. So what can a restaurant do?

Special Requests

GUESTS AT ALL KINDS OF RESTAURANTS may ask for a particular table, a high chair, flowers, a cake, joy buzzers, Champagne, and so on. A diner might have dietary restrictions or allergies. Note this clearly and inform management.

These extra efforts often mean a great deal to customers, so every effort should be made to accommodate them cheerfully. Some restaurants add a special touch to the reservations system by putting out a table card with the customer's name on it. If the request seems especially unusual or difficult, the reservationist should explain to the guest that it would be noted as a request, and that every effort will be made to honor it.

SPECIAL SERVER REQUESTS

Guests sometimes prefer a particular waiter. While this is not always possible due to scheduling or station assignments, a good host will try to accommodate

Gift Certificates

Very often, someone will call reservations with a request for something special to be given to another guest. Unless the customer is well known to the establishment, there are many opportunities for misunderstandings in such transactions. A safer approach is to recommend a gift certificate. A sample order form is shown below.

GIFT CERTIFICATE ORDER FORM

Manager's name: _____

Restaurant name: _____

Telephone number: _____

Email address: _____

Name of recipient/reservation: _____

Description of gift: Amount: $ _____

Special comment or occasion: _____

From: _____

Bill to credit card holder: _____

Telephone number: _____

Email address: _____

Would you like us to mail you a receipt? (circle) Yes No _____

Address:

Credit card: (circle) Amex Visa MC Other: _____

Credit card number: Expiration date: _____

Signature:

Please mail the gift certificate to (circle) Purchaser Recipient

Address: _____

Please fax or send this form to: when completed.

Thank you.

(restaurant name)

Try to Seat the Most Desirable Tables in the House First, Gradually Moving to the Least Desirable

Best can mean great view, quietest, or most visible, and *worst* can mean terrible view, nearest the kitchen, or in the back where no one can see you—it all depends on the restaurant. For example, in waterside restaurants, the window tables should go first, then the next row in, and so on. If the best tables are turned over earlier, guests arriving later can also enjoy them. When the dining room manager is assigning the sections, he or she tries to divvy up assignments to the best tables to avoid a slam. If several good tables are available, try to offer the guests choice: "Would you like to sit where you can watch the chef in our open kitchen, or would you prefer to be by the window?"

them. Professional servers can develop their stations as if they were their own businesses—acting as entrepreneurs in promoting their own repeat customers.

SPECIAL TABLE REQUESTS

At fine dining restaurants and bistros, one of the most common requests, especially from regular customers, is for a special table. In most cases the reservation desk cannot make guarantees on the spot, but the person on duty can note the request for the maître d'. When such a table request is made, the reservationist should immediately check to see if that table has been booked already within a certain seating time frame. A good host will try to fulfill these requests whenever possible (especially if given sufficient notice), because of the personal bond it can create between the guest and the restaurant.

Sometimes a particular table has a better view, or has some other distinguishing and desirable feature. Some restaurant managers, finding that these specific tables are always in demand, have taken to adding a surcharge when those tables are reserved. In order to defuse any resentment a guest might feel at being charged an extra fee, the restaurant generally offers some special service—perhaps a card, or unusual dessert, or bottle of wine—to make the evening more memorable.

GROUP RESERVATIONS

In sizable restaurants, a banquet manager may be on staff to book all large parties; this position would be a luxury for most medium-size establishments. Large groups (10 to 20 percent of a restaurant's seating capacity) require meticulous handling.

In order to allow smooth flow in the dining room and kitchen, consider the following suggestions:

- Recommend that the party arrive early, before the bulk of the other customers, or later, when the crowds are dwindling.

- Large groups make special demands on the kitchen and dining room staff, so try to establish a set menu in advance—one that is satisfactory for both the guests and the staff. If the group is small (5 to 10 percent of seating capacity), a select menu could offer two or more options per course, but not the entire menu.

- If the group is large (greater than 15 percent of seating capacity), it is best to offer a fixed banquet menu. Kitchens can handle set menus more quickly and efficiently than à la carte for groups. Guests, on the other hand, do not have to deal with the delays and confusion that result when many people attempt to make decisions simultaneously. Guests will enjoy faster service, too.

- Consult with the host to preselect wines that complement the meal. This way you ensure there will be an adequate quantity of wines, readily available at the correct temperature, at the correct time.

- Print the menus for each guest in advance to alert the kitchen about any allergies or other problems.

- Before the group arrives, establish a plan for gratuities and payment of the check. Gratuities for large groups range from 15 to 20 percent.

It is advisable to take a deposit of 25 to 50 percent for large groups. Some restaurants require payment in full, while others divide the bill into three equal payments. This protects restaurants in the event some guests do not show up as the restaurant often loses those covers. The number of guests in the group may need to be guaranteed the day of the party. If fewer show, there could be a per-person charge for each no-show. All of this should be in the contract or written agreement that you should provide each time a special party reserves a table.

Juggling reservations for a large group along with normal reservations can be a complex matter. The clearer the details before the engagement, the more enjoyable the experience for all. When booking large groups, keep in mind that they tend to linger longer, possibly overlap into a second seating, take a number of tables, can disturb other guests, and generally take longer to be served cocktails, order, and eat. At the same time, they often spend more, often buying additional bottles of dessert wine or port. Groups may also introduce your restaurant to new customers who could become regulars.

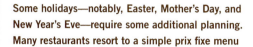

Holiday Booking Form

Some holidays—notably, Easter, Mother's Day, and New Year's Eve—require some additional planning. Many restaurants resort to a simple prix fixe menu with set seatings, while others require a more detailed reservation, essentially a contract. An example of a holiday reservation request is shown below.

Restaurant name: _____

Address: _____

Telephone number: ( ) email address: ( ) _____

Name of party: _____

Date of party: Time of reservation: _____

Party of (number of people): _____

Contact person: _____

Telephone number: ( ) email address: ( ) _____

Menu sent by date: Any allergies? _____

Specific dislikes: Special requests: _____

Full names of guests in party (including your own) _____

_____

_____

The price for dinner is $ per person. Deposit per person.

Cancellation must be made 48 hours in advance for refund of deposit.

How would you like us to handle the payment? (check one)

    Present at table

    Hold at front desk for your signature

    Charge to credit card and mail receipt to your address

Name of credit card holder: _____

Credit card: (circle) Amex Visa MC Other: _____

Credit card number: Expiration date: _____

Signature: _____

Please fax or send this form to: when completed.

Thank you.

(restaurant name)

An inexpensive but effective way to make a birthday presentation (especially at the last minute) is to pipe "Happy Birthday" and the guest's name in meringue on the rim of a plate, then brown lightly in the salamander. Tempered chocolate can be used instead of browned meringue. The guest can order any dessert, which is served with a candle, on the specially prepared plate. Sparklers should never be used indoors—they are toxic, smelly, and messy; the ashes may drop onto food; and they can pose serious risk of fire or burns.

BIRTHDAYS, ANNIVERSARIES, AND SPECIAL OCCASIONS IN THE DINING ROOM

Whether the service staff gathers together to harmonize on "Happy Birthday to You" or your waiter simply wishes you congratulations, acknowledging birthdays is an excellent way to engender goodwill with customers. Noting anniversaries and special events is important, too. With computerized reservation systems, it is possible to have birthdays and anniversaries pop up automatically. Reservationists should convey such information to the staff. Moreover, the front desk should be familiar with taking cake orders, quantities needed for different parties, pricing, and so on.

Restaurants should establish a cancellation policy for cakes and special requests. This might include a credit card deposit or a clear written arrangement stating what happens if the reservation is canceled on short notice, such as the day of the party. Some restaurants still charge for the entire cake but suggest the client pick it up. Others may decide to sell the cake to regular customers and charge the party a partial fee of 25 to 50 percent of the original price. It should be written in triplicate copy, with one going to the chef, one to the reservation book, and one to the customer.

Waiting Lists

IF YOU HAVE DECIDED TO GO with a first-come, first-served system, you will find that it is relatively easy to work with—until the room fills up. Now you have to figure out how to implement a waiting list. Have you ever wondered how hosts are able to look at a list of names and confidently tell you that it would be twenty minutes for a table? To tell you the truth, they may wonder how they do it, too—it is a skill that comes largely with experience.

ESCOFFIER ROOM AM
DAILY RESERVATONS

Today's Date	July 3, 2017						

Time	# in Party	Name	Res #	Table	Ck-In	1/2 Hr Total	Comments
11:30	4	Phillips, Deirdre	447996		▼		$40 Deposit, Grill Rm/Window if pos
	3	Pucci, Eileen	448531		▼		$30 Deposit
	2	Calderon, Josh	448587		▼		Student dining with San Antonio student
					▼		
					▼		
					▼		
					▼		
					▼		
					▼		
					▼		
					▼	9	
12:00	9	Riddle, Phillip	442025	71	▼		$80 Deposit, library
	2	Salber, Lee	448015		▼		
					▼		
					▼		
					▼		
					▼		
					▼		
					▼		
					▼		
					▼	11	
12:30	2	Caggainello, Gary	447466		▼		$20 Deposit
	2	Rand, Renata	447829		▼		$20 Deposit
	2	Koppel, Steven	447983		▼		$20 Deposit
	2	Guadango, Victor	448264		▼		
	4	McInerney, Michael	448611		▼		
	2	Carrano			▼		Alex's parents
					▼		
					▼		
					▼		
					▼		
					▼	14	
1:00	2	Reid, Janet	447961		▼		
	6	Montelione, Michael	448243		▼		5 adults + 1 infant
					▼		
					▼		
					▼		
					▼		
					▼		
					▼	8	
1:30					▼		
					▼		
					▼	0	
	42	Total Covers for the Shift				42	

Yes
Cancelled
Walk-in

Example of a reservation list

The Value of a Seating Chart at the Front Desk

A seating chart marked with each station's designated tables is a useful tool at the front desk. This can assist in seating parties in alternate stations so one waiter does not get slammed, followed by the next waiter, and so on. Some managers keep the seating chart covered with clear plastic—marking the tables already assigned with china markers, and erasing as necessary with a wipe of a paper towel.

The more experience the host has in your restaurant, the more accurate those estimates will be. The estimate is based on many factors: average guest stay, number of large parties, how fast the kitchen is sending out plates, and even the unquantifiable factor of how the place simply feels that night. The best hosts will take all of the available criteria, analyze them, come up with an accurate estimate, and then add five minutes to play it safe. The more accurate the estimates are, the more business you will do; people who decide to wait and are able to sit down on time will be happy with the result and will probably return. The ones who decide not to wait might well come back someday to see what the hubbub is about, and they might stay that next time.

If, however, the host consistently underestimates wait times, it will eventually hurt your business. Guests who have to wait an hour instead of twenty minutes will be very upset once they get to the table. Even worse is when people walk out because the wait was longer than they expected—they may decide never to come back.

If you are going with a no-reservations system, the operative word is, of course, *system.* Maintain the wait list on a legal pad, sure, but next to the guest's name, write the current time and the quoted wait time. When the table is ready for the guest, some hosts will walk through the bar calling the guest's name while other restaurants, like the Hilltop Steakhouse in Saugus, MA, have a public address system. Still other restaurants have electronic pagers that they will hand to the guest once their name has been logged. When the table is ready, the host pushes a button and it sends a signal to the pager. It's not a foolproof system, because guests sometimes misplace the pagers, but it can cut down on the number of annoying announcements. There are also apps available through which you can send a text to your guest that their table is ready.

REGULAR GUESTS WITHOUT RESERVATIONS

What if you have a reservation policy, but you also have a lot of regulars who have specific tables that were "theirs." You may get no notice or very short notice when they decide to come to the restaurant, expecting "their" table and may have already seated a party at that table. You might simply offer another table nearby and let them know you appreciate their understanding. For very important regulars, a restaurant might actually keep the guest's favorite table open when that this person is in town to create an extremely loyal clientele. Is it worth it? It might be, if you calculate that around two-thirds of your business comes from that select group of regulars who make up around one-third of your clientele.

OTHER GUESTS WITH NO RESERVATIONS

What if you have a reservation policy, but guests arrive without them? Every restaurant will have guests coming through the front door without reservations. If there is a free table, of course they should be seated and served. If there is not any unreserved space, they can be offered a seat at the bar to wait for a cancellation or no-show, with the caveat that this might not happen. When the walk-ins are regular customers, it is a good idea to get them a table as soon as possible.

Do not get into the habit of referring out loud to people who arrive unannounced as *walk-ins,* as in, "Could you seat these walk-ins at table nine?" How would you like to be called a "walk-in" instead of your real name? It is best to ask the guest's name. You may want to keep track of how much walk-in business you do on any given night, so after you write their name in the reservation book, write "NR" for "no reservation" rather than "WI." This might help avoid referring to guests as walk-ins.

Conclusion

GREETING AND SEATING THE GUESTs is a critical moment in establishing remarkable service in the guests' mind. It is where first impressions are made, where the nature of the dining experience is first suggested, and where the warmth of their relationship with the restaurant is established.

6

Serving Guests

THE ABILITY TO REMAIN
CONFIDENTLY in control of the guest's
dining experience, without being overbear-
ing, is a skill one learns gradually, practicing and improvising with each encounter.
Proper table maintenance, reading the
table, and taking the order correctly are
all critical in any successful dining room.
Additional important aspects of remarkable service, such as dealing with delays or
mistakes and handling difficult guests and
children, are discussed in this chapter.

The Soft Skills of Remarkable Service

REMARKABLE SERVICE IS THE COMBINATION of hospitality and service skills. Before going on to the hard skills of table service, the soft skills of hospitality should be described so that you can incorporate them into all service situations. Empathy, communication skills (including making suggestions or recommendations and upselling), and reading the table are some of the most important skills any professional server can develop.

EMPATHY

The entire dining room staff should treat each guest as they would like to be treated themselves. The best way for a server to accomplish this is to emphasize with the guest. Empathy, the ability to put yourself in another's situation and feel what that person is feeling, allows you to anticipate the guest's needs. This will certainly impress the guest as well as make your job easier, since you are in a better position to control the flow of work, rather than responding to one situation after another.

COMMUNICATION

Communicating with the guest is a two-way street. When speaking to guests, it is important to sound sincere and avoid repeating a few stock phrases and responses. When the guest talks to you, it is important to listen carefully, making eye contact with the speaker. Providing accurate and honest information is the goal, but in order to do so, you need to be certain you have understood the real question. When you speak to the guests, avoid putting them on the spot. Asking, "Is everything alright?" forces them to mentally review the entire meal. You may even see them look up and to the left as they conduct an internal survey before responding. Instead, ask a specific question—"Isn't the rosemary in the lamb wonderful?"—or offer a bit of information about the dish: "The chef goes to the market every morning to select the fish."

More often than not, customers will have questions about the menu for the waiter to answer. They might want some advice from the waiter to select an appetizer that complements their main course particularly well or from the wine steward to suggest a wine for the table. There can be clear signs that guests might need more information. They may ask to have the name of a dish pronounced or simply point at the menu rather than embarrass themselves. Guests who are clearly comfortable with the menu selections, on the other hand, might ask leading questions about dishes or pronounce the names of more obscure dishes or ingredients correctly. Once you have an idea of what the guest is comfortable with or worried about, you can assist in finding a dish that is familiar for the nervous guest or suggest something an adventurous guest might not have tried before.

Sometimes the waiter can feel conflicted about offering advice: "Should I tell them that the vichysoisse is cold and the steak tartare is raw, or will it come across as an insult to their intelligence?" One way to give your guest a subtle hint about an order is to repeat back the order in a descriptive manner. Rather than saying, "So you will start with the vichysoisse and then have the tartare as your entrée?" you can rephrase the order like this: "So you will start with the cold potato-leek soup, and then move on to the chilled raw beef for dinner?"

READING THE TABLE

Everything that happens in the dining room, if done well, should be exactly the same all of the time—except for one variable: the guests. Every guest is different, and has different needs. Some are in a hurry, while some want to enjoy a leisurely dinner. Some want a four-course meal, others would prefer three appetizers, and still others are on restricted diets. The professional server interprets body language and other nonverbal cues from the guest, a skill known as *reading the table*. This permits the server to control the pace of the meal, suggest additional items, and occasionally even steer the guests away from certain items.

You should begin reading the table from the moment you come in contact with the guests. A little conversation when the guests are first seated can provide the kind of clues you need to do your job well. A series of carefully phrased questions can clue you in about what you can suggest to the table to make them feel special.

Some aspects of reading the table are straightforward. You read the table after each course or beverage is served to make sure that glasses are full, flatware is set, and the table is properly cleared. If someone is fiddling with his water glass while everyone else is eating, he might not have the steak knife he needs for his entrée. If a guest tastes the food, then pushes the plate away, something is wrong. By reading these signs, and acting on them, servers can do more than fix an existing problem; they can actually improve the entire dining experience for the guest.

Other aspects of reading the table may be less direct. For instance, a guest may appear impatient or even irritated. You can see the behavior as she crosses and uncrosses her arms and stares fixedly out the window. Maybe she is late for an appointment, or maybe she is simply lost in thought. What the remarkable server should do is try to uncover the source of the impatience and make appropriate adjustments, perhaps by approaching the table with some additional service. If she is late for an appointment, her expression probably will not lighten at the sight of you. Now you need to ask some questions to find out how you can help improve the situation. If she was simply lost in thought, her expression most likely will change, so if there is nothing else required, you can simply refill a glass or retreat from the table.

Servers have to step close enough to the guests to be able to hear them as well as to serve food and drinks. You should keep in mind that people have a *zone of privacy* that can only be entered by their most intimate friends and relatives. The size of the zone varies from culture to culture, as well as from one situation to another. If anyone other than these intimates intrudes into that private space, the person will become uncomfortable. There is also a privacy zone that surrounds the table's conversation. Some guests are happy to converse a bit with the server; others are not inclined to chat. Signs that you have stepped too close include leaning back, shifting a chair, stiffening up, and stepping away. Retreat if you can and let the guest recover.

SUGGESTIONS, RECOMMENDATIONS, AND UPSELLING

This time and effort spent reading the table for clues about ways to improve service can do more than simply enhance the guest's experience, it can also generate sales for the restaurant. For example, an initial dialogue might run as follows:

Server: Would you like to see our cocktail menu?

Guest: No, thanks, we'll just be drinking wine tonight.

Server: How about a wine list, then?

Guest: Sure, but we're not sure what we're going to be eating yet.

Server: May I suggest, then, a glass of Champagne while you make up your minds?

Guest: That sounds perfect!

The waiter followed the lead of the customers, guiding them toward a decision that will make them happy and make a nice sale for the house.

SUGGESTIONS

When answering the guests' questions, you may either suggest, which means that you are offering information without an opinion, or recommend, which means that you are offering an opinion. The more time you spend getting familiar with your menu and the more you know about customer reactions to the dishes, the more confident you will be when it is time to suggest or recommend items to the guest. You can now do more than just list the ingredients or cooking methods of the dish—you can describe its subtleties or personality.

A helpful, effective suggestion depends on your having enough information at hand to describe menu items accurately. If a guest indicates an allergy to something, you can suggest alternatives that do not include the offending item or check whether the order can be modified in the kitchen. Making a suggestion is relatively safe, since it is primarily a statement of fact. To improve your skill at making suggestions, try mentioning a particular dish and see how guests react. If they frown or shake their heads, mention something else.

RECOMMENDATIONS

Recommendations are a bit more risky; if the guest accepts the recommendation and is not pleased, the waiter is at fault. When the guest asks, "Which shellfish appetizer should I have?" you cannot just keep reciting the menu offerings over and over. When you offer a recommendation, try to include a description of a specific ingredient or quality of the dish (wild mushrooms or smoked eel, spicy or smoky, and so forth). If the reaction is negative, move on to something else.

UPSELLING

Upselling is that act of getting the customer to buy either more items than originally intended or more expensive versions of the items they order. Keep in mind that the primary motivation behind upselling is improving the guests' experience. It is true that upselling will result in a higher check average (better for the restaurant and better for you), but keeping the guests' interests at heart is important if you want to use a suggestion or a recommendation to upsell without appearing pushy. Open-ended questions such as, "What would you like for dessert?" cannot be answered with a simple yes or no. They are more effective for upselling than closed-ended questions like, "Do you want dessert?" Here are some ways to upsell (and thereby increase the check average):

- Use appetizing words, such as steaming, sweet, spicy, juicy, fresh, savory, and refreshing.

- Suggest premium liquors when guests order generic drinks.

- Suggest side orders that complement entrées (e.g., "The roasted potatoes are especially good with the steak").

- If the entrée takes some time to prepare, suggest an appetizer.

- Suggest a fresh fruit plate if the guest hesitates while considering desserts.

- Suggest definite menu items ("Would you care for a dessert or perhaps some espresso or cappuccino?") rather than asking, "Will there be anything else?"

- If a guest especially likes something he or she ordered and it is available for takeout, suggest an extra portion to take home.

The Steps of Service

WHILE INDIVIDUAL ESTABLISHMENTS DEVELOP house rules to cover all aspects of service, from greeting to actual service to the presentation of the check, most restaurants include some of all of the following as part of their basic sequence of activities:

- Greeting

- Seating

- Water

- Beverage service

- Menu/wine list presentation

- Taking the order

- Bread and food service

- Clearing

- Check presentation/payment

- Farewell

- Resetting tables

The order in which these individual steps are completed can vary. Some of them may not be appropriate for a given situation; for example, you would not automatically serve bread at breakfast. You might present the menu before anything else is put on the table or you might bring bread and then present the menu. Although the particulars of what happens, when it happens, and who is responsible for what may vary, there are some standards of service that apply to most situations and establishments:

- Come to the table to greet guests promptly. Some establishments have a thirty-second standard.

- Serve children first, then ladies, starting with the eldest woman at the table and then moving clockwise around the table, followed by gentlemen; if there is a specific host at the table, serve that person last, regardless of age or gender.

- Serve all guests at the table at once; do not serve just one or two guests and leave the others to wait. (An exception is made when the guests do not all order the same number of courses.)

- When serving a table, try to avoid showing the guest the back of your hand by serving foods from the left with the left hand and clearing from the right with the right hand, except for bread and butter plates.

- Avoid reaching across the guest. Imagine a line that runs down the middle of the guest's face and chest, and plan your actions so that line is not crossed. If the only alternative to reach across the guest because of the seat's location, acknowledge that you are doing so by apologizing for the breach of protocol and reach open-handed.

- Serve all courses in the order specified or requested by the guest.

- Clear courses after everyone at the table has finished, unless a guest asks you to remove a plate before the rest of the table is finished.

- Remove all items from the tabletop that are not required for the course that is about to be served.

- All soiled dishes should be removed from the patron's right side with the waiter's right hand and transferred to the left hand—except bread and butter plates, which should be picked up from the left side. Do not scrape dishes in front of the guest or stack dishes or utensils on the table.

GREETING

Guests should be greeted by the host, maître d'hôtel, or manager within thirty seconds of their arrival with a warm smile and good eye contact. A timely and appropriate verbal greeting should accompany the smile. Even though you may greet several people every night, it is important that the greeting sound sincere, rather than rote.

Welcome guests with a sincere smile and verbal greeting.

If possible, greet the host or the person holding the reservation by name and ask if they will be dining with you as well as the number in the party. If you do not recognize the guests, asking them, "What was the name of the reservation?" is friendlier than "Did you have a reservation?" If guests do not have a reservation, this is an opportunity to add them to the reservation system. Take the customers' names and discreetly note some characteristic to help remember them later ("White hair, lapel pin on suit"). Avoid using judgmental descriptions—and never give the impression of being confused or disorganized.

Once the reservation is confirmed, the maître d' may alert the server if the table needs to have extra place settings and chairs should be added or removed prior to seating, if there is enough time. This gives guests the impression that the table was set just for them.

SEPARATE ARRIVALS

When several guests are going to be dining together, they may arrive separately. You can use the reservations book to keep track of these split parties, but what do you do with them while they wait?

You may choose to seat guests as they arrive, and in fact, some guests do prefer to be seated rather than wait at the door or in the lounge. However, some establishments have found it necessary to ask guests to wait until the party is complete before seating them, especially on busy nights. Imagine that you have put together two four-tops to accommodate them. If two members of a party of eight arrive early and are seated at an eight-top, and then two others call to cancel after they arrive, you have two empty seats. This can be costly to the restaurant if you must turn away guests because there are not enough tables.

SEATING

Each restaurant should have a predetermined method for assigning tables and filling the room. The benefits of such a plan are efficient distribution of guests throughout the dining room and a balanced workload on servers. By paying attention to the distribution of seated guests in the dining room, the guests' perception of the room is that it is nicely filled, while at the same time leaving them a comfortable amount of physical space to enjoy their meal. It also permits the servers to prepare each table for arriving guests with minimal disturbance of nearby guests, and gives servers a balanced workload without getting "slammed."

After the reservation has been verified (see Chapter 5), the guests are seated at their assigned table. The maître d' or a server can lead the guests to the table and assist in seating the guests. Since the person doing the seating can only seat one guest at a time, another server might assist by pulling out additional chairs. It is traditional to seat women first. If the number of guests is fewer than the number of place settings, the maître d' should indicate this to the captain or waiter with a predetermined signal, such as placing the butter knife on top of the folded napkin, so that the waiter can remove the extra place settings. Remember to reposition the centerpiece toward the empty place setting when the number at the table changes.

Once they are seated, the server should greet guests as soon as possible, or at least acknowledge them. Allow them to place their napkins on their own laps.

CHECKING COATS AND BAGS

The guests' reception is more pleasant if it includes an offer to take their coats, hats, umbrellas, or shopping bags (rather than sending them to the coat-check room). They have not come to your restaurant to be sent to the cloakroom. The coats could be handed to the coat-check person in exchange for the coat claim check numbers. This way the guests don't wait for their coats to be hung up. The check numbers should be given to the coat's owner or to the men—unless guests indicate some other preference.

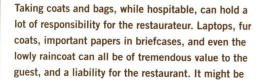

Taking Coats and Bags

Taking coats and bags, while hospitable, can hold a lot of responsibility for the restaurateur. Laptops, fur coats, important papers in briefcases, and even the lowly raincoat can all be of tremendous value to the guest, and a liability for the restaurant. It might be smart to post a sign at the coat-check stand stating that the staff cannot be held responsible for lost or damaged items. To be certain, managers and owners should talk to a lawyer and insurance agent to make sure the restaurant is covered.

Every establishment should have a policy on checking furs and other valuable items. There are legal implications that vary from state to state. Some restaurants have the guest sign the fur in when checked and require the same signature when the fur is retrieved. The coatroom should never be left unattended.

Assuming that guests have not been kept waiting, the host should ask them if they are ready to be seated—they may want to stop at the bar first. This may not always be desirable, especially if a party is late. The host may politely nudge them toward their table by saying, "We don't want you to be rushed, so perhaps you'd like to have your cocktails at the table?"

The host should lead the guests to the table, rather than offering the guests a choice. Actually, it is not all that important who seats guests, as long as there is a host to take care of them from the moment they arrive.

A customer is shown to her seat by a server.

In the more polite past, men always seated women in their party by pulling out their chairs. Today, such courtesy is rare. The task is usually performed by the maître d' in fine dining establishments, and by the floor manager in bistros. If guests bring their coats to the table, the host should repeat the offer to check the coats for them. This is both gracious and practical— waiters can trip on coats while carrying trays, or accidentally spill on the guests' jackets.

Women are generally seated with their backs to the wall, facing the dining room. Men may face the women, with their backs to the dining room. If you sense that there is a problem with the seating arrangement, ask if the table is satisfactory. Most problems with seating arrangements can be worked out by the guests once they are at the table, but the maître d' should remain nearby to help with reseating. If the guests request another table, they should remain at the table while the maître d' checks the reservation book to determine if another table is available.

PRESENTING THE MENU

Once guests are seated, menu presentation can begin.

The menu may be presented by the maître d', headwaiter, captain, or server. A conscientious server presents the menus, right side up, in the most convenient manner for the guest. Since most fine dining establishments take some care with the cover of the menu, it is generally preferable to present the menu closed. Use the same service standard for presenting the menu as you do when serving the food or beverage, present from the right with the right hand or from the left with the left hand.

Some restaurants feel it is a good idea to get something to eat or drink on the table as soon as possible: a premeal drink, water, bread and butter, or a complimentary snack (classically known as an *amuse-bouche*). Other restaurants prefer to take the order before any food is offered in order to sell more.

Before the guests begin to read the menu, inform them of any specials that are being offered during the meal period, and any unavailable items or substitutions. This can prevent disappointment if the menus are presented for the guests to make a decision while the server is getting beverages.

Often, a guest will listen to the server's recitation of the day's specials, and then ask, "What was number three, again?" If you always recite the special items in the same order, you can respond more easily without having to repeat the entire specials menu.

This can be done successfully when you know the menu thoroughly, as opposed to having merely memorized it. Servers should provide a full explanation of menu items that might be unclear or foreign to new guests, or new items that might be unfamiliar to regular guests.

Present a closed menu to highlight a carefully selected menu cover.

BREAD AND WATER

The appropriate server brings bread and butter and water to the table according to house standards. If your restaurant offers bottled waters, you might ask the guests if they prefer iced water or bottled water.

When water glasses are part of the standard cover, the server can bring a pitcher and pour iced water for each guest. If they are not, the server might bring empty glasses on a tray, set them in, and then pour, or the server might bring filled water glasses on a tray to serve the guests.

When pouring iced water from a pitcher, position it two or three inches above the glass to avoid touching and chipping the glass. It is important to make sure

Position the pitcher several inches above the glass, and use a towel to guard against splashes.

that glasses are refilled frequently. (See Chapter 7 for more about beverage service.)

As the bread and butter plate is to the left of the cover, bread is served from the left. Note the use of the fork and spoon for serving the roll as shown here. The same technique is used in Russian/French service. You may hear this style of service referred to as *pincé,* the French world for "pinch." To execute this maneuver, make an "OK" sign, turn the wrist with the palm of the hand toward the ceiling, rest the spoon on your pinky, ring, and middle fingers and use your pinky finger to grip the handle. Place a fork between the index finger and thumb. The tines of the fork should be up for sliced bread and down to better grasp rolls.

Sometimes a basket of bread and a dish of butter are placed on the table. For tables with six or more guests, two baskets and two butter plates are more convenient.

Note, however, that in some establishments, the house standard may specify that bread be served after the order has been take so the guest will not "fill up" on the bread. In restaurants where olive oil is offered with the bread, waiting to serve the bread helps avoid getting oil on the menus.

Using the pincé style of service, bread is pinched between a spoon and fork and served on the guest's bread and butter plate.

BEVERAGES

No matter which meal of the day, guests generally want something to drink soon after they arrive at their table. If there is a house specialty beverage or daily special drink, the server should be sure to mention it. Many guests prefer to order wine as an apéritif, so be prepared with a wine list. Chapter 7 gives additional information about beverage order taking and service. Traditional apéritifs are designed to stimulate the appetite, so serving the cocktail before the menu is presented can encourage a more adventuresome, and possibly larger, order.

WINE LIST PRESENTATION AND THE WINE ORDER

After the food order has been taken, the wine list is presented to the host by the sommelier, maître d', headwaiter, captain, or server. When the wine list is simply placed on the table when the menus are presented, it can be overlooked, but handing the wine list directly to one of the guests will initiate the ordering process. If the restaurant serves wine by the glass, it is best to offer all guests this wine list. Presenting

Napkins should not be replaced unless they become excessively soiled or if they fall to the floor. If guests leave their seats, do not refold their napkins, it is unsanitary for both the server and the guest—folded napkins are always unused napkins. When they return, their chairs should be pulled out to seat them. Napkins should not be touched by servers unless they have become extremely soiled and in need of replacement. Only lift soiled napkins by the corner, and then wash your hands immediately.

the wine list separately from the menu is a good way for the captain or waiter to break into the conversation. It helps the staff identify the table's host, and it brings some attention to the list, influencing the guests to look at it and perhaps order from it.

The wine order is usually taken after the food order because the selection of wine will depend on the choice of food—unless, of course, the host wants to select a bottle of wine instead of cocktails.

If only one wine has been ordered, the server could suggest a special wine or a multiwine meal, such as a split of Champagne, or a half bottle of white and a half bottle of red, with the main course instead of a full bottle of one or the other. This will most certainly enhance the meal by creating a new wine experience for the guests without necessarily increasing the check average. Suggestions might include a light wine for starting the meal, a full-bodied wine for the main course, and possibly Champagne for dessert.

The server should record all pertinent information concerning the wine order—such as name of the wine, vintage, winery and/or bin number. Finally, the server should inquire as to when the host wants the wine served. (Wine ordering and wine service are covered in greater detail in Chapter 8.)

TAKING THE ORDER

The server observes the table for cues—such as closed menus—that the guests might be ready to order, or waits a reasonable amount of time (five to ten minutes), and then asks politely, "Would you care to order?" or "Do you have any questions about the menu?" If the guests need more time, the server withdraws and returns in a few minutes.

Sometimes guests are so engaged in their conversation that they do not notice that the server is ready to take their order. While it might seem rude to interrupt (the guests' pleasure is foremost, of course), tables must be served if a restaurant

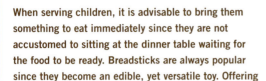

Serving Children

When serving children, it is advisable to bring them something to eat immediately since they are not accustomed to sitting at the dinner table waiting for the food to be ready. Breadsticks are always popular since they become an edible, yet versatile toy. Offering children coloring books and crayons can keep them entertained for a while, but they may soon get bored. Stocking inexpensive, colorful toys is yet another successful ploy. Tie a string to the child's spoon and the high chair so it does not reach the floor if it falls.

is to stay in business. Since the guests cannot be served if they do not order, the server is presented with a dilemma. Here are some solutions:

- ❑ The server should try to make eye contact with one of the guests, who may inform the rest of the table that they should order.

- ❑ The server may be able to find one of the guests who is not actively involved in the conversation. The server can quietly ask if the guest would like to order.

- ❑ The server can also offer to come back when they are ready. Very often, this will stimulate an urge to order in the talkative guests.

- ❑ Finally, the server can explain that a large group is expected shortly, and if they postpone their order it might be further delayed by the impending volume of business. This allows the guests to become allies of the server, and feel that they are exercising some control over the timing of their order.

When requesting the order for a table, it is important to establish eye contact to see who will order first. It was once the tradition for couples that the male ordered for the female and then followed with his own order. For larger parties, etiquette suggest that you begin with the guest seated to the left of the host and then continue to take orders in sequence, moving clockwise around the table. The host orders last. When you cannot determine who the host is for the table, you should walk to the table, stand near seat number one, address the table, and make eye contact.

When both guests are of the same gender, the elder is usually first to order, followed by the younger. When there are four or more guests in a party, each one usually orders separately.

WRITING THE ORDER

All of the data in the information box at the top of the guest check should be filled in before approaching the table, typically including the table number, the number of guests, and the server's initials. Other information may be necessary as well, depending on the house standards.

The near ubiquity of point-of-sale (POS) systems has changed the way waiters take orders. Handwriting is not as important as it used to be; there is no longer any need for "waiter's shorthand," and waiters do not have to go into the kitchen to place an order. However, the existence of such systems means that communication between front and back is more important than ever, and waiters have to send a lot of clear, accurate information to the cooks.

Along with getting solid training on the house computer system, waiters have to realize how important the process of correctly placing the order is. If the order is clear and free of errors, the server can push the send button and then move on to other chores. An unclear or mistake-riddled order, however, will require the attention and talents of the expediter, the waiter (who now has to go into the kitchen), and potentially the chef, manager, bartender, or cashier—none of whom has time to spare on such matters. The irony is that just a few more moments is all it takes to make the order unmistakably clear. Even with a POS system, you will still need to write the order down in enough detail so that you can complete the order at the computer.

Using PDAs to place the order electronically at the table can increase the speed of service, but small screen and stylus can also result in more errors. While the PDAs may seem too impersonal to some, it may increase "face-time" with the guests rather than spending time facing the POS terminal at the server station.

The order is generally taken from the right of each guest, but as with all dining room procedures, it should be taken in whatever manner will disturb the guests the least.

Stand near guests as they order so no one has to shout across the table. Take the complete order, getting each person's appetizer, soup, salad, and entrée order, in that sequence, before moving on to the next person.

Any guest preferences, such as doneness of meat or sauce on the side, should be noted at this time. If salad is to be served after the entrée, the salad order is written after the entrée order. The waiter should take the menus from each guest after they order.

It is advisable to repeat the names of any order as it is recorded if there is some possibility of confusion to make sure that the information is being interpreted correctly. For example:

Guest says, "I'll have the scallop main course."

Server says, "So that will be the sautéed sea scallops."

This step is important to avoid a mistake; perhaps the customer meant the escalope of veal. Clearing up any potential confusion must be done now, rather than allowing the wrong menu item to be prepared and delivered to the table. One simple question while taking the order can avoid a big problem down the road.

Once all of the orders are taken, you have another chance to clear up any potential confusion. If there is even a glimmer of doubt in your mind when putting the order in, it is imperative to go back to the table to clear up that doubt before the kitchen starts work on it.

WHEN GUEST ORDERS ARE NOT IN SYNCH

If some guests have ordered two courses while others have ordered three, this should be pointed out to the guests so they can either modify their orders to match each other's, if they wish. Even if they do not want to adjust their order, they will be prepared for awkward moments when only a few members of the party will have food in front of them. There are ways the alert server can minimize those moments by writing the order appropriately. For example, if two of four guests order a salad and main course, and the other two order appetizers, salads, and main courses, it is best to forgo classic dining structure and the order should be written so that you can serve the two salads with the two appetizers so all four guests have a first course together. Then the other two salads can be served after the appetizers have been cleared.

WAITER'S SHORTHAND

The purpose of writing dupes is not only to help remember the order but also to communicate the guests' needs to the kitchen or bar or to another server. Consequently, establishments often have their own system of dupe writing with standardized

Using Waiter's Shorthand

These are some common abbreviations for food.	SOS: sauce on the side
BLK&BLU: black and blue (a very rare steak)	STK: steak
R: rare	CX OR CHK: chicken
MR: medium rare	OM: over medium
M: medium	OW: over well
MW: medium well	OE: over easy
W: well	SCR: scrambled

abbreviations. This is true even if the restaurant uses a POS system; you may even see some of them as part of the POS system itself.

CARRYING PLATES

Simple activities such as carrying plates or glasses need to be perfected to a point of automation so you do not need to concentrate on them. That leaves you free to concentrate on developing and delivering the finer points of service and hospitality.

When picking up the dishes in the kitchen, the server picks up the plates in the reverse order in which they will be served. That is, the last plate to be served in each trip should be picked up first. Either two or three plates can be carried in the left hand. The kitchen staff takes extra effort to remove any thumbprints on the rim of the plate, so be careful not to leave thumbprints on the plates. One way to accomplish this is to hold the plate between the knuckle and the meaty base of the thumb rather than the thumb itself.

The ability to carry four plates at the same time (three with one hand and arm and the fourth in the other hand) means that you can serve a four-top without any assistance. Some more formal restaurants require their servers to carry no more than one or two plates at a time to avoiding anything that resembles plate stacking. For synchronized service, servers carry only one or two plates at a time so that the plates are presented to all of the guests at the table at the same time. Carrying fewer plates is more elegant and it also allows the staff to perform synchronized service described on page 159, where the food is placed in front of all guests at the table at the same time.

THE "PEACE SIGN" TECHNIQUE

1. Make a peace sign with the left hand, lay it flat toward the floor and turn the palm side up to the ceiling. Rest the plate on the index and middle fingers with the thumb knuckle on the rim of the plate. The second plate makes a three-point landing resting on the base of the thumb, the ring and pinky fingers and the forearm.

2. Rest the plate on the index, middle, and ring fingers and secure it with your thumb and pinky on the rim.

3. Rest the second plate on your wrist and support it with the tips of your thumb and pinky.

The peace sign technique uses the index and middle finger as support, with the remaining fingers as stabilizers.

Peace sign technique

THE "SPIDERMAN" METHOD

Place the plate in your left hand with the plate resting on the index, middle and ring fingers. The thumb and pinky secure the plate from the top of the rim. The second plate balances on the base of the hand and forearm. Although it is not elegant, it is possible, for smaller, room-temperature plates, to carry a third plate.

In the Spiderman method, the second plate balances on the base of the hand and forearm.

Spiderman method

THE INTERLOCKING METHOD

Hold a plate in the left hand with the index finger supporting the right side of the bottom of the plate, thumb knuckle on top, take a second plate and slide its rim slightly underneath the right side of the first plate with the index finger between the two plates, the middle finger below the rim of the plate on the right and the middle and pinky fingers on the bottom of the plate.

With this method a third plate could be carried by turning the wrist of the left hand toward the body and making a three-point landing for the third plate on the rim of the second plate, the forearm and the base of the thumb. For smaller, room-temperature plates it may be possible to balance a fourth plate on the middle finger.

CLEARING MULTIPLE PLATES

Rest the plate's base on your index finger and grip with your thumb knuckle on the rim. Slide the left rim of a second plate under the right rim of the first to rest the base on your middle finger.

Fan your ring and pinky fingers under the second plate. Turn your wrist slightly toward your body and rest a third plate on the wrist, forearm, and outer edge of the second plate.

If you are carrying plates that are heaped high (e.g., a steamed mussel appetizer), use the high carry as shown in the photographs (to the left/right/below).

PRESENTING THE PLATE

It is part of the server's job to present the kitchen's food in the best way possible. The plate should be accurate as it was described to the guest. The chef will determine the actual placement of food on the plate. When setting-in, the server should place the plate in the alignment chosen by the chef. Be sure to find out what that alignment is, if you are unsure.

To make service as smooth as possible, servers need to take an extra second before picking up the plate to make sure their thumbs are in the right area. The plate in the right hand will be served first so the thumb should be placed about three o'clock. The thumb on the plate in the left hand should be placed about seven-thirty so when it is passed to the right hand, the right hand thumb is in its correct position at three o'clock. Simply,

For the interlocking method, the index finger serves at the center support of two plates.

Interlocking method

Spiderman technique is a modified peace sign technique that allows a server to carry heaped plates.

hold the plates with the six o'clock position to your belly so they will also be toward the guests' bellies.

THE FIRST COURSE

Before the appetizer is served, all required utensils must be set in place, if they have not been preset. Clean flatware is carried to the table on a clean dinner plate and napkin (STP, the silverware transport plate; see Chapter 5) by the server. Several appetizer covers are described in Chapter 4 on page 97.

Appetizer utensils must be set in place before the course is served.

The appetizer fork is placed to the left of the dinner fork, with the left hand. The appetizer knife or spoon is placed to the right of the dinner knife, blade toward the center of the setting with the right hand. If wine is to accompany the appetizer, it must be served before the food; this is usually done by the person who takes the wine order. After the wine has been poured, the appetizer is served from the right with the right hand. All courses are served according to the standards of service of the house, but generally, women are served first. Any accompanying sauce may be served by the server from the guest's left. Bread and rolls, water, and wine should be checked and, if necessary, replenished at this time.

SOUP

The appropriate soupspoon is set in place to the right of the dinner knife, with the right hand. A round bouillon spoon is needed for soup served in a cup and an elongated soupspoon, similar to a tablespoon is needed for soup served in a flat soup bowl. Once this has been done, the soup is served. As usual, soiled dishes and flatware are removed from the right using your right hand (proper handling of flatware is discussed in Chapter 4).

SALAD

According to custom, most American restaurants serve salad before the main course. American diners generally choose soup, salad, or appetizer—not all three—so, in effect, the salad is a form of appetizer course.

Presenting the appetizer.

European-style Salad Service

In Europe, salad greens are served after the main course. This alternative service sequence is said to enhance the guest's appreciation of the main course. Greens have a lightening and relaxing effect on the stomach, so their consumption after the main course helps to prepare the guest for dessert. By this point, guests will have consumed a considerable amount of food, so they need a little rest. If salad is to be served after the main course, leave the bread and butter plates on the table and then remove them as you clear the salad plates. When the salad course is finished, the plates should be cleared from the right, salt and pepper removed, and the table reset for the fruit and cheese course, rather than the main course.

As with the appetizer and soup courses, all necessary tableware must be set in place prior to the service of the salad. Set the salad fork to the left of the place setting with your left hand, then move to the guest's right side before setting the salad knife to the guest's right, with your right hand. The salad itself should be served from the right side of the guest, with the right hand. A pepper mill may be offered or left on the table.

After the guests have finished their salads, the table must be prepared for the main course. All dishes and flatware that were set for the salad should be removed whether they were used or not. Only what might be needed for the rest of the meal should remain, the guests should not need two knives for the main course.

Grinding pepper on a guest's salad

Show Plates or Chargers

Many operators, especially those using expensive show plates, instruct their staff to remove the show plate before serving the appetizer to avoid having the show plate scratched by the underside of the appetizer plate. Otherwise, the show plate is typically left in place until the appetizer, soup, and salad courses (if served before the main course) have been served and cleared.

THE MAIN COURSE

The main course is the high point of the meal. It usually takes more time to be consumed and a leisurely air at the table ensures optimum enjoyment. By the time diners have reached the main course, their appetites have been appeased and their thirsts quenched. Sometimes, all that is needed to revive the patron's appetite is a simple but well-designed plate, offering pleasing contrasts in color, texture, and contour, and presented with flair and style.

At other times (and other restaurants), special presentations, such as sous cloche, en papillote, and flambé or other forms of tableside cookery help to stimulate the palate. If a guéridon is to be used for preparing, finishing, or plating the main course, the server must check to see that it is equipped with all needed serviceware.

If wine is to accompany the meal, it should be poured before serving the appropriate course. If, as the meal progresses, the guests require more of the same wine, it might be appropriate to offer the "wine by the glass" list, to permit some of the guests to try a different wine (the details of wine service are covered in Chapter 8).

If the flatware for the main course has been set prior to the guests' arrival; there should be no need to set it now unless the guests have used or dropped it, so it is wise to double-check before the food comes out from the kitchen. When the main course calls for a special utensil, such as a lobster pick or steak knife, it should be placed in position before the main course is brought into the dining room. (*See Covers, page 94, for more information.*) Flatware should only be held by the handle, never by any area that will touch food or the guest's mouth. It should be brought to the table on an STP.

As the main course progresses, bread and butter should be replenished as necessary, and water and wine repoured as needed. After the guests have completed the main course, the table should be cleared in the

Plates should be served from the right side and with the right hand.

In cases where the server cannot serve from the customer's right side, it is best to serve with the left side with the left hand.

Synchronized Service

This style of service is efficient, elegant, and much simpler to perform than it is to describe.

True synchronized service calls for one waiter for each seated guest. The waiters carry only one plate each. All the plates are set on the table simultaneously upon a signal from the lead waiter. Plate covers, if used, are lifted simultaneously.

As the waiters arrive at the table from the kitchen or the guéridon, the first server walks to the guest farthest away from the kitchen or guéridon. As the succeeding waiters bring a plate or plates to the table, they position themselves to the right of the first guest they will be serving.

When the situation demands it, synchronized service can also be done with one waiter for every two seated guests; in this scenario, the waiters carry two plates. They set the first plate in front of the guest, and then walk around the table to the next guest to set down the second plate.

It is possible to perform synchronized service with one waiter for every three guests, if the area is too crowded to accommodate a large number of waiters walking around the table. In this case, waiters carry two plates in the hand they will not use for service, and one more in the hand used to set the plate down.

Synchronized Service Diagram for an Oval
Eight top serving from the right.

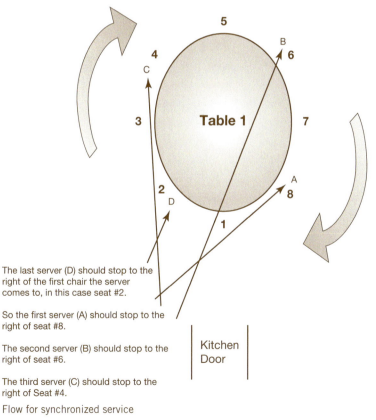

The last server (D) should stop to the right of the first chair the server comes to, in this case seat #2.

So the first server (A) should stop to the right of seat #8.

The second server (B) should stop to the right of seat #6.

The third server (C) should stop to the right of Seat #4.

Flow for synchronized service

French/Russian Service

In French/Russian service, the main course is presented to the entire table so the guests can view the platter arrangement. When plating the food, the server moves swiftly, yet gracefully, to plate the main course first, and then any accompaniments, such as vegetables or potatoes.

The server should place the food on the plate in a manner that will facilitate cutting and eating by the guest. The main course item should be placed so that the guest does not have to reach over the accompaniments to cut the protein.

Generally, the main course is served with the protein in the lower, center portion of the plate (the six o'clock position). If accompaniments are served on separate dishes, they are placed on the table, to the guest's left, after the main course is set.

same manner as in the previous courses. Bread and butter plates and butter knives are left on the table only if they will be used during a salad course that follows that main course or when there is a cheese course.

TABLESIDE PRESENTATIONS

In the United States, those restaurants that offer fruit and cheese at the end of a meal generally serve them together. In France, guests typically do not like to mix foods; they prefer to have them *sans mélange,* or pure and unblended. Normally, a cheese board of as few as three or four contrasting cheeses (a total of three to five ounces of cheese) is adequate for even the most discriminating diner.

A simple cheese course is offered in some establishments along with the salad, especially if a respectable Stilton or Roquefort is available. This simplifies the cheese course, but does it with style.

There should also be variety in the accompanying fruit. Only fresh, ripe fruit should be offered. Due to seasonal variations and fluctuating market availability, it is not generally a good idea to specify on the menu exactly which fruit or cheese will be served—but the server should always know what is available each day.

Before the cheese and fruit cart is presented to the table, the server should set a knife and fork in the appropriate places. The cart should be arranged in a neat and organized fashion. The mise en place should be checked: knives to portion cheese and carve fruit, a bowl of clean water to wash certain fruits, service forks and spoons, plates, and clean napkins. Each guest makes a selection of fruit and cheese. Carefully slice and plate the desired cheeses.

Some fruits, such as grapes, may be rinsed in the dining room, since washing them too far in advance can affect their quality and flavor. Using a fork to hold a small cluster, the grapes should be dipped into clean water. The server then places them onto a clean linen napkin atop an appropriately sized plate, serving from the right.

Much food has been consumed by this time, so portions should be modest. If, after completing their first serving, guests desire more, they should be accommodated, of course.

Some restaurants have a cheese and fruit course that is plated in the kitchen, in place of tableside service. It is faster, involves less service, and allows better portion control—although it is less elegant.

After the guests have completed the fruit and cheese course, everything that will not be used with dessert should be cleared from the table: bread and butter plates and knives, bread baskets, butter dishes, salt and pepper, empty wineglasses from previous courses, and any other soiled flatware and dishes.

DESSERT

Ending the meal with a superb dessert is as important as beginning it with a quality appetizer. The insatiable sweet tooth of the American public makes dessert a popular course and the profit margin on most desserts makes this sale quite desirable from a management viewpoint.

A simple and effective approach to merchandising dessert is to offer a separate menu listing desserts and after-dinner beverages. The more unique the presentation of dessert, or even the idea of dessert, the greater the likelihood of the sale. Dessert on the main menu reminds the guest of the amount of food, both in terms of calories and cost, they have just consumed. A simple dessert card or separate dessert menu will arouse the patrons' interests and set them up for a sale. A dessert display or cart, which visually stimulates and lures the guest to order, is even more effective. Merely carrying a tray of available desserts to the table can sometimes be an irresistible presentation.

As with any course, the table must be made ready before dessert is presented and served. After the plates, glassware, and condiments are removed, the table is de-crumbed and the flatware necessary for dessert set in place. If the original table setting included dessert flatware above the cover (as it would for a banquet setting), move the guest's fork down from their left with the left hand, then with the right hand, from the guest's right, the dessert and coffee spoons should be moved down. Wine or Champagne to accompany dessert should be served at this time to the guest's right with the right hand.

All food should be arranged neatly and appetizingly on a dessert cart before presenting it to the guests. Make sure the cart is stocked with all necessary equipment, including serving forks and spoons, napkins, dessert plates, and clean knives for cutting. A container of warm water may prove useful on the dessert cart. Dipping a knife into warm water and then drying it before slicing a cake or pie prevents icing from sticking to the knife.

The dessert cart should be presented and the guests invited to make a selection. Some restaurants offer their guests a sampler plate, so they can try small portions of several different desserts. If the sampler is served family style, bring enough serving utensils to the table. Each dessert order should be plated, and then served open-handed.

AFTER-DINNER BEVERAGES

Guests often enjoy hot beverages, such as tea or coffee, and after-dinner drinks (Cognac, cordials, or dessert wines) at the conclusion of a satisfying meal. A wide selection of coffees and teas can be stocked and controlled in the pantry or cold-food section of the kitchen. A special house blend of American and French roasts can be created by the coffee purveyor. A selection of herbal and regular teas, easily stored in boxes or tins, can also be offered to the guest.

Hot beverages containing liquor, such as café diablo or Irish coffee, can be offered in place of a heavy dessert. This type of selection increases the check average and adds style at the conclusion of the meal.

Before serving after-dinner beverages, all necessary flatware, empty cups, and accompaniments must be delivered to the table. Coffee should be poured at the table from the patron's right side. Orders for after-dinner drinks should be taken in the same manner as before-dinner cocktails. The drinks should be served from the right. (For more detailed information on serving coffee, tea, and after-dinner drinks, sees Chapter 7.)

Table Maintenance

THERE ARE FIVE ASPECTS of table maintenance that a server must consider, aside from the actual serving of food and drinks. We only want to have on the table what might be used in the rest of the meal.

1. Glassware

2. Flatware

3. Clearing

4. De-crumbing

5. Trash

The goal is to keep the table neat, clean, and running smoothly—and to do so as unobtrusively as possible.

CLEARING THE TABLE BY HAND

Depending on the style of the house, clearing of dirty plates begins only after all of the guests have finished that course. In other operations, it is acceptable to clear plates as each guest finishes. If a guest asks for a dirty plate to be removed, it should be done no matter what the house rules. Clear cracker wrappers or sugar packets whenever possible.

In some restaurants, you can use the same method as previously described for carrying plates from the kitchen to the table when you are ready to pick up plates and deliver them to the dish room. There is also a method whereby the plate with the most uneaten food is picked up with the right hand and transferred to the left, and then subsequent plates are stacked on the heel of the hand, balanced with the left ring finger or pinky. In formal restaurants, clearing is done the same way as delivery—no more than two plates at a time.

CLEARING THE TABLE WITH TRAYS

Trays should be placed on a stand, not a table when guests are present. Never stack more than one tray on the tray stand or jack stand. It is very difficult to separate stacked trays when the top one is laden (some establishments get around this problem by inverting all trays except the uppermost tray). The dirty plates should be scraped onto one plate (only when out of the guests' view—and not too close to another table). Never stack more than four plates (and no more than two stacks per tray). Flatware is piled on one side of the tray or separated by type to make it easier to sort in the dish room. Cover the entire tray of soiled dishes and flatware with a serviette.

Glassware should be transported on a separate beverage tray, with the tallest items in the center of the tray. Empty bottles should be laid down so they will not fall over and possibly fall off the tray.

For sanitary reasons, when picking up used glassware it should always be carried upright by the stems, never the rims. Servers should avoid using "the claw," grasping glasses with the fingers inside the glasses. Flatware must never be placed in glasses because it can create invisible hairline fractures that cause the glass to shatter in the heat of the dishwasher.

A bus tub is easier to use, and there is less chance of breakage, if it is placed on a cart. Separate tubs should be assigned for flatware, china, glassware, and waste. Bus tubs should not be placed on the seats of chairs since they may soil or dampen the seat.

DE-CRUMBING THE TABLE

Before dessert (or whenever necessary), the table should be de-crumbed. A special de-crumber or brush may be used to remove the crumbs from the tablecloth into or onto a folded napkin on a six- to ten-inch plate. An alternate approach is to use a folded linen napkin to brush crumbs in, but this method tends to be less effective. Do not sweep crumbs onto the floor or into your bare hand.

To de-crumb a square four-top, imagine a large + on the table running from guest to guest. Begin de-crumbing on the left side of one guest, and then de-crumb the right of the next. Move clockwise around the table repeating this procedure three times to com-

Using a crumber to prepare the table for dessert service

plete the table. The table should not be de-crumbed if no crumbs are present, but should be done at other points in the meal if needed. When de-crumbing a round table, imagine the surface divided into wedges, the point from the center of the table to the middle of each guest. De-crumb from the narrow point to the wide edge of each section.

NOTE: If something liquid, like a drink or soup, spills and dampens a large area of the tablecloth, a half cloth or dinner napkin can be temporarily used to cover the area, rather than replacing the entire cloth during the middle of your guests' dinner. For surfaces that are not covered with linen, a simple wipe with a clean cloth is sufficient.

MONITORING GLASSWARE

The monitoring of glassware is a good example of anticipating the customer's needs. A server should always remember, and practice, the Three Rs.

- ❑ Refill: If a glass or cup is empty, refill it. (In table service, it is not pessimistic to consider a half glass of water empty. It should simply be refilled.)

- ❑ Replace: If a beverage is finished, sell the guest another, or refill it (coffee or tap water). If a cocktail glass is empty, ask the guest if he or she would like a fresh cocktail before you remove the glass by naming the cocktail "Would you care for (like) another martini?"

- ❑ Remove: If the guest does not want a refill or replacement, remove the glass or cup.

Check Presentation and Payment

AFTER THE LAST COURSE HAS BEEN SERVED, and the meal nears completion, the guests should never be abandoned; a server must be available, for example, to offer additional beverages. Many operations instruct their service personnel to present the check only if the host requests it. However, if it is obvious that the patrons are waiting for their check, the server should approach the table and determine if any further services are required.

It is considered inattentive to ask, "Can I get you anything else?" It is better to approach the table with some service to offer, such as the water pitcher or coffee pot and ask, "Would you care for some more. . .?" At which point the host will more than likely request the check.

The correctly totaled guest check should be presented in a book or in a simply folded napkin on a dinner plate.

No matter the type of restaurant, most guests find having to wait for their check especially frustrating. Some of the nonverbal methods a guest might use to "ask" for the check include

At some restaurants, the check is presented with a plate of small sweet items, "mignardises", designed to leave a "sweet taste" in the customer's mouth.

- ❑ Looking around the room, as if searching for something.
- ❑ Making a "checkmark" in the air.

- Writing with an imaginary pen in the air.

- Placing a credit card on the table.

- Reaching for a wallet, or placing it on the table.

- Returning napkins to the table.

- Fidgeting.

- Part of the party getting up to leave (This can be a sign that the guests feel the server has been tardy in presenting the check.)

If no one at the table has specifically requested the check (or is hosting the party), or if there is an argument about who is going to pay, it is best to place the check in a neutral zone not too close to anyone. In some restaurants, the guests are expected to take their checks to the front desk or register—if that is the house policy, the server should politely inform the guests. The server does not leave the table immediately after delivering the check. If guests are ready to leave, they may wish to pay immediately. If they do not indicate that they are ready to pay the check, the server withdraws a short distance and waits for a sign that they are ready.

Friands ("dainty tidbits") or *mignardises* may accompany the check. Like dessert, these *lagniappes* ("something extra," in Louisiana Creole) are meant to leave a sweet taste in the patron's mouth at the completion of the meal—literally and figuratively.

At this point, the server should thank the guests and tell them to whom the check should be paid, if necessary (i.e., to the server at the table or to the cashier). When picking up the paid check, the server stands next to the host, writes the total amount of monies received from the guest on the check, and then excuses him- or herself by saying, "I'll be right back with your change." The server should never assume that the change is a gratuity, or examine or count the tip in front of the guest. The receipt and any change should be returned in the same manner that the check was presented, either in a book or in a napkin on a plate.

The server should be prompt, but not overly hasty, in retrieving the payment once it is placed with the check. If payment is in cash, the money is discreetly counted before leaving the table. The plate is taken to the cashier, and then returned to the table with the

Entering payment into point of sale system.

change and receipt. If the payment is not in cash, the server takes the credit card for processing, and then returns the voucher and the credit card to the guest, along with a plain pen. With the increase is theft and technological advances, many restaurants have the capability of the server swiping the credit card for authorization tableside.

Pens should be "click" type—not capped—to eliminate any temptation to remove the cap with the teeth, and should contain no advertising printing—with the possible exception of the restaurant's name or logo.

It is unprofessional for a server to comment on or show in any way that a tip is expected or that it was not as much as desired. If the server suspects the guests were displeased based on the amount of tip, it should be brought to the attention of the manager to approach the guests if necessary.

The service staff should be prepared to provide any general information that might be requested, such as other available facilities and services, the location of the restroom and telephones, and suggestions as to entertainment areas in the city.

It is not uncommon for guests to choose to take home a portion of their meal therefore state and local sanitation laws will need to be integrated into operational practices for service staff. Several methods of packaging are commonly employed, from the guest self-packaging their food items themselves at the table, the server packaging the food items out of sight and bringing the packages to the table while guests are finishing their meal, to a slightly more "attentive" model, where in addition to packaging food out of sight the packages will be placed in the foyer/entrance/exit with a coat-check style of identification for retrieval upon their departure. Of course this more elaborate style of left-over handling would need to be explained to the guest when giving them their package identification number or tag. The service staff should assist with departure of the guests—as it does with their arrival—helping with parcels, wraps, and any personal items left on the table. The final farewell to the guest should be as engaging as the first hello. Establishing a friendly and lasting impression, in a sincere manner, encourages the guests to return.

Resetting the Table

EACH ESTABLISHMENT HAS ITS OWN POLICY concerning the resetting of tables. It is often disconcerting for those guests still in the dining room at the end of a meal period to find themselves in a kind of demolition zone. It is generally better to reset each table as it is vacated than to reset all of the tables for the next shift at one time. At the end of the evening, glasses can be inverted (to avoid gathering dust) if the surface is sanitary.

Handling Complaints and Other Special Situations

ANTICIPATING GUESTS' COMPLAINTS is as important as anticipating their needs. After serving any food or beverage, servers should not disappear. Servers should stay long enough to observe the guests' behavior and reactions and then return after a minute to make sure everything is still satisfactory.

The truth is that, most likely, someone will have a complaint or other concern. When they do, it's somebody's job to fix it. Problems tend to fall into one of several categories, which need to be addressed in different ways.

When the Table Lingers

How should one deal with those diners who never seem to leave? Usually, these folks are having such a good time that, after the meal, they sit and sip endlessly, as if they are in their living room. Meanwhile, the party waiting for that table might be fuming at the bar. What is a restaurateur to do, especially in a fine dining restaurant or bistro/trattoria, where clients are not very forgiving about waiting?

Jean-Claude Baker, of Chez Josephine in New York City, shares some thoughts about dealing with customers who never leave.

A lot has to do with the price of the restaurant. If you are at Le Cirque in New York or maybe Valentino in Los Angeles, where dinner could be $100 or more per person, customers should be able to linger as long as they like. In a more casual place, like Chez Josephine, with a $37 average check and only seventy seats, you have to rotate the tables to survive. We have a payroll of twenty, and we would starve if we did not.

Early diners are usually no problem. However, the 8:00 to 10:00 P.M. seating is where people can come late, order late, and sit over coffee or after-dinner drinks. Waiters are not usually aware of the

timing problem—but managers and owners are, and they start to panic. They have to do something!

If I know the customers, I might say, "Please, you have to save my life!" Who doesn't want to save somebody's life? "This table was booked at 10:00 P.M. and I have some people waiting at the bar for twenty minutes. Could I buy you a Cognac at the bar so you could save me?" I do not offer cheap dessert wine that comes in tankers; Cognac may cost me money but it keeps the customer happy. By sharing my problem with customers, they become part of the solution. You will find that most people will be very nice about it. Most have no idea such problems exist.

If I do not know the people, I might have to be more firm and professional. "I'm sorry, but sometimes we have people waiting for tables that they have reserved at a certain time." I might offer them something at the bar. It is a double-edged sword, really. If you approach people in the wrong way, you could destroy the relationship that you have had for the past two or three hours.

Jean-Claude Baker, Chez Josephine, New York City

FOOD AND BEVERAGE PROBLEMS

Either there is something wrong with the product and it needs to be replaced, or the guest does not like it and it has to be replaced. If an unsanitary foreign object is discovered in a guest's food or beverage, the server must immediately apologize and replace the item. Most people understand that such things can happen—even in the most fastidious establishments—but a mere glimpse of a misplaced hair or insect can spoil the appetite of the most reasonable of people. Some guests may wish to order something different. (Once, a guest found a slug in her salad—and was afraid to order anything from the responsible kitchen. The maître d' was able to calm her fears by guaranteeing that he could provide a plate on which there was "no place that anything could hide.") If the server handles a problem like this quickly and calmly, the guest will usually be forgiving. As soon as the problem has been resolved to the guest's satisfaction, the server must inform the chef and manager. Always give the guest whatever replacement is requested—and make sure the offending item is removed from the bill.

When a steak is gristly or the Champagne is flat, anyone can see that the product is not up to standard. Normal guest recovery procedures (see Guest Recovery, page 171) can be followed: getting a replacement for the substandard item and perhaps doing a little something extra for the guest. It is not as easy when the guest is not happy with a perfectly good menu item or bottle of wine. Staff members can feel irritated or even angry when a guest complains about, say, a steak that to most observers is cooked perfectly. Unfortunately, medium-rare is a relative term, and the guest's perception is the reality in this case. No matter who explains that the meat is perfectly prepared, the customer will not be happy.

In the vast majority of cases when a guest is unhappy it is because what is on the plate or in the glass is not what they expected. The best solution is to apologize and then bring the guest something pleasing. The truth is, if the customer expects one thing and gets another, the quality of the wrong food does not matter. Part of the solution is a menu that is clear and easy for guests to understand.

The other part is the ability to read a guest's uneasiness during the ordering process or spotting the potential problems with certain types of dishes. Whether real or perceived, guests' disappointment with food that has been served to them must be dealt with swiftly. Disenchantment can turn into annoyance very quickly.

If a guest seems dissatisfied with the food, beverage, or service, or if the server perceives any potential problem with a guest, it is wise to notify the dining room supervisor or manager after handling the problem. When a food item is returned because it is overcooked, undercooked, served at the wrong temperature, or unacceptable in any way, the guest is not usually charged for a fresh item, if the kitchen or dining room is at fault. However, an additional charge may be made if the guest ordered incorrectly in the first place, as when a customer asks that a fresh steak be prepared rare, even though he ordered one well done. In some cases, it may be better to appease the guest by not charging for the item—even if the restaurant was not at fault—in order to keep, or develop, a regular customer.

Anytime an additional item needs to be served, it should be entered into the POS system or added to an error check for inventory and accountability records.

DINING ROOM CONDITIONS

One guest says it is too hot, but another thinks the same dining room is too cold. One guest says that the room is too noisy, while another says she cannot hear the music well enough. Someone complains that the sun is in his eyes, and another person then summons the waiter to ask that the shade be lifted because she cannot see the sunset.

Every dining room has its own foibles, and listening for certain repeated complaints will help you to pinpoint specific problems that need your attention so that you can address common complaints before they happen. Some situations seem constant from restaurant to restaurant. Here are a few:

- Elderly guests tend to feel cold more easily than younger guests do. When possible, seat them away from any known drafts, and when that is not possible, turn down the air-conditioning a bit.

- Most customers do not like to sit next to the swinging kitchen door. Either do not put a table right next to the door or, if you can't afford not to, at least face the table away from the door or make it a four-top; deuces are more easily distracted because fewer people are talking.

- Sitting next to the band or in front of the sound system can be unbearably loud for most guests. Nowadays, audio system designers tend to distribute a larger number of small speakers around the dining room, which allows for lower volume levels but still ensures that the music can be heard throughout the room.

□ Dining rooms that are too dark make it hard to read the menu. Well-aimed lights over the tables or raising the overall light level somewhat will not only solve that problem but also make it easier to see the carefully presented food. In dimly lit dining rooms, servers should carry penlights for the guests as part of their mise en place.

SERVICE ISSUES

Many service problems can be avoided if the manager or captain rarely leaves the dining room. The waiters are, because of the nature of their jobs, moving around the restaurant—picking up drinks from the service bar or running into the kitchen to clarify an order or inform the kitchen that a guest has just gone to the restroom and to please hold the food a minute. The best solution is to have someone whose main responsibility is to watch the room and the guests within it. In most cases, it should be a dining room manager, but in restaurants where the tip pool is big enough, you may see additional headwaiters or captains. The captains can add to the tip pool by selling wine, upselling the menu, and providing more immediate service than the waiter is able to.

When a guest has to wait a long time for anything, the waiter is aware of the problem but may yield to the temptation to hide from the guest rather than deal with the problem. This, of course, adds to the guest's frustration. If the waiter instead goes directly to the guest and explains the delay, the guest, while still somewhat inconvenienced, usually relaxes a bit. In fact, saying something like, "The chef wasn't happy with the quality of your main course and is preparing another one for you," can make the guest feel particularly well taken care of—it is nice to know that the chef is watching over you. The key here is, of course, for the waiter not to avoid the problem—it won't go away by itself, but don't blame anyone else on the team.

GUEST RECOVERY

The term *guest recovery* implies that you had the guest at some point but lost them somewhere along the way, and in a sense that is exactly what happens when there is a problem, whether it is with the food, the service, or the dining room environment.

You can sense when it happens—everything is going along nicely, but then the guest gets the wrong food, or it is cold, or it takes too long, and the atmosphere at that table suddenly changes. Many waiters will avoid the guest at this point, apparently hoping that the problem will go away if they ignore it, but the only reliable way to get a customer back is to address the problem and the guest directly. Avoidance merely exacerbates the problem. When something has gone wrong, the best time to correct it is at the beginning, before the guest has had a chance to become annoyed or resentful.

So how do you bring the annoyed guest back? You communicate with him honestly. For example, a guest tells you that his steak is overcooked. The kitchen immediately puts another steak on the grill, but it will take ten minutes to reach medium-well, the doneness the guest requested. The waiter could avoid the guest altogether, figuring that the steak will eventually arrive. For the guest, those ten minutes can seem like hours, especially if they are not aware that the kitchen is working on the new steak. The guest spends the next ten minutes darting annoyed glances around the room, wondering when the food is going to arrive. It would be better to let your guest know how long it will be until the steak arrives. The guest might be a little miffed but will at least know what is causing the long wait for dinner, and perhaps will be happy to get a little something free out of the deal.

The basic steps of guest recovery are as follows: apologize, correct the problem, make it up to the guest, and finally, follow up to make sure that the situation is amicably resolved.

APOLOGIZE

Apologizing is one of the easiest things to do, but too often, the power of a simple apology is ignored in favor of much more elaborate schemes. When the slipup is not too serious, sometimes an apology is all you need to appease the guest. In the example just given, the waiter could go to the guest, apologize for the anticipated delay, and perhaps bring the guest a little something to munch on during the wait. The foundation of an effective apology is, of course, sincerity. To show sincerity, the server should

- Make eye contact.

- Use the words "I'm sorry" or "I apologize for the error or the inconvenience".

- Avoid blaming others.

Making eye contact is not the easiest thing to do. Eyes are indeed the windows to the soul, but not everybody wants to look in there. Even if you cannot muster the courage to look straight into the eyes of someone who does not, for the moment, like you very much, saying you are sorry goes a long way.

Having apologized to the guest, blaming someone else for the slipup can instantly bring into question the sincerity of the person who is apologizing. Most guests realize that the waiter is not personally responsible for the undercooked chicken, but a server taking the blame can bolster the reputation of the entire staff.

CORRECT THE PROBLEM

There is a series of basic steps that are key to correcting any problem:

1. *Find out the guest's version of the problem.* Do not assume you know what has upset the guest. A veal chop that is still a bit pink in the center is not necessarily the problem. It could be that the guest was not expecting the broccoli rabe.

2. *Remove the offending item.* If there is something on the table that is causing a problem, whether it is food, flatware, china, or glassware that is causing a problem, the sight of it will only upset the guest more. Get it off the table right away.

3. *Take steps to remedy the situation.* Go directly to the person who can accomplish that. For example, if the manager or maître d' is the only person allowed to talk to the chef, then go find him or her—quickly.

4. *Give the guest an accurate timeframe for the replacement.* Do not forget that when everybody else at a table has their food, an extra five minutes to bring a replacement for one of the guests can seem like a lot longer. Once the wheels have been set in motion to correct the problem, you should go to the guest to let them know how long it will take. An honest and accurate estimate will help you to build your credibility. Be conservative, that is, overestimate the time needed. If the replacement item comes out sooner than you said, the guest should be even happier.

5. *Replace any flatware that was removed with the plate.* It pours salt into the wound if the guest has to wait again for the flatware to eat the corrected plate.

6. *Bring the replacement personally, if possible.* First, it shows personal concern. Second, it allows the waiter to confirm the guest's satisfaction, or lack thereof, immediately. If a nameless, faceless runner brings the dish to the table, this cannot take place.

MAKE IT UP TO THE GUEST

Here is where professional judgment and experience can really come into play. The most important thing to recognize is that there are different kinds of problems, of varying degrees of seriousness. There is no single answer to the question, "What should I do to make the guest happy?" A couple of suggestions:

- Consider each situation on an individual basis.
- Do not always assume that offering a free dessert is the best solution.

The response should match the situation in scale and nature. Before choosing a remedy to the situation, consider both the seriousness of the problem and the type of problem. If the guest is unhappy with a cocktail, a glass of wine chosen by the waiter or sommelier to accompany the guest's next course is both more appropriate in style and closer in proximity to the problem than a free dessert at the end of the meal. If the guest complains that the appetizer was lackluster, you might ask to have a plate of risotto sent out along with the main courses— the risotto that you overheard all of the guests discussing, though nobody actually ordered it.

When an entire dinner is ruined by interminable delays, the response needs to be different. Sometimes, it takes a grand gesture such as buying the whole dinner and inviting the guests back for another visit on the house, so they can see what the experience is supposed to be like.

FOLLOW-UP

Arguably, follow-up is the most important part of the guest recovery process. You could carry out all of the previous steps, but it is for naught if the guest never gets the replacement steak or the drinks that you promised to remove from the check are still there. Any goodwill that you engendered by offering to take care of the guest's bad experience is gone when the guest doesn't get what was promised. The more often you carry out these steps in guest recovery, the more precise your judgments will be.

Conclusion

REMARKABLE SERVICE MUST BE CONSISTENT AND LOGICAL, yet flexible. There is no single way to serve a meal. Actually, there are three ways: the correct way, the wrong way, and the best way.

The correct way is to adhere to the rules as established by management. The wrong way is to disregard house policy for no obvious reason. The best way is to adapt the rules to adjust to unique or unforeseen circumstances. For example, most operations instruct service personnel to clear soiled dishes from the patron's right side; this is the correct way. The wrong way would be to remove the soiled dishes from the left side of the patron arbitrarily. However, if two adjacent guests are leaning toward each other, engaged in conversation, the only way to remove the soiled dishes of one of the speakers without disruption is from the left side.

The prescribed procedures for service should not be taken as gospel. Circumstances will always arise that require service personnel to make instant decisions that alter their customary way of doing things. At first, these exceptional situations might prove unnerving—but with experience, they will be handled as second nature.

This chapter has discussed the basic tasks and processes that comprise the service of a meal. However, certain parts of the meal will need a bit more explanation—for example, beverage service, the subject of the next chapter.

7

Beverage Service

AN EXCEPTIONAL DINING EXPERIENCE always includes prompt, knowledgeable, and responsible beverage service, whether you are serving water, soft drinks, cocktails, wine, coffee, or tea. Beverages should enhance the dining experience.

While a great dining experience is always the goal of remarkable service, you should keep in mind that beverage service can be profitable for an establishment. Beverages sales can account for as much as 25 or 30 percent of gross restaurant sales and they often have. They have a better profit margin than food sales. (Note: For information on wine service, see Chapter 8.)

Water

IN MANY RESTAURANTS, water is often the first item brought to your guests after they are seated. Many of your guests will take it for granted, but you should not. Whether you serve only tap water or have a full menu of bottled waters, the way you serve water can set a standard of quality for service throughout the meal. And if you do serve a selection of bottled waters, it can also be an opportunity for a sale. There is a difference between all of the different brands of bottled water. Some contain a higher mineral content, which contributes to a mineral, almost briny taste. Other bottled waters are very low in mineral count, leaving a very clean taste. In most establishments, one sparking and one sill water choice is enough. It can be perceived as an extra level of service if you offer several different styles of bottled water.

TAP WATER

The quality of your tap water depends on the quality of the water in your municipality. Many restaurants now have installed their own filtration and carbonation machines. Depending on your establishment, this might be a greener option than serving bottled waters.

Some establishments serve water automatically and others serve it only upon request which is common in areas with issues of drought and severe water shortages.

It is acceptable to wrap a serviette around a water pitcher to absorb any condensation on the outside of the pitcher from dripping onto guests.

If the table is not preset with water glasses, serve tap water and all other cold beverages in one of the two following ways:

SERVING TAP WATER: METHOD 1

1. Bring empty glass to the table on a beverage tray and place them above each guest's knife.

2. Fill each glass two-thirds to three quarters full with ice water poured from a pitcher, leaving the glass on the table when pouring.

Saving Steps and Improving Service

If your house's standard is to pour guests only after the guests make a request, you can be more efficient and provide the entire table better service if you ask all of the guests whether they, too, would like water.

3. Keep the pitcher's mouth two to three inches from the water glasses and refrain from allowing the pitcher to come in contact with the glass at all times for safety and sanitation purposes.

4. Refill water glasses frequently and never let them get less than one-half full. Alternatively, some restaurants simply leave a pitcher or carafe of water on the table so that guests can refill their own glasses.

SERVING TAP WATER: METHOD 2

1. Bring filled water glasses to the table on a beverage tray in the left hand and place a glass above each guest's knife using the right hand.

2. Refill glasses, pouring from a pitcher, according to the instructions above.

BOTTLED WATER

If you serve bottled water in your establishment, the servers should always recommend it before mentioning iced water. Here's one way to make the offer that gives guests both a free option and an upscale alternative without sounding pushy.

Server: "Would you care for bottled water or ice water?"

Bottled water comes in two varieties:

Still (nonsparkling) bottled water: Noncarbonated water, usually bottled spring water. Still water can also be filtered and bottled water from a municipal source. Not to be caught off guard, many guests will also refer to still water as flat water.

Sparkling bottled water: Carbonated water, which is water containing either naturally occurring or added carbon dioxide. Most sparkling waters contain added carbon dioxide. Another term for sparkling water that is frequently also used is "gas".

If some guests at the table have sparkling and some have still water, it is a good idea to provide different glass styles for each so that all service staff know which type of water the guest is drinking. This will avoid the error of someone pouring still water into a guest's glass of sparkling water.

SERVING BOTTLED WATER

Serve bottled water in a glass that looks different enough from the tap, or "iced", water glass; you do not want to pour tap water into a glass that holds bottled water. Observe these standards for serving bottled water:

□ You may open bottled water at the table.

- Serve bottled water without ice, unless you make the ice from bottled water or the guest specifically requests it.

- Large bottles can be left on the table or, preferably, placed in an ice bucket.

- Although refills on glasses of ice water are always free, be sure to ask guests before bringing additional bottles of water to the table.

Cocktails

AFTER THE WATER HAS BEEN SERVED, the guests may order one or two cocktails (or other alcoholic beverages) as they look over the menu and consider their order.

While many guests will have a favorite standard cocktail, a specialty cocktail menu can be fun for guests and profitable for the restaurant. If there is a house specialty beverage or daily special, the server should be sure to mention it. Many guests prefer to order wine as an apéritif, so be prepared with a wine list.

TAKING THE ORDER

Waiters should know the primary liquor used in drinks to offer better service to their guest as well as to upsell by offering the choice of a better-quality liquor. They should also be aware of all of the possible variations on the drink (perfect or dry, for example), the proper garnish (twists, olives, or cocktail onions, for example), and ways in which the drink may be served (up, on the rocks, or frozen, for example). If a guest orders a specific brand that is not carried or is out of stock, it should be brought to the guest's attention, asking if he or she would care to make another selection.

Every establishment may have a distinct method of requesting the cocktail order. Some more formal options for addressing the guest include:

"Would anyone care for a cocktail before dinner?" *or*

"Would anyone be interested in an aperitif?"

In a more casual setting such as café or bistro, you might use the following:

"Can I get you something from the bar?"

Sometimes the host orders for the entire table, otherwise the server should take orders from women first as follows:

- Begin with the woman seated to the left of the host.

- Proceed clockwise around the table, finishing with the host's order.

- While recording the cocktail order, repeat the name of each cocktail as it is ordered, including garnish.

It is more pleasant for all of the guests if children are also served a drink that makes them feel special. To be safe, ask the host or a parent so he or she can help children choose a suitable beverage, rather than asking young children directly what they want to drink.

- Write standard abbreviations on the dupe pad.

- Excuse yourself from the table by addressing the host, but maintaining eye contact with the entire table, "Thank you, I will be back with your order." It is important that this promise be kept.

- Serve guests their beverages within two to three minutes of the time that they were ordered. With the advent of handheld electronic ordering devises such as small tablet computers that send the order to the bar at the instant that you record it, it is possible that the back waiter can bring the drinks to the table while you still at the table explaining the specials or answering questions about the menu. Using correct seat numbers is crucial.

SERVING COCKTAILS AT THE TABLE

Most cocktails are served from a cocktail tray. When picking up the beverage order from the bar, check to see that the drinks are placed on the tray in the order in which they will be served (women first, for example), carefully noting the position of any similar-looking drinks. A gin and tonic and vodka tonic, for example, can be distinguished by placing two stir sticks, or two lime wedges, in the vodka tonic, since *vodka* has more letters than *gin*.

The tray should be carried on the fingertips of the left hand (this method is much more stable than carrying with the thumb hooked over the edge). The tray should never be held above a guest's head. If you feel that the tray is about to fall, try to have it collapse on you. It is better for you to get wet than the guest.

Observe the following guidelines when serving cocktails at the table:

- Balance the tray on the fingertips of your left hand.

Carry the cocktail tray on the fingertips of the left hand for added stability.

Tipped Trays

Your guests may, on occasion, try to lift drinks from the tray themselves. This is never ideal, and can actually lead to accidents, because only the server can feel whether the tray is balanced. If a guest should reach for a drink, stabilize the tray by grasping its edge with your right hand.

- Position yourself to the right of the first woman to be served with your body at a right angle to the table.

- Bend slightly at the knees as you reach to place the glass on the table to avoid bending at the waist and to help keep the tray level.

- Remove one glass at a time with your right hand.

- Place each drink to the right of each cover or directly on a cocktail napkin, if no tablecloth is used.

- Mention the name of each drink as it is served to eliminate possible misunderstandings with the order.

- Before serving the first course, move the cocktail to the right of the first service glass, and remove the cocktail napkin and any used garnishes.

- If the guest is not finished with the drink by the time the first course arrives, then the drink should be left in place, but, as soon as the guest has finished it, remove it from the table.

Cocktail Napkins

If you use cocktail napkins, place them down on the table so that the restaurant logo is facing the guest. Cocktail napkins are appropriate whenever you serve drinks on table that has no tablecloth. It is a common rule that you should not set paper on linen.

Club Service

Some restaurants offer club service, which means the server mixes simple drinks (such as scotch and soda) at the table in front of the guests. The server should ask if the guest would like the drink mixed. If the answer is yes, the server pours the liquor into the glass, typically over ice, then pours the mixer until the combined liquid fills half the glass. The drink, along with the remaining mixer, is served to the right side of the guest.

Built cocktails are often served over ice, or "on the rocks".

TYPES OF COCKTAILS

Cocktails—distilled alcohol mixed with other beverages—take a variety of forms, depending on the primary liquor. Most cocktails are mixed in or poured into a special cocktail glass. It is important for you to be able to distinguish one cocktail glass from another. All waiters and dining room staff need to know information about cocktails.

Cocktails are mixed in one of five ways:

Build: Pour each ingredient into the glass, one at a time.

Muddle: Place flavoring ingredients like citrus wedges, herbs, berries, and sugar in a mixing glass (or in the glass the drink will be served in). Use a

Flavoring ingredients are added to the bottom of a mixing glass for muddled drinks.

Muddling, or crushing, items, in the bottom of a glass helps to release flavors and aromas.

Stirred cocktails are mixed with ice, which is strained out before serving, known as served UP.

Shaken drinks, like Margaritas, are often strained over ice, known as served ON THE ROCKS.

muddler, a small wooden bat, to crush these ingredients and release their flavor. Add spirit and stir. Add ice and mixer. Garnish if desired.

Stir: Mix ingredients by stirring them with ice in a mixing glass, and then straining the cocktail into a chilled serving glass; this process keeps a drink from becoming diluted by melting ice.

Shake: Mix the ingredients in a hand shaker (Boston shaker) by shaking vigorously; this process is used for cocktails that include cream, fruit juice, or other difficult-to mix ingredients.

Blend: Mix ingredients in an electric blender to blend the ingredients, often including ice, to make drinks such as with frozen strawberry daiquiris and margaritas.

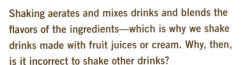

Shaken or Stirred?

Shaking aerates and mixes drinks and blends the flavors of the ingredients—which is why we shake drinks made with fruit juices or cream. Why, then, is it incorrect to shake other drinks?

Part of the enjoyment of many alcohol-only cocktails (such as a martini) is the crystal-clear appearance of the liquor. Shaking such a drink introduces thousands of tiny bubbles that can make the drink look cloudy. In addition, shaking drinks made primarily of liquors could easily dilute them. Instead, drinks like a Manhattan or Rob Roy should be stirred, with good-size ice cubes to chill the drink and give it a noticeable viscosity for a satisfying mouthfeel, without introducing too much water, as shaking might do.

Ice is an important part of any well-made cocktail. The quality and size of the ice cubes used can make a huge difference in the final quality of the drinks that the bartender can produce. A good-size ice cube (1¼ to 1½ inches) allows the bartender to make better drinks. If the drink is shaken or stirred, the lower surface area of the larger cubes will allow the drink to be chilled with less dilution. For rocks or highball drinks, the larger cubes will last longer, keeping a scotch on the rocks from turning rapidly into a scotch and water. Ice should also be free of any foreign objects and should be neutral in taste.

Table 7.1 presents the type of barware to be used for various drinks.

TABLE 7.1 Barware

Glass Type	Capacity	Typical Use
Beer glass	10–23 ounces	Beer
Carafe	0.5–1 liter	Wine, sangria
Cocktail glass, martini glass	4.5–6 ounces	Martinis, Manhattans
Cordial glass	1–4 ounces	Sherry, liqueurs, cordials
Collins/cooler/iced tea	16–23.5 ounces	Iced tea, Collins
Margarita	7–60 ounces	Margarita, tropical drinks
Highball	7–12 ounces	Gin and tonic, rum and Coke, whiskey sour
Mixing glass/pint	16–20 ounces	Beer (traditional Irish beer glass)
Mug/stein/tankard	10 ounces–1 liter	Beer
Pilsner	6–22 ounces	Beer
Pitcher	34–96 ounces	Beer/soda
Port	3–4 ounces	Port
Pub glass/pint	12–19.5 ounces	Beer (traditional English beer glass)
Rocks glass/old-fashioned glass	5.5–10 ounces	Whiskey, scotch, cocktails
Sherry glass	1–4 ounces	Sherry
Shot/shooter	1–2 ounces	Whiskey
Snifter	5.5–7.0 ounces	Brandy

COCKTAIL TERMS

In order to serve your guests, you want to be familiar with a few key cocktail terms:

Apéritif: A dry alcoholic beverage such as Campari, Lillet, or Dubonnet served before a meal, ordered immediately upon seating.

Vodka can be made out of fruits, grains such as rye or wheat, or potatoes. Vodka is filtered through charcoal, diamond dust, quartz, and/or paper before it is bottled, and it is not aged. Despite the common belief that vodka has no flavor, the different ingredients used to make vodka give each variety its own distinct flavor profile. Potato-based vodkas generally have a sweet finish; rye-based vodkas have a slight spiciness; wheat-based vodkas have a soft flavor profile.

Flavored vodkas have become increasingly popular and may include a wide range of fruits from lemon to passion fruit to black currant. Other popular flavors include vanilla, chocolate, and pepper.

Vodka (flavored or not) can be served neat or straight up, as well as in a number of cocktails, including the following:

Bay breeze: Vodka, pineapple juice, and cranberry juice, served on the rocks in a highball glass.

Bloody Mary: Vodka and tomato juice with many savory spices (or bloody Mary mix), served with a wide variety of garnishes (most notably, celery or olives) in a Collins or hurricane glass.

Cape Codder: Vodka, fresh lime juice, cranberry juice, and sugar, served in a highball glass with a slice of lime.

Cosmopolitan: Vodka, Cointreau, fresh lime juice, and cranberry juice shaken with ice, strained into a cocktail glass, and served with a lime wedge.

Greyhound: Vodka and grapefruit juice served on the rocks in a highball glass.

Madras: Vodka, cranberry juice, and orange juice served on the rocks in a highball glass with a lime wedge.

Salty dog: Vodka and grapefruit juice served on the rocks in a highball glass with a salted rim.

Screwdriver: Vodka and orange juice served on the rocks in a highball glass and garnished with an orange slice.

Sea breeze: Vodka, grapefruit juice, and cranberry juice, served on the rocks in a highball glass with a lime wedge.

Vodka gimlet: Vodka and lime juice (preferably Rose's lime juice), served in a cocktail glass and garnished with a slice of lime.

Vodka martini: Vodka and dry vermouth (see Chapter 8 for more on vermouth), either shaken or stirred into a chilled cocktail glass, served straight up, and garnished with cocktail olive or lemon twist (or, occasionally a cocktail onion).

Sour apple martini: Vodka, Sour Pucker Liqueur, shaken and served with a maraschino cherry.

GIN

Gin is an unaged spirit made from grains, flavored with juniper berries and other botanicals. Depending on the botanicals used in making the gin, each has a distinctive flavor profile. Some are more herbaceous while others have a more pronounced juniper flavor. The three basic categories of gin include London Dry, American-style, and Holland or genever. London Dry gin tends to have a more pronounced juniper flavor. American-style gins have a wide range of flavors; they can have light herbaceous notes or very pronounced juniper flavor. Holland or genever gin has a different flavor profile than London dry gin. Genever has malty aroma and flavor.

The type of cocktail determines the correct gin to use. Gin-based cocktails including the following:

Aviation: Gin, lemon juice, maraschino liqueur, crème de violette.

Bronx: Gin, dry vermouth, and orange juice shaken with ice, strained into a cocktail glass, and served with an orange slice.

Gibson: Gin and vermouth, stirred with ice, strained into a cocktail glass, and garnished with cocktail onions and onion juice.

Gimlet: Gin and lime juice (preferably Rose's lime juice), served in a cocktail glass and garnished with a slice of lime.

Gin and tonic: Gin and tonic water served with a lime wedge in a highball glass on the rocks, and stirred.

Martini: Gin and dry vermouth, either shaken or stirred, strained into a chilled cocktail glass, served straight up, or on the rocks and garnished with a cocktail olive or lemon twist.

Negroni: Gin, sweet vermouth, and Campari bitters, stirred with ice, strained into a cocktail glass nearly filled with cracked ice, and garnished with an orange slice.

Tom Collins: Gin, fresh lemon juice, and superfine sugar shaken with ice cubes, strained into a Collins glass nearly filled with ice, and served with club soda, a maraschino cherry, and an orange slice.

RUM

Rum is produced from the fermented sugarcane juice or molasses. Rum is made in over 200 different countries and is a source of great national pride and each claims theirs is the best rum in the world. The two basic styles of rum are light and aged.

Aged rums tend to have a caramel hue, which may be from the type of barrel in which the rum is aged, although may also be the result of adding caramel for coloring.

Light rums have a light flavor and are clear in color; amber rums are darker in color with a more pronounced flavor; dark rums have the strongest molasses flavor. Premium rums have complex flavor profiles and should be reserved for serving on the rocks or in a brandy snifter.

Rum is used in cocktails such as the following:

Bacardi cocktail: Bacardi light rum, lime juice, simple syrup, and grenadine syrup shaken with ice cubes and strained into a cocktail glass.

Cuba libre: Light rum and cola, served on the rocks with the juice of a lime rubbed on the edge of a Collins glass and squeezed into the drink and served with a lime slice.

Daiquiri: Light rum, fresh lime juice, and sugar shaken or mixed in a blender, strained into a Collins glass or martini glass.

Jamaican rum punch: A blend of various types of rum, pineapple, orange, and lime juices, and grenadine syrup, mixed in a blender or punch bowl and served on the rocks.

Mojito: Mint, lime wedges, and sugar are muddled together in a cocktail shaker, then ice is added, followed by a light rum. The cocktail is shaken to dissolve the sugar, then poured into a Collins glass and topped with chilled seltzer.

Piña colada: Light rum, coconut cream, and pineapple juice blended with crushed ice and poured into a Collins glass.

Aromatic Cocktail Bitters

The term *bitters* refers to a mixture of herbs and other aromatics (such as citrus) dissolved in spirits, resulting in a bitter or bittersweet flavor. The purpose of bitters in cocktails is to add depth in flavor and balance out the sweetness of the drink. They are essential for preparing cocktails including Manhattans and old-fashioneds. Bitters have concentrated flavor, which is why you only need a couple of drops in a cocktail. Angostura and Peychads are two of the best-known bitters, but there is a wide range of bitters on the market and many bartenders and mixologists have started to make their own "house bitters."

Rum and Coke: Rum (usually light rum) and Coke (or other cola brand) served with ice in a highball glass.

TEQUILA

Tequila is a spirit produced in seven different areas of Mexico, mostly around the town of Jalisco. Authentic tequila can only come from these regions and is made from the agave plant known as *Agave tequilana weber azul* (blue agave). The finest tequilas are made from one-hundred percent blue agave. Mezcal, another alcohol spirit from Mexico, is made from more types of agave than tequila. Mezcal tends to have a slight smoky, earthy taste. Even though Mezcal is made throughout central Mexico, its center of production is Oaxaca.

There are a few different categories of tequila; each is used and served in specific ways. Silver or "plata" tequilas are not aged and are most often used to prepare cocktails such as those in the list below. Reposado tequila has an earthy profile that can be enjoyed both neat and in cocktails. Aged tequilas ("añejo" or extra "añejo") tend to have a more pronounced, complex flavor than non-aged varieties. Premium and ultra-premium tequilas should be served as you would fine brandies—either on the rocks or in a brandy snifter.

Tequila is featured in the following cocktails.

Margarita: Tequila, triple sec, and fresh lime juice shaken with ice, and either strained in a cocktail glass or served on the rocks, garnished with a lime slice. Guests may request that the glass be salt-rimmed.

Tequila sunrise: Tequila, orange juice, and grenadine syrup served in a highball glass over ice with a stirrer, straw, and cherry or orange slice garnish.

WHISKEY

Whiskey is produced from fermented and distilled grain mash and aged in oak barrels. It is the barrel-aging that gives whiskeys their color and characteristic flavor and differentiates them from clear grain spirits like vodka or gin

There are four basic styles of whiskey—American, Scotch, Canadian, and Irish.

AMERICAN WHISKEYS

There are three distinct styles of whiskeys produced in America: bourbon, corn whiskey, and rye whiskey.

Bourbon, a distinctly American whiskey made mostly from sour mash including at least 51 percent, but no more than 80, percent corn, as well as malt, wheat, and/or rye. It is aged in new oak barrels, contains no coloring additives, and traditionally comes from Kentucky; however, bourbon may be produced elsewhere in the United States.

Corn whiskey has become popular in the last couple of years, corn whiskey is an unaged whiskey that includes least 71 percent corn. Sometimes called "legal moonshine," this spirit has a distinctive, buttered popcorn flavor.

There are rye whiskeys made in the United States. They can be utilized for Manhattans and are the essential whiskey for a Sazarac (rye whiskey, absinthe, sugar, Peychads bitters).

SCOTCH WHISKY

Scotch whisky (note that Scotch whisky is always spelled without the *e*). is the most distinctive style of whisky, with each brand delivering a unique flavor ranging from a soft honey or caramel taste to a heavy smoky iodine taste. These distinct flavors are due to the manner in which the malt is handled and as well as the source location of the peat used to fire dry the malt, lending to the characteristic and pervasive smoky flavor. Scotches that are aged near saltwater often take on a briny taste. Scotches may also be made from a single malt or a blend of malts.

A single-malt Scotch whisky is distilled at a single facility and labeled to indicate to the region of its origin. Blended Scotch whiskys may be distilled at several different facilities and, therefore, may be less expensive. They are known for their consistency and the relative simplicity of their flavors compared to single-malt Scotches.

CANADIAN WHISKEY

Canadian whiskey is a spirit made from several different grains, including rye, giving it its nickname, "rye whiskey." Canadian whiskey must be aged at least three years in oak barrels.

IRISH WHISKEY

Irish whiskey is made predominantly from barley, sometimes with the addition of wheat, corn, and rye, and aged a minimum of three years in used bourbon barrels. The flavor of Irish whiskey is usually lighter than Scotch and is served neat or on the rocks.

Whiskeys of all sorts are commonly served neat or on the rocks. It is also often served mixed with water or soda. Whiskey-based cocktails include the following:

Manhattan: Bourbon or whiskey, sweet vermouth, and Angostura bitters served in a cocktail glass with a cherry or orange slice garnish.

Sours: Bourbon or whiskey, fresh lemon juice, and superfine sugar shaken and served in a whiskey sour glass with an orange slice and cherry.

Blood and sand: Scotch whisky, vermouth, cherry brandy, and orange juice.

Rob Roy: Scotch whisky and sweet vermouth.

BRANDY

Brandy is a distillate made from grapes or other fruit, and then aged in oak barrels from just a few years to as many as forty years. Cognac, the best-known brandy in the world, is double-distilled and produced only in the Cognac region of France; Armagnac is a single-distilled brandy from the Armagnac region of France; and Calvados (an apple brandy) comes from Normandy.

Brandy is categorized as V.S. (very superior), V.S.P. (very superior pale), V.S.O.P. (very superior old pale), and X.O. (extra old, a luxury category). Brandy is served neat in a snifter, often as an after-dinner or dessert drink, or it may be mixed into cocktail.

Brandy is often served neat in a snifter.

used, the degrees of grain toasting, type of yeast used, and the type and amount of hops added that make up the unique characteristics of beer.

Water makes up 95 percent or more of beer and hence is extremely important to the end product. Ironically, it is not uncommon for breweries to use municipal water with minimal filtration versus natural sources.

Malt is the ground grist of selected grains that have been germinated and then toasted to a desired taste profile and developed color. The flavor is affected by the degree to which the malt was roasted with darker roasts developing more sweetness. Most of the malt's sweetness is lost when the naturally occurring sugars convert to carbon dioxide and ethyl alcohol however, some beers, notably porters, and stouts, do retain some sweetness.

Hops are the bitter tasting seed cone flowers of the hop plant, or Humulus lupulus. In beer hops help balance the sweetness of the malt, lend stability to the structure of the beer, and aid in preservation.

Yeast is the kicker for fermentation and the production of carbon dioxide and ethanol alcohol which adds to the flavor and preservation of the beverage.

Unlike spirits, for which you double the percentage of alcohol by volume to get the proof, beers are labeled simply with their percentage alcohol—generally 4 percent for a light beer, 6 or 7 percent for most other beers, and up to 14 percent for a few varieties.

TYPES OF BEERS

Though there is debate as to the number of types of beers, for simplicity most group beers as either lagers or ales, and the primary differences are as follows:

Lagers: Lagers are fermented at cooler temperatures than ales, a process known as "bottom fermenting." As a result, they have a crisp, clean taste. The most popular American brands of beer sold are lagers. Pilsners and bocks are the two varieties of lager that customers prefer most. Lagers usually have an alcohol content of about 4 percent. Serve pale lagers at 45° to 50°F. Dark lagers should be served at 55° to 60°F.

Ales: Ales are fermented at slightly higher temperatures than lagers in a process called *top fermenting*. They tend to have a fruity, full, complex taste, although the taste ranges from bitter to almost sweet (as is the case with porters and stouts). The color, too, can vary from blond to almost black. The most popular varieties of ales include India pale ale, stout, porter, and lambic, and all have a slightly higher alcohol content than lagers with most in the range of 6 to 8 percent. Serve light ales at 50° to 55°F; serve dark ales at 55° to 60°F. A general rule is the higher the alcohol content, the higher the serving temperature; however, too high a temperature risks shortening the beer's life span, and too low induces cloudiness.

SERVING BEER

Serving beer to your guests demands the same care and attention as you would give to the service of any other food or beverage. The style of beer determines the type of glassware that should be used, the ideal service temperature, and the type of head. Aficionados will expect that your beers are carefully selected to accompany the restaurant's cuisine, that beers are carefully stored and chilled, and that the beer has the correct color, body, and aroma, Some of your guests may prefer to pour their own beer to achieve the desired head.

Serve beer in a perfectly clean glass—without any oil or detergent residues—so as not to destroy the flavor and head of the beer. A pilsner glass has traditionally been the glassware of choice for serving beer, but fine ales are often served in goblets because of their more complex aroma.

The size of foam *head* that should result from pouring each type of beer varies. Traditionally, lagers should have a 1-inch head, ales a ¾-inch head, and stouts only a ¼-inch head. The longer a beer is poured straight down into the center of the

Tip the glass at a 45 degree angle and pour straight into the bottom of the glass.

Slowly pour the beer while the glass sits flat on the table.

.08 percent, a person might have slurred speech and blurred vision. However, driving may be impaired with a BAC as low as .05 percent (three to four drinks per hour for a large person; two drinks per hour for a small person). One drink is defined as one and a half ounces of 80-proof spirits, three ounces of 14-percent wine, six ounces of 6-percent wine (including most white wines), or twelve ounces of 4-percent beer.

CHECKING IDS

Always check IDs, and check them carefully, even for patrons who appear to be well older than the legal drinking age of twenty-one. If you suspect that a customer is trying to pass a false ID, ask the patron to show a second form of ID or verify the information on the ID, such as asking middle name, date of birth, and address. Politely but firmly refuse to serve customers who do not have any ID, appear to possess a false ID, or do not resemble the picture on the ID.

Coffee and Tea

COFFEE ORIGINATED IN AFRICA, where, according to legend, it was discovered by a ninth-century Abyssinian goat herder, who observed lively behavior in goats that had nibbled the coffee berries from the shrub. Cultivation of the coffee shrub began in the fifteenth century and the beverage arrived in Europe in the seventeenth century. Coffeehouses quickly became social and political gathering spots.

Tea has been in use for about 5000 years. The Chinese legend says that Emperor Shen Nong issued a mandate that water for drinking be boiled first. One day, some leaves fell into the water as it boiled. The emperor was intrigued by the smell and sampled the brew. Another legend, this from the story of Siddhartha's journey from Nepal to China, tells us that Siddhartha had pledged to forgo sleep on that journey, but he fell asleep anyway. When he woke up, he cursed his eyelids, tore them from his face, and threw them on the ground, whereupon they grew into tea bushes.

Today, your coffee- and tea-drinking guests may be highly sophisticated about their favorite hot beverage. Reputations can be made or lost on the basis of a cup of coffee or a pot of tea. In fact, an entire restaurant category—coffeehouses—caters to the almost religious experience of coffee drinkers consuming an excellent cup of coffee. Tea shops provide the same experience for tea lovers. Restaurants that can provide not only an excellent product but also excellent service have a distinct advantage when it comes to word-of-mouth recommendations.

To create a coffee beverage, the green coffee beans are first roasted, a process that affects the color, flavor, and intensity of the brewed coffee (long roasting makes for a darker, stronger, less bitter, more robust coffee than does a shorter roasting time). Arabica beans are considered by many to be the best in quality of flavor though commonly more expensive than Robusta beans. Dark- and light-roasted beans can be combined into special blends, in order to achieve an almost infinite variety of flavors. After roasting, the beans are ground, either finely or coarsely, depending on how the coffee will be brewed.

Decaffeinated coffee (which contains only about 3 percent of the caffeine of regular coffee) is now so popular that, in some restaurants, guests request it twice as often as caffeinated coffee. Decaf coffee beans are either soaked in water or exposed to a chemical gas to extract the caffeine from the beans; water extraction (often called "the European method" or "the Swiss water process") is the less toxic—and, in the opinion of many people, has the best flavor—and is requested most often among discerning coffee drinkers. Be sure decaffeinated coffee holding and serving vessels are well marked in order to easily differentiate products for servers as well as is the case in many casual-style restaurants, to visually reassure the guest. Common signs are the use of different colored coffee pot handles such as green or orange.

Oils in the beans flavor the coffee, but those oils oxidize easily, which is why ground coffee is vacuum sealed; after the seal is broken, ground coffee should be stored in airtight containers. Whole beans can be stored at room temperature for only about two weeks, but last far longer than ground coffee. For this reason, fine restaurants grind whole beans each day as needed to achieve the freshest, most flavorful coffee.

AMERICAN COFFEE

The best coffeemakers brew the grounds at 205° to 207°F and hold it at 185°F—but do not leave brewed coffee over direct heat for more than twenty minutes. Many establishments use a series of small coffeepots (ten to twelve cups) as transport vessels instead of one or two large industrial-size coffee urns, so that the waitstaff can serve directly from the brewing pot at the table, instead of pouring the coffee in the kitchen and carrying full cups on a tray to the guests.

Making Cappuccino

1. Fill a pitcher about one-fourth full with milk.

2. Position the pitcher so that the tip of the steaming nozzle is at the surface of the milk and turn the steam on.

3. Continue steaming, lowering the pitcher to keep the tip of the steamer at the surface of the milk until the milk has doubled in volume and filled the pitcher.

4. Prepare the espresso as described in steps 1 through 3.

5. Use a spoon to hold the foam back and pour steamed milk into the espresso. Spoon the foam on top of the espresso. Garnish with cinnamon, cocoa, or shaved chocolate.

6. Wipe down the steamer spout between uses!

7. Remove the spent grounds from the filter and clean it between uses.

8. Return the empty arm to the machine.

as is soy milk for customers who either cannot or prefer not to consume dairy products. Skim milk foams better than whole milk, but whole milk adds flavor and the froth is more stable. The milk must be cold in order to create the foam. Many baristas now make it with one-third espresso and two-thirds steamed milk in a graduated foam method, though appearing similar to a latte. Although it is not traditional, cinnamon, cocoa, or chocolate shavings may be added to the top of the foamed milk.

An espresso machine brews one or two cups of specialty coffee at a time, and although it does much of the work for you, the coffee has to be ground to the right consistency and properly tamped into the machine. Most coffee suppliers have developed prepackaged, preground espresso servings that are said to produce a more consistent product with a cleaner process. Available in the form of pods, cartridges, or capsules (according to the brand of espresso you use), this style of coffee requires an adapter arm that is provided by the supplier. Some of these preground, preportioned espresso servings are less likely to make a long-lasting crema, but advances are being made continually to the quality of these convenient products.

For cappuccino, the machine should heat the milk as it is foamed, to no more than 158°F to avoid a scalded taste. The top of the espresso machine should be used only to warm espresso and cappuccino cups. The elements in making a good espresso are the quality of the beans, the coarseness of the grounds, the amount of grounds, the correct pressure applied when packing the grounds, a clean espresso machine, the quality, pressure and temperature of the water, preheated brewing arm, preheated cups, and length of time for the extraction. The espresso machine should not be turned off overnight, to preserve the heating element. The machine should be cleaned and backwashed daily.

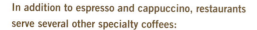

Other Specialty Coffees

In addition to espresso and cappuccino, restaurants serve several other specialty coffees:

LATTE: Espresso with more steamed milk than a cappuccino and no foam.

MACCHIATO: Espresso with a dollop of steamed milk on top.

LATTE MACCHIATO: Steamed milk with a dollop of espresso on top.

DOPPIO: Double espresso.

RISTRETTO: Espresso made with a little less water, thereby producing a much stronger flavor.

LUONGO: Espresso made with a little more water.

FREDDO: Iced coffee served in a tall glass; espresso freddo (or caffé freddo) is iced espresso; cappuccino freddo is iced cappuccino.

CORRETTO: Espresso that has been "corrected" by adding a little alcohol, usually Sambuca or grappa.

HOT TEA

All tea comes from the same plant, the *Cameliasinensis*. The way the tea is picked and processed determines whether the final product is known as green, black, oolong, or white, as well as herbal teas, also known as *tisanes*:

- Green teas come directly from un-oxidized tea leaves. "Their" flavors are best developed when steeped between 165° and 180°F.

- Black tea, the most popular form of hot tea consumed by Americans, is fully oxidized before it is dried, and is best steeped at 190° to 210°F for no more than five minutes.

- Oolong tea is lightly fermented before it is dried and is best steeped at 175°F to 190°F for five to eight minutes.

- White teas are from tea leaves and buds that are allowed to wither in natural sunlight before they are lightly processed to prevent oxidation and is best steeped at 180°F for five minutes.

- Herbal teas are not really tea at all but dried herbs and flowers. There are no widely agreed to standards for steeping herbal teas, although steeping at about 190°F is a safe guideline.

Store all teas in a clean, dry container, away from moisture, light, and strong-smelling foods.

8

Wine Service

WINE IS THE CLASSIC COMPLEMENT TO A FINE MEAL, but many diners lack confidence in their ability to choose wines that enhance the flavor of their meals. A knowledgeable server can alleviate a diner's apprehension about wine choices—and will be rewarded for doing so, given that wine can total as much as 35 percent of the check for some diners, resulting in a much larger gratuity. For this reason, be sure to ask, "Would you like to see our wine list?" or "Will you be having wine this evening?" as soon as guests are comfortably seated. This chapter shares the basics of wine production, styles of wines you may find on the wine menu, and best practices for serving wine to your guests. *For information on serving other beverages, see Chapter 7.*

What Is Wine?

WINE, OR THE FERMENTED JUICE OF GRAPES AND OTHER FRUITS, has been recognized as long as there has been written recordings of human civilization.

Originally, yeast, a living organism found on the skin of ripe grapes, transformed the sugars naturally present in grape juice into alcohol and carbon dioxide whereas today many wine makers choose specific strains of yeast in order to better control and predict fermentation. During the process of wine production, the grapes go through several stages. First they are harvested, either by hand or machine, sorted, and then crushed. The resulting grape pulp, known as *must,* is then placed in large vats for a process known as *primary fermentation*.

The next stage is the separation of the juice from any solids (known as the lees) and transferring of the juice to clean containers such as vats or barrels for a secondary fermentation and bulk aging, a process that is typically slower than the primary fermentation. During this secondary fermentation, some or most of the sugar in the wine is consumed by the yeast.

Following the secondary fermentation, wines may be blended to achieve a particular style or flavor and finally, they are bottled or capped, and labeled. Many wines are further aged in the bottle before release and consumption.

GRAPES

Wines, or the grapes they are made from, obtain their distinctive characteristics as a result of terroir, which includes the geographic location, climate, soil type, sun exposure, altitude, and irrigation. Grapes do not ripen as well in colder regions as in warmer regions. That means that wines from colder growing areas produce wines that are lighter-bodied and highly acidic. Wines made from grapes that grow in warmer, southern regions tend to be full-bodied with less acidity. See Table 8.1, Major Wine-Producing Grapes.

Styles of Wine

THE SPECIFIC VARIETY OF THE GRAPE, the condition of the grapes when they are picked, the age of the vines, the control of the fermentation process, and the storage techniques used after fermentation play a role in final quality of the wine.

TABLE 8.1 Pairing Food and Wine

APPETIZERS	
	Dry, light-bodied wines; sparkling wines such as CHAMPAGNE or PROSECCO

PASTA	
Fettuccine Alfredo (cream sauce)	Frascati, Sauvignon Blanc
Lasagna (tomato sauce)	Chianti, Cabernet Sauvignon
Spaghetti primavera (light sauce)	Soave, Sauvignon Blanc

FISH AND SEAFOOD	
Grilled or broiled fish	Chardonnay, Sauvignon Blanc
Fresh shellfish	Sauvignon Blanc, Johannisberg Riesling
Fried fish	Chardonnay, Johannisberg Riesling

POULTRY	
Chicken with light cream sauce	Chardonnay, Johannisberg Riesling
Barbecued chicken	Gamay Beaujolais
Sweet-and-sour chicken	White Zinfandel, Johannisberg Riesling

BEEF	
New York strip steak	Cabernet Sauvignon, Merlot
Filet mignon with béarnaise sauce	Cabernet Sauvignon, Merlot
Beef stroganoff	Merlot, Pinot Noir

PORK/VEAL/LAMB/HAM	
Roast pork	Chardonnay, Gamay Beaujolais
Glazed ham	White Zinfandel
Grilled pork chops	Gamay Beaujolais, Zinfandel
Veal parmigiana	Zinfandel, Chardonnay

LIGHT ENTRÉES	
Fruit salad	Johannisberg Riesling
Quiche Lorraine	Sauvignon Blanc, Chenin Blanc
Chicken Caesar salad	Sauvignon Blanc, Chardonnay

Winemakers, known as *vintners,* can adapt and intervene in the process at several points in order to create an array of different wine styles:

- Red, white, or rosé (blush) wines
- Still
- Sparkling
- Fortified

Wine drinkers often use a specific vocabulary to discuss various characteristics of wine that, taken together, are meant to describe a specific wine's flavor as well as its style.

RED, WHITE, OR ROSÉ WINES

Grape skins contain most of the fruit's pigment and tannins. The pigment determines the color of the skin: red or white. The tannins contribute two characteristics to the wine's character: astringency and bitterness.

The color of the skin and the length of time the skin stays in contact with the juice from the grape during fermentation have a direct impact on color of the finished wine as well as its flavor. In general, white-skinned grapes produce white wines and red-skinned grapes produce red wines. However, if the red skins are kept away from the pulp during processing, the resulting wine will be white, even though the grape's skin was red.

Red wines are made from red-skinned grapes. The longer the skin stays in contact with the grape juice, the deeper the color of the wine. If the skins are left in the pulp as it ferments, the result is a deep red to purple color. If the skins are removed relatively early in the process, the result is a pink or blush color, often known as rosé.

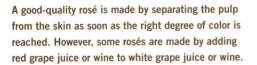

About Rosé Wines

A good-quality rosé is made by separating the pulp from the skin as soon as the right degree of color is reached. However, some rosés are made by adding red grape juice or wine to white grape juice or wine.

While this technique is usually associated with less expensive wines, rosé Champagne, a notable fine wine, is an exception to this general rule.

STILL WINES

During fermentation, yeasts consume the sugars in the wine and produce alcohol and carbon dioxide. If the carbon dioxide gas escapes from the wine during fermentation, the product is called *still* or *table* wine. The European Union, however, defines table wine as any wine that does not meet the appellation standards and is the least distinctive legal category for wines. This has led some people to assume that the term *table wine* means that the wine is somehow inferior to other wines. In the United States, table wines may contain from 7 to 16 percent alcohol. Table wines in Europe may have an alcohol content of 7 to 14 percent. See Opening Still Wines on page *224* for opening and serving instructions.

SPARKLING WINES

To make a sparkling wine, the carbon dioxide produced during the fermentation process must be captured in the bottled wine. When sparkling wines are served, you can see, hear, and feel the fizziness in the wine. Although most sparkling wines are white, they can also be red or rosé. The alcohol content of most sparkling wines ranges from 8 to 14 percent. See Opening Sparkling Wines on page *225* for opening and serving instructions.

Sparkling wines range from very dry to very sweet on the following scale: extra-brut, brut, extra-dry, sec, demi-sec, and doux and are produced in one of three ways:

Méthode champenoise: As with most wines, the fermentation process begins in a large vat, but the wine is then bottled and fermented again, remaining in that bottle until it is opened by the consumer (look for a label that says, "fermented in this bottle"). During the second fermentation process, sugar and yeast are added to the bottle to produce more carbon dioxide and develop additional flavors. This process produces a sediment that must be expelled before shipping the wine, and when the cork is removed to expel the sediment, more sugar may be added.

Transfer method: Due to the trouble inherent in removing sediment from the bottles, some sparkling wine is transferred to a pressurized machine that removes sediment quickly after the second fermentation process is complete. From there, the wine receives a sweetening dosage and is rebottled. The label will say, "fermented in the bottle." The difference between that statement and "fermented in this bottle" reflects the differences in method, and often, in quality and price between method champenoise and the transfer method.

The more wines you taste, the more knowledgeable you will be when guests have questions about the wine list. If your establishment does not offer wine-tasting sessions for servers, ask the dining room manager whether such events can be scheduled. When tasting wines, keep a notebook in which you record the wine's name, vintage, cost, description, and personal impressions.

To taste wine, you first hold the wine up to the light (or a white background) to note its color; then swirl the wine in the glass (do not swirl sparkling wines). Next you smell the wine with your nose down in the glass. Finally, taste the wine, and note the impression left in the mouth after swallowing or spitting the wine out. When going through this process, note the color and clarity, body, aroma and bouquet, and taste of the wine.

Charmat or bulk method: With this method, the wine is kept under pressure in large tanks and it is also given sugar and yeast in order to produce more carbon dioxide, before the sediment is filtered out and the wine is bottled.

FORTIFIED AND AROMATIZED WINES

Fortified wines are wines "fortified" by adding grape brandy or other additional alcohols in order to either stop the fermentation process (which thereby changes the flavor of the wine) or simply to increase the alcohol content of the wine. Compared to still and sparkling wines, the alcohol content of fortified wines is significantly higher—between 17 and 22 percent.

Apéritif wines are a type of fortified wine also known as aromatized wines because they have been flavored with aromatics such as herbs, spices, flowers, or bark. They are usually served before a meal and may be either sweet or dry. Vermouth is one such example of an apéritif or aromatized wine.

Some dessert wines, including port, sherry, and Madeira, are also fortified to produce a sweet, full-bodied wine that is served after a meal.

Wine Labels

THE MAIN WINE LABEL gives you four important pieces of information about a particular wine: the type or name of the wine; the vintage; the region; and the producer. The vintage may also be listed on the neck label, if there is one, which makes the vintage easier to identify. Wines sold in the United States must also list the alcoholic content (as a percentage), state whether it is a still or sparkling wine, and must also include a printed warning about the dangers of alcohol consumption.

A wine's vintage wine tells you the specific year that the grapes used to produce a wine were harvested. Some vintage years are considered "exceptional," which means that wines can be left to age in the bottle for longer periods than wines from unexceptional vintage years. Most wines, even the unexceptional ones, include a vintage (date) on the wine label indicating when the grapes were picked. A vintage chart lists the quality of grape harvests. Although this chart cannot give you a sense of the quality of the wines from a given year, it can give you a general idea about which years are better than other.

The shape of wine bottles varies depending on the type of wine contained within.

Wine Storage

Storing wine properly is essential for maintaining its flavor. Wines have corks, or caps, to protect them from contact with air. Air will cause the wine to oxidize and lessen in quality. The bottles must also be kept at a constant temperature (and not extremely hot or cold), away from sunlight, free from vibration, and away from herbs and other foods with strong odors. Keep all wines in a well-ventilated, dark, odor-free, vibration-free area that is temperature controlled (between 55° and 60°F (13° and 16°C), with no fluctuations).To help prevent the corks from drying out, the humidity in the wine storage area should be 70 percent. If it is too high, this could increase the chance of mold on the corks.

Store all wines horizontally (on their sides) to prevent the cork from drying and shrinking, but avoid having bottles roll around the storage area—instead, hold them still in racks or bins.

For easy identification and to avoid disturbing the sediment, keep labels up, facing the ceiling. Some establishments also use a numbering system that corresponds to a wine list—wine bottles are tagged with numbers that match those on the list.

Convenient access to the wine storage area from the dining area is essential; otherwise, keeping a par stock (a supply equal to the amount normally needed) in the dining room is advisable. The area that you store the wine should have limited access in order to discourage theft.

The Wine Menu

THE WINE EXPERIENCE in the dining room begins with the wine menu, which includes a listing of wines available in a variety of formats such as the full- or half-bottle or carafe, as well as wines available by the glass. While some restaurant menus may combine the food and wine offerings into a single menu, a separate wine menu is common for a restaurant with an extensive list.

The timing of the presentation of the menu varies from place to place. Historically, one wine list would have been presented to the host at the table (typically a man) by the sommelier. Today, many restaurants simply present the wine menu along with the regular menu. Some prefer to wait until the guests have indicated that they would like to see it. Some establishments may have the server address the table along these lines: "Would you care to see our wine list?" or, "Will you be having wine this evening?"

If there is an identifiable host at the table, hand the menu to that person. If there is no clear host, you can ask the table who would like to see the menu, or place it in the center of the table. A menu that offers an extensive selection of wines by the glass can be offered to all of the adult guests at the table.

Taking the Wine Order

WHETHER DONE BY THE SOMMELIER, maître d', or server, the wine order should be taken with elegance and grace. Do not offer suggestions unless asked, but do answer all questions completely. If guests are struggling with which wine to order, you may want to ask, "What type of wine do you normally enjoy?" You can then suggest similar wines from your list.

Ask the host (or individual guests) whether they want the wine served before or with the meal, as well as which course the wine is meant to accompany.

PAIRING FOOD AND WINE

The adage that red wines should be paired with red meats and white wine with "white" foods such as poultry, pasta, and fish is no longer considered gospel. Instead, discerning wine drinkers are encouraged to choose the wine flavors that they enjoy most.

If guests ask which wine they should order, ask about their tastes and preferences, as well as their price range. Keep in mind that a table of four people is likely to order different foods, so a finely tuned wine pairing goes out the window anyway, unless you only go with wines by the glass.

Some establishments offer guests wine charts that match wine varieties to the foods with which they are best paired. At other establishments, those charts are only for the staff and include the wine number (for easy identification in the storage rack), name, pronunciation, year, bottle size, price, type (red, white, rosé, sparkling, fortified), origin, serving temperature, characteristics (body, flavor, bouquet), and recommended accompanying dishes. Other restaurants don't have charts at all, so it is wise to know as much as possible about the wines offered at your establishment.

If the wine selection in your establishment is well chosen but simple, you will be able to help guests make wine selections without a copious amount of additional wine education. In establishments where the wine selection is vast, a sommelier (wine steward) assists guests in selecting wines. If your establishment does not employ a sommelier and has a large wine list, you may be educated about the wines your restaurant carries through tastings and seminars. In addition, the manager may suggest wines to go with each day's special menu offerings in pre-service meetings.

When Guests Bring Their Own Wine

Some establishments allow guests to bring their own wine, either as a general policy or for some special occasions. Keep in mind, however, that the lost revenue may be substantial. Corkage fees are common in establishments that allow guests to bring their own wine—these fees cover the cost of handling, uncorking, and serving the wine, as well as washing the glasses. Fees may be charged per person or per bottle, but generally range from $2 to $5 per person or $15 to $50 per bottle. Not all states allow guests to bring their own wine. Check with your state and county beverage laws.

Some basic wine "flavor" understanding and terminology can help service staff navigate the wine menu in order to best assist guests in determining the most enjoyable selection for their dining experience.

Wine flavors are described in the following terms:

Fruit: when most people say a wine is "fruity", they usually mean it's sweet. Fruit flavors in wine can actually mimic sweetness, so technically dry wine (one with no residual sugar) can seem sweet. Grapes themselves have a broad range of esters (flavor molecules) that can mimic the flavors of other fruits. Add to this the fact that fermentation also creates other flavors, and you can wind up with aromas of green pepper or strawberry. Remember, most of what we think is taste happens in the nose—so smells turn into flavors. While you might think that you taste sweetness, you are experiencing the aroma of something else (like peach) that is sweet.

Tartness: The acidity of grapes both preserves the wine and flavors it. The prevalent acid in grapes is malic acid, which is also found in apples. A tart wine helps balance rich foods that are high in fat content. Wines that are high in acid can make your mouth water.

Tannins: Tannins are found in the skins, pits, and stems of grapes, and although they act as an excellent preservative (they were once used to tan leather), they also can add a bitter, astringent flavor to wines, as well as drying sensation on the sides of the mouth. Red wines have tannins than white, and because tannins soften with age, older red wines tend to have a softer mouth feel, and somewhat less bitterness.

Body: Body refers to the weight, or feeling, of a wine in your mouth. For dry wines, this sensation is usually related to the percentage of alcohol since glycol, an alcohol related sugar, makes the wine feel thicker. The more alcohol there is, the more glycol there is, and the thicker the wine feels. Body can be important when matching wine with food—big wine (such as Napa Valley Cabernet) overpowers light food (such as boneless chicken breast) and light wine (like Muscadet) tastes watery with big food (like grilled salmon).

Balance: Balance refers to the combination of fruit, tartness, tannins, and body; that is, how all of the proceeding flavors work together. A wine that is neither too fruity nor too tart, with a nice complexity of flavor, gives you a well-rounded drinking experience.

COMPLEMENTING AND CONTRASTING FLAVORS

Aside from sticking with a wine one is conformable with, complementing and/or contrasting flavors of dishes and wines is a means of truly enhancing a meal.

Matching intensity of wine with food includes matching all facets of the experience—matching the body of the wine with the general body of the dish, general intensity or impact of flavor, texture, or predominant flavor profiles. Primary ingredients, cooking methods, and dish accompaniments and garnish are all equally important to the wine paring.

Mise en Place for Wine Service

THE RIGHT GLASS FOR WINE SERVICE can do more than simply hold the wine. The shape of the bowl of the glass can affect the wine's bouquet and taste. Knowing the style of wine you are about to serve will guide you to the appropriate mise en place for opening and pouring wines, as well as the correct glassware.

To teach yourself about the capacity of the various wineglasses used in your restaurant and to make it easier to pour consistently for an entire table without either under- or overpouring, practice filling wineglasses with a measured amount of ice tea so you can tell by looking how much wine you have poured.

Still wines generally call for a corkscrew, a coaster and a serviette. Sparkling wines typically call for a wine bucket and a napkin. Some red wines may be decanted prior to service, which indicates the need for a wine basket, decanters, a candle, and matches or a flashlight.

GLASSWARE

Wineglasses in different shapes and sizes are meant to serve different wines. The best design for a wineglass for still wines is a stable-based, stemmed, bowl-shaped glass with the rim turned in slightly. The bowl of a white wineglass has a smaller opening to capture and hold the aroma and bouquet; the opening for a red wineglass is generally wider in order to promote aeration of the wine. Sparkling wines are generally served in stemmed glasses known as *flutes* that have tall, relatively narrow bowls, meant to prevent the wine from losing its bubbles too quickly. You should know which glasses your establishment has in stock and as well as which glass pairs with which wines.

Most wineglasses have a capacity of about 8 to 24 fluid ounces. Very large glasses may hold as much as 16 fluid ounces. However, a typical wine pour ranges

Uniform pours in different wine glasses. From left to right: champagne flute, white wine, red wine, and dessert wine.

from 3 ounces when poured at the table to 5 ounces when poured at the bar or for sale "by the glass." Why is there so much extra room in a wineglass? The larger the bowl, the more room left for aromas to accumulate and the more opportunity for the drinker to evaluate and appreciate the wine's aromas. Unfortunately, oversized glasses filled with a standard pour can give the impression that your pour is rather meager, so some restaurants prefer to serve wines in standard-size glasses, but reserve the extra-large glasses for guests who specifically request them.

Glassware for wine must be impeccably clean, because the aroma and taste of wine can be affected by foreign substances and soap residue. It can even diminish the effervescence of a sparkling wine. You should always *steam and polish glasses prior to service* as described on page *83.* Whether or not you have steamed and polished glasses, check glasses for spots before bringing them to the table and remove any spots you find with a clean, lint-free cloth.

After the guest orders the wine, but before you bring the wine to the table, set the appropriate wineglasses on the table, either by carrying them on a tray or carried by the stems between your fingers (see page 85). Whether you are bringing clean glasses to the table or removing used glasses, remember to handle the glassware either by the stems, never put your hands around the rim of the glass.

If separate wines are served for different courses, bring all of the required glasses to the table at once and set them at each place, with the first glass to be filled closest to the tip of the main course knife's position. Remove the glass used for the first wine only after the second wine has been poured. If there is still some wine remaining in the glass, ask the guest if he or she would like to keep the glass or have it cleared.

CORKSCREWS

A captain's corkscrew (also called a *waiter's tool*) it is the most popular because it folds up so that you can keep it in your pocket. Be sure yours has a spiral worm with at least five curves, with the outsides of the curves are grooved to provide a strong grip on the cork. Bordeaux corkscrews will have two levers for longer corks.

MAINTAINING THE WINE'S TEMPERATURE

Chilling takes approximately fifteen minutes. However, sparkling wine bottles are thicker than white wine bottles, so they require more chilling time:

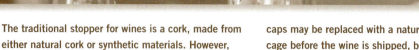

About Wine Corks and Other Stoppers

The traditional stopper for wines is a cork, made from either natural cork or synthetic materials. However, there are a variety of other stoppers you may encounter.

NATURAL OR SYNTHETIC CORK Natural cork is easier to remove than synthetic or plastic stoppers, is biodegradable, and can be used to reseal an open bottle. However, cork may allow some air into the bottle and may introduce trichloroanisole (TCA), the compound chiefly responsible for musty flavors and aromas. Synthetic or plastic stoppers are inexpensive but they are nonbiodegradable and are more difficult to reinsert in a bottle.

METAL SCREW CAPS Metal screw caps make a virtually air-tight seal and can be used to reseal an opened bottle. To remove screw caps, hold the bottle in your non-dominant hand. Wrap your other hand around the cap so that it is inverted with your thumb pointing toward the floor, and twist sharply to break the seal. Twist the cap off at this point.

CROWN CAPS Effervescent wines may be sealed with crown caps like those used to seal sodas or beer. These caps may be replaced with a natural cork and a wire cage before the wine is shipped, but some producers do not replace them. These caps are an effective seal, but do not provide the "show" guests often expect during sparkling wine service, since you simply pop them off the bottle with a lever-style bottle opener.

GLASS STOPPERS Glass stoppers are covered by a capsule and a screw cap. Once the capsule and cap are removed, the stopper is pulled from the bottle; no tools are required to remove or reinsert the stopper. These stoppers offer excellent protection from oxidation.

ZORK The Zork looks like a traditional bottle stopper covered with a capsule. The stopper itself consists of three parts; a clamp that holds the cap securely onto the bottle, a sheet of metal foil that seals the bottle, and a plunger. To remove the Zork from a bottle, pull on the plastic "ribbon" holding the cap in place. Pull the cap away from the bottle to open the seal and lift out the plunger. The plunger recreates the sound of a cork's "pop" during the opening ceremony and seals the bottle up when the Zork is reinserted.

- White and rosé wines are served chilled and, once opened, are held at the table either on a coaster or in a holder. They do not need to sit in ice after they are opened because they are best at a serving temperature of 44° to 54°F (7° to 12°C).

- Sparkling wines are served chilled and, once opened, are held in a wine bucket to maintain a serving temperature of 41° to 47°F (5° to 8°C).

- Red wines are served at room temperature and, once opened, are held at the table on a coaster or in a wine holder, never in a wine bucket. Light red wines are best served at 50° to 55°F (10° to 13°C) and full-bodied red wines 55° to 65°F (13° to 18°C).

WINE BUCKETS

A wine bucket can be used to chill wines before they are served as well as to hold opened bottles of white, sparkling, and some fortified wines. Some wine buckets are meant to sit directly on the table while others are set up to the side of the table on a stand.

To set up a wine bucket for service, fill it with a mixture of two parts ice and one part water. Drape a cloth serviette over the top of the bucket.

An ice bucket can be placed near the table to keep open wines chilled during service.

COASTERS AND HOLDERS

Coasters and holders are used to hold opened bottles on the table. Coasters may have a lip or rim to help the bottle sit securely in place and are often lined with cork so the bottle does not slip. Holders are typically made of a material that will help maintain the wine at an appropriate service temperature without cooling it any further.

BASKETS AND DECANTERS

The process of decanting a red wine separates the wine from the sediment that settles in the bottom of a bottle of wine. This sediment comes from tannins and color

A wine holder helps to keep wine at an appropriate temperature during service.

pigments that have an unpleasant, bitter taste. The older a red wine, the more likely it is to have some sediment. Some restaurants make it a policy to decant all Bordeaux red wines, while others reserve this style of service for delicate older red wines. In addition to keeping the sediment out of the guests' glass, decanting "aerates" the wine before it is served to the guest.

To decant a bottle of wine, you need a scrupulously clean glass decanter to hold the wine and a candle to help you see when the sediment is beginning to flow toward the neck of the bottle. If the wine is old or fragile, you will need a wine basket to carry the wine to the table but remove the bottle from the basket (wine cradle) as you decant the contents. Follow these steps:

1. Lift the wine gently out of the storage rack, keeping it in the same orientation as it had in the rack. In other words, the label should be facing up toward the

Present the wine to the host for review.

Position the bottle over the candle and pour into the decanter.

Decanted wine is poured from a carafe.

Using an electric light to decant wine.

ceiling. Do not tip the bottle upright, since that will disturb the sediment and swirl it throughout the wine.

2. Present the wine by holding it in the basket at a comfortable reading level for the host.

3. Set the decanter and light on the guéridon or table. Light the candle or flashlight. Open the bottle while in the cradle then carefully remove the bottle from the cradle. Hold the shoulder of the bottle in front of the lit candle so that you can see through the bottle clearly. To avoid rolling the bottle as you pour, you need to keep the label facing up to the ceiling (the same orientation it had in the rack), so this is the only time you may place your hand over the label as you pour.

4. Pour the wine into the decanter, stopping as soon as sediment appears in the shoulder. Leave both the decanter and the empty wine bottle on the table.

Many establishments ban the use of open flames in the dining room. In that case, use a small electric light as shown here.

The Sequence of Wine Service

VERIFY THE INFORMATION on the order against the information on the label to be sure you have the wine that your guest ordered. The wine list may not reflect wines actually in-house; they may have a different vintage, for example. Check this before bringing bottle to table; if wine in your hand doesn't match the wine ordered, let the guest know and ask if the available vintage is acceptable of if the guest would like to order something else.

PRESENTING THE BOTTLE

To present a bottle of wine, carry it to the person who ordered it by approaching from the right side. Hold it in front of the guest, making sure that the entire label is visible to the guest as you review the vintage, name, and producer. Since the bottle's label may be new to the guest, and since different producers list the information in different places on the label, it is appropriate to recite and indicate these three pieces of information to the guest.

OPENING STILL WINES

Both natural cork and synthetic or plastic wine stoppers are used to seal still wines. They are of a traditional size and shape meant to be removed with a captain's corkscrew (waiter's tool). When your guest indicates approval, place the bottle back in the bucket, on a guéridon or hold it mid-air, according to your establishment's wine opening standards, as you remove the cork.

1. Present the bottle to the person who ordered it, cradling it in a serviette so the entire label is visible and can be read.

2. With the bottle on a flat surface, in an iced wine bucket, or held in the air, remove the capsule covering the cork by cutting around the front of the neck of the bottle just below the band of glass.

3. Cut the foil around the back of the neck just below the band of glass.

4. Peel away the top of the foil, lifting it away using the blade from the corkscrew and holding the neck of the bottle with the left hand. Put foil in your pocket.

Before opening the wine, present the bottle to the guest who ordered, making sure the label is visible for the guest's review.

OPENING A WINE BOTTLE IN A WINE CRADLE FOR DECANING.

Insert the corkscrew, allowing the worm to grip the cork.

Rest the lever against the second lip near the mouth of the bottle.

Straighten the corkscrew while the lever rests against the bottle.

Wipe the mouth of the bottle before pouring.

5. Insert the corkscrew slightly off center at a slight angle and straighten it up with one or two turns.

6. Tilt the corkscrew so that the top notch in the lever will rest on the lip of the bottle. Hold it in place with the index finger while bracing the neck of the bottle.

7. Pull the corkscrew straight up while continuing to hold the lever in place and brace the neck of the bottle. Be careful not to touch the lip of the bottle.

8. Twist the cork, holding it in a napkin to release it from the bottle.

OPENING SPARKLING WINE

Sparkling wines have a special closure to keep the contents, which are under some pressure because of the carbon dioxide in the wine. The cork is secured with a wire cage to keep it in place.

If the Cork Breaks

From time to time, you may break a cork as you open a bottle of wine. As long as it does not fall into the bottle, you can simply twist the broken piece from the corkscrew and then reinsert the corkscrew into the remaining cork. Twist the worm into the cork with enough pressure to allow the worm to catch the cork, but be gentle so that you don't end up pushing the cork into the bottle. Turn the worm as far as possible, connect the lever, and lift.

If either the entire cork or a piece of the cork does fall into the bottle, use a cork retrieval tool to remove it before serving the wine.

Keep the bottle in the wine bucket as you open it, held at a 45-degree angle as you work. Be sure to direct the cork away from the guests. Remember that a loud pop or flying corks are a sign that the bottle was not opened properly.

1. Cover the top of the bottle with the serviette, remove the foil covering the wire cage.

2. Hold your thumb over the cork as you untwist (six turns) the wire cage that holds the cork in place. When the cage is open, pull it away from the cork.

3. Hold the base of the bottle in one hand and keep the serviette over the cork.

4. Hold the cork still while you twist the bottle. The pressure inside the bottle will help to push the cork out, so hold it tightly. The cork should come out slowly and make a slight "shhh" sound.

5. Gently remove the cork from the bottle.

PRESENTING THE CORK

The purpose of presenting the cork is to give the host an opportunity to confirm the name of vineyard and also to make sure the cork is dry on one end. Crown caps and screw caps will not provide the same type of information and they are not typically presented. However, some establishments have abandoned the practice of presenting corks of any sort on the theory that if there are faults with the cork, the server should be able to identify them and takes steps to correct the problem.

What is the server or host looking for when examining a cork? One thing to look for is the name of the winery. Most wineries print their names on their corks to avoid counterfeit wine. That means that the name on the cork should match the name on the label.

The second thing to consider is the condition of the cork itself. If wines are properly stored on their sides with labels facing the ceiling, the cork should be wet on one end and dry on the other. A cork that is wet on both ends indicates that the

Pull on the tab to unzip the foil.

Twist to loosen the wire cage.

Use a serviette to cover the cork, and grasp the bottle with the opposite hand.

Hold the cork tightly while twisting the bottle. Allow the pressure inside the bottle to gently push the cork out.

cork was not tight enough to prevent wine from leaking out and air from leaking in. A cork that is dry on both ends indicates that the wine has been stored standing upright and there is the possibility that air had seeped into the bottle in this case as well. In both cases, the result is often a wine that is oxidized or "corked."

If it is the practice in your establishment to present the cork to the host, present it on a small plate just to the right of the glass of the person who ordered the wine.

Pouring Sparkling Wines

1. Use a serviette to wipe the water from the bottle.

2. Pour about an ounce, slowly, into the glass. Let the foam subside in the glass. (priming the glass)

3. Continue pouring the sparkling wine into the glass, adding another 2 to 3 ounces to each glass.

Handling Rejected Wines

The guest might reject a wine when you present it if the label does not contain the anticipated wine. The vintage or producer might not be what the guest anticipates, for instance. In that case, you may need to present the wine list again so the guest can make another selection or call in the dining room manager or wine steward to help find a suitable replacement.

A guest might also reject a wine at the point of first tasting it. If your guest does not approve the wine, make the necessary corrections and return with a different bottle. If a guest complains that he or she either does not like a wine or that it tastes bad, you should offer to replace the bottle and immediately remove the rejected bottle from the table.

Chances are, if the guest complains, it is a bad bottle. The truth is that about one in ten bottles goes bad and must be discarded. One fault that can affect wines is cork mold (called *corkiness*) or some other form of mildew or mustiness in the wine. This can be the result of holding wines in a storage area that is too hot and the wine is cooked (a situation referred to as *volatile acidity* or *madeirization*).

If the wine is unacceptable because of a fault in the wine, your wine distributor may give your establishment a credit for that bottle. If nothing is wrong with the wine, you can sell the rest of it by the glass to cover the cost or use it for a staff tasting at the end of the night.

THE TASTING POUR

After the cork is removed, wipe the lip and mouth of the bottle and pour about one ounce into the host's glass, keeping the label facing the guest; this is known as the tasting pour. At this time—as well as each time you finish pouring any wine—lift and twist the mouth of the bottle to avoid dripping wine down the side of the bottle.

Slowly pour about an ounce of wine into the glass.

Once the guest approves the wine, proceed to pour 3 oz. to the women, then men, then the host last.

FILLING GLASSES

If the wine is accepted, pour wine for all guests (women first, then men), pouring last to the person who ordered. At this point, remove the cork from the table.

Each restaurant has its own standards for pouring wine, usually about 3 fluid ounces, which means that you should be able to pour eight glasses from a standard 750-milliliter (25.3 oz.) bottle. However, the size of the pour should be adapted to suit the situation. Wineglasses should never be filled more than half full in order to leave space for the wine to be swirled and to release its bouquet.

Keep the following factors in mind as you pour:

□ Size of party (you should be able to pour the same amount into each guest's glass without running out of wine).

□ Guest preference (some may ask for more, some for less than your establishment's standard pour).

□ Number of courses to be paired with a particular wine (slightly smaller-than-standard pours might be appropriate if the same wine is to accompany both the first and the main course, for instance).

If separate wines are to be served for different courses, the next wine should be poured before the previous glass is removed. Depending on the style of service, the house rules may allow the server to ask the guest if the old glass may be removed.

Conclusion

REMARKABLE WINE SERVICE DEPENDS on the server's ability to understand the house wine list and the characteristics of the wines. With that knowledge in hand, making helpful suggestions to the guest concerned about which wine to choose for the table, or even an individual guest's selection of a glass of wine to enjoy with an entrée, is much easier.

Once the wine is selected, the service of the wine should be a pleasure for the guests. Learning to use a waiter's tool and other bottle-opening devices, as well as the other accoutrements of wine service—buckets, baskets, and decanters—means that you can make the show of presenting and opening the wine smooth and elegant. Preparing and setting the correct glassware is yet another key to success. When it is finally time to pour the wine, you should be able to gauge just how much to put in each glass so that every glass has the perfect amount.

9

Banquet Service in the Restaurant

FROM THE GUEST'S PERSPECTIVE, any dining experience in a restaurant could be a special event. From the restaurant's perspective, any dining event that represents a change in the normal structure of service is a special event. These events might include such occasions as large parties with ten or twelve guests, seated at a single large table for a larger group that fills an entire section of the restaurant (station). A banquet or special event that fills the entire dining room is often referred to as a buyout. Throughout this chapter, we consider the aspects of properly managing a banquet in the restaurant. *If you are interested in learning more about service for large banquets and catered events, you will find a list of resources in Appendix I or the Remarkable Banquet Service book.*

Banquets and Special Events

A SPECIAL EVENT DIFFERS from a large group reservation in some important respects and has some distinct advantages for the business as a whole as well as for the dining room and the kitchen staff. There may be some negatives to consider as well: Small groups that you planned to seat in a single section of the dining room often spill over into the entire restaurant. If they become loud and boisterous, other diners will be affected. Service can be difficult if they spend a lot of time mingling at tableside and standing in the service aisles. If the event closes only a portion of your dining room, your regular patrons may be disappointed that their favorite table is unavailable. If the entire restaurant is closed, they will simply take their business elsewhere. Repeatedly turning guests away from an à la carte restaurant might easily encourage them stop trying to dine at the restaurant at all if they are not confident that it will be open and available to them.

ADVANTAGES OF BANQUETS AND SPECIAL EVENTS

There can be some specific advantages to banquets for the restaurant, the kitchen staff, and the servers. For the restaurant, it is an opportunity to bring in more money without incurring additional expenses. If the restaurant would otherwise be closed, special events are a great way to bring in business during those unproductive hours. However, if you are planning an event during your normal hours of operation, you must consider whether you will be losing other business.

A significant advantage of offering banquets or special events in your restaurant is that your client will undoubtedly bring guests to the event that have never been in your restaurant before. This is a chance to introduce yourself to a pool of new, potentially regular, guests. These events are a chance for servers to discuss the history, concept, and philosophy of the restaurant with the guests and to begin a relationship with them. It is a good idea to have copies of the regular menu available for guests who are interested in seeing it, as well as to offer assistance making a reservation for another visit to the restaurant.

Any special requests the client may have, such as a podium or special linens, can be rented and then charged directly back to the client. This means you do not have to add items to your inventory that you may never use again. Since most special events require an initial cash deposit, this money is immediately available to underwrite any upfront costs you may have, leaving your working capital untouched. Profits from these events can even help avoid the necessity of raising menu prices, since the profits can be used to help pay for upgrades and improvements.

Staff in the kitchen and in the dining room have some assurances and advance information. Unlike a typical reservation, banquet and special events are booked in advance. Consequently, the number of guests and the amount of food to be served are all known beforehand. Having this information allows you to make more accurate forecast sales and profits. Both the dining room and the kitchen are in a much better position to have the right number of staff on hand to do the additional work.

Banquets are also traditionally considered a good way for servers to earn good money. Most banquet servers receive a flat hourly or "event" rate that is significantly higher than for regular à la carte service, which means that servers are assured of a specific amount of income. Some contracts also specify a gratuity, typically 15 to 20 percent. In that case, servers also receive a guaranteed tip. A server may also earn additional tips from the host or the guests for special service, since there is usually more time for interactions and conversations at a banquet than à la carte service.

While a large group typically orders from the standard menu, a booked event often includes a set menu with either no choices or one with limited choices. This makes the order-taking process much simpler for both the guests and the server. The kitchen staff can be more efficient in the ordering, production, and plating of the food. Servers know exactly when they are working and how much gratuity they can expect.

BOOKING CONSIDERATIONS

If you are booking a small group of up to 25 percent of the seating capacity, try to time the booking so that it is not at the same time as your regular dinner reservations, although you might still accept reservations that fall before or after the group is seated. This permits the service and kitchen staff to dedicate their time to preparing and serving out food specifically for the event. A service charge may also be included in a banquet contract. This money may go directly to the restaurant or the management may decide to split it among the service and kitchen staff.

When approached about closing the dining room for a buyout, consider the income the restaurant might typically bring in for the night and use that as a way to determine whether the booking will be profitable or to adjust your rate for the buyout. For example, if you typically turn tables in your restaurant three times on a Saturday but only once on a Monday, a Saturday-night buyout might carry a fee that is three times more than a Monday, or the Monday night booking could be presented as one-third the fee for a Saturday night booking.

Planning for Remarkable Banquet Service

IT IS IMPORTANT TO KEEP in mind that no matter how routine banquet service is for the server, for the guests it is a special, perhaps once-in-a-lifetime event. The entire staff should work together to make it perfect for them.

The flow of the entire banquet is of paramount concern. The sequence of service should be consistent and timely for all tables and should follow the standards established ahead of time. Careful planning is required, no matter which service styles are employed. You will need to modify your à la carte service standards for a banquet or special event as well as brief service personnel on the changes well before the event. For example, your standard cover for à la carte may call for just the entrée knife and fork, a water glass, and a napkin. At a special event with a set menu, you may set the entire cover, or even preset the plated first course before the guests are seated. It all depends on the menu and service style the client has requested.

The timing of courses should be coordinated with the host or master of ceremonies to allow enough time for toasts or opening speeches, ceremonies or awards, or presentations. The information must be communicated with the chef and the kitchen staff before as well as throughout the event.

THE BANQUET EVENT ORDER (BEO)

As you plan a special event for your restaurant, you want to keep track of all the details. The client may only be concerned with the date, the time, the menu, and the wine list, but you will be thinking about staffing, scheduling, the schedule of billing, and a host of other factors. To keep all the detail and responsibilities in mind, you can borrow a tool used by successful caterers known as a banquet event order (BEO). As you complete the document during the planning stages with the client, it becomes the blueprint for the entire event.

This document has two parts: an external component prepared for the client and an internal component for the staff. The external component becomes a contract between the establishment and the host and includes details concerning costs as well as personal information about the clients, such as personal contact information. The internal component provides details that the staff needs to have in order to provide the best possible service to the host and his or her guests. All of the client's personal information and details concerning the billing or other financial matters are removed from this internal component. The BEO should include the following information:

- Name of client

- Type of event

- Date, day, and time of event

- Description of event

- Menu

- Special requests

- Guaranteed minimum/maximum number of guests

- A menu prepared specifically for a banquet has distinct advantages over simply offering the entire à la carte menu to the party. You may offer a select menu that includes some, but not all, of the items from that night's regular menu in order to allow guests choice, or you may create a predetermined set menu for the group.

- The advantage of a select menu is that the guests have a degree of choice. The disadvantage is that if the group should arrive late, or not order in a timely manner, the group can throw off service for all of the patrons, especially if its food order coincides with the à la carte orders from the rest of the dining room.

- A set menu makes service flow more smoothly, since the kitchen knows exactly what and how much to make of each item. However, if there are any special dietary needs or considerations, you must coordinate with the host and then communicate all special requests to the kitchen and the servers.

STAFFING FOR A BANQUET

The number of service personnel needed for a banquet depends on the total number of guests and the style of service:

- American service requires one server for every twenty guests.

- French/Russian service requires for two servers for every thirty guests.

- Buffet service requires one server for every thirty guests.

- Butler service for hors d'oeuvre and drinks requires one server for every thirty to forty guests.

A meeting for the service staff is usually held prior to the catered affair to ensure that all servers have been briefed about their duties and have the information they might need to perform well before, during, and after the event. The banquet manager's and the client's planned schedule of events should be fully understood by the banquet headwaiter, the chef, the bartenders, the band, the photographer, and the videographer. Last-minute changes to the schedule on the day of the event must also be communicated to all concerned.

Particular points to be covered prior to the function are:

- Menu, wines and other beverages available

- Floor plan

- Number of tables and covers per waiter and per captain, if applicable

- Sequence of events, including food and beverage service, entertainment, or ceremonies

- Mise en place requirements for side stands, pantry, and backups, with attention to special equipment

- Specific points to remember, such as specialty presentations, styles of service, or special requests

- Sample banquet cover and tabletop setting

Arranging the Room and the Tables

YOUR CLIENT MIGHT HAVE SOME SPECIFIC requests regarding table arrangements. Wedding receptions, for instance, might call for a head table. Your client might have asked for a dance floor or a large antipasti display. Arranging the dining room on paper first lets you review the placement with the client as well as to work out any issues related to service aisles or setting up a podium or screen.

Square footage allotments for banquets vary, depending on the specific service details, such as size of dance floor, placement of cake or gift table, and so on. For sit-down affairs, from 12 to 15 square feet per person should be allowed. Buffet service requires a little less space, 10 to 12 square feet per person.

The seating chart should be drawn up prior to the affair. The host may wish to create the seating chart, or prefer to review and approve it once generated by either the maître d' or the event organizer. The seating chart becomes an important organizational tool to check that all necessary arrangements have been made, such as ordering the correct number of floral arrangements and so forth. It also allows the management to station servers effectively as well as to plan solutions for any difficulties that might arise.

The head table or podium should be positioned for optimal visibility by all of the guests. In some cases, the head table or podium is placed on a raised platform, known as a dais, to be visible from all parts of the room.

Guests at the head table are generally seated on one side of the table, facing the room. The rest of the tables are arranged according to the type of function, the size and shape of the room, the number of guests to be seated, and the preferences of the organizer. Round tables, for example, are ideal for banquets, since they allow for easy conversation among guests, but may be too wide to place in your dining room.

All tables, with the exception of the head table, should be numbered. Table numbers can be mounted on stands and should be visible to guests as they enter the room. Guests can obtain their table numbers from either a master seating chart or from a table that holds cards with the guest's name and assigned table number.

Any good seating plan has an allowance for extra guests. A good rule of thumb is to anticipate that there may be a minimum of 5 to 10 percent more guests than the number the of RSVPs the host received, but this number is always discussed with the host or organizer ahead of time.

DECORATIONS

Consulting with the florist, or event planner is part of the planning process. It is imperative to know the layout of the décor ahead of time, so that any potential disruption to the placement of serving pieces can be resolved. Servers need to know how to set the tables in conjunction with the decorations on the table. Generally, the florist is scheduled to arrive just after the tablecloths are laid but before covers are in place, so the centerpieces can be set up. The florist may require assistance or may deliver the centerpieces off earlier in the day for the servers to place them.

Display on buffet

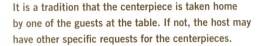

The Centerpiece

It is a tradition that the centerpiece is taken home by one of the guests at the table. If not, the host may have other specific requests for the centerpieces.

Before you remove the centerpieces, find out if there are such plans.

Servers should be careful to avoid spilling the water from the vases or disturbing the floral arrangements. If there are any spills while setting up the room, you may need to replace the cloth and completely reset the table. Centerpieces should be either short enough to fall below eye level or positioned on stands that are well above eye level so that the guests can see each other across the table.

Garland runners may be used for rectangular banquet tables or the head table. If there are place settings planned for the end position of the table, the runner should not extend the full length of the table, but should leave enough room for the cover to be set without forcing you to place dishes on top of the flowers. Garlands may be used along with centerpieces, but they need to be placed prior to other items, such as the salt and pepper shakers and candles. If lilies are used, carefully remove the yellow-orange stamens as they can permanently stain fabric.

CANDLES

The florist may also supply candleholders. Candles should be lit before the guests arrive at the banquet. Whenever candles are used, servers need to be especially watchful: guests often toss their napkins or programs too near the candles when they rise from the table to dance or speak with friends. Placing candles in hurricane lamps or small glass vases keeps them visible but takes away the danger of an open flame at the table. Check with local fire department. Local fire codes may prevent the use of open flames altogether. In such cases, battery-powered candles offer an attractive option and decrease the risk of fire.

SETUP FOR BUFFETS

Buffets can be as elegant or informal as the client wishes. Foods are arranged on tables, which may include floral or edible arrangements, ice carvings, and other special decorative touches, such as fountains.

The size and placement of a buffet line depends on the configuration of your room and the number of guests you are feeding. You may create more than one line by setting up the buffet so that both sides of the table are identically filled or by adding

Setting up buffet (include skirting and drap-
ing, creating height)

Use hot water to fill the chafing dishes

more tables throughout the room. If the buffet line requires electricity, that might determine its placement. Allow about 2 feet of space around all sides of a buffet line.

A variety of techniques for arranging and setting up a buffet is shown below. Particular concerns of buffet service setup include the following:

- If space for the length of the buffet line is limited, create wider tables by setting additional eight-foot tables on four-inch-square blocks behind and overlapping the other eight-foot tables. The blocks should have small, notched holes for the feet. The holes prevent the legs of the table from sliding off the blocks, which could cause the entire table to collapse. Using deeper holes in the front can provide a slight sloping of the table toward the guests.

- If skirting is not available for the table, use tablecloths. Most tables are 30-inch high. Most six foot and eight foot tables are 30-inch across, so an 85- or 90-inch cloth will cover the tabletop and drape to the floor on both sides of an eight-foot table. Another cloth of the same size will cover the other end of the table to the floor and the tabletop. This economical way of skirting can be disguised by using colored 45-inch squares placed at an angle on top of the overlapping cloths, creating a bent diamond over the edge of the table.

- To add height and create more visual interest, place items on the table on a variety of improvised platforms, including inverted empty glass racks, wine crates, or inverted empty milk crates covered with a cloth.

- Use underliners beneath sauces and dips to catch any drips. A soiled underliner can be replaced more quickly and easily than the entire cloth. Keep sauces and dips close to the table edge so that guests won't have to reach very far for them; this will result in less spillage.

- Hand-wipe plates for the buffet line before service. Dishwashing machines do not always get all of the food off the plates. It is very unappetizing for a guest to pick up a plate and find dried food adhering to it or even dried water spots.

- Either place flatware at the buffet line (preferably at the end rather than the beginning so that the guests do not have to carry them through the line with them) or preset it at the tables. Extra china and flatware should always be available.

TABLE SETTINGS

The table setting should reflect the occasion as well as the menu. All tableware should be laid according to the style and sequence of service. Its placement should be extremely precise. There may be a lot on the tabletop, so it is important to do your best to make each cover as neat and compact as possible to give guests enough room to enjoy their meal as well as to permit servers to do their work efficiently and safely. Be sure to set up a complete place setting for the servers to refer to as a guide so that no time is lost re-setting tables.

A number of variables go into establishing the place setting for an event:

- Type of menu (set menu or one with options, for example)

- Number of courses

- Inclusion of printed materials such as programs or menus

- Charger plates

- Preset appetizers or salads

- Number of wines

If guests are ordering from a menu with options, the covers should be set in the same way that they normally are for regular service as described in detail in Chapter 4. If there is a set menu for the group, the table should be set with all necessary flatware and glassware. If space at each place setting does not allow all the flatware to be preset, it may be necessary to mark or place in some pieces between courses, which may slow down the service.

In either case, part of the dining room setup should include preparing STPs with appropriate silverware for the menu items that might be served so that you are prepared in case someone drops a piece of silverware or uses the wrong utensil for a course. You will also be ready to supply the appropriate silverware to any guest with a special request for an alternative meal (vegetarian, gluten-free, nut-free, and so forth) once you know where that particular guest is sitting.

Place the napkin in the center of each place setting first, if you are not using a charger plate. If a charger plate is included in the cover, place the charger first in the center of the setting. If there are printed materials to include in the setting, place them in the center of the setting or on the charge plate and top them with the napkin. If serving a preplated first course, place the serviette above the setting, to the left of the setting, or under the forks.

Place the main-course fork and knife to establish the width of each place setting; setting them 12 inches apart and about ½ inch from the edge of the table, as a general rule. The fork should be on the left, with tines facing up, and the knife on the right with the edge of the blade toward the center of the setting. If salad is served after the main course, place the salad fork and knife first, rather than the main course silverware.

With the appropriate fork and knife in place, set the remaining flatware pieces required for each course, except for the dessert course. The flatware on the far right and the far left is used by the guest first. The server sets the flatware from the inside out. The guest uses the flatware from the outside in.

Set dessert silverware above the place setting. Position the fork just above the place setting with its handle to the left. Place the dessert and beverage spoons above the dessert fork with their handles to the right. If space at each place setting does not allow all the flatware to be preset, it may be necessary to mark or place in some pieces between courses, which may slow down the service.

Typical place setting for three-course banquet and two wine glasses

If your restaurant has a bar and if the size of the party does not mean that bar service for other patrons is affected, you may simply work out of your existing bar. If you need to set up a "satellite" bar just for a specific event, use the following guidelines:

When a facility has no physical bar, two clothed and skirted eight-foot tables can serve as front and back bars. Arrange bottles and back-ups on the back bar. Use the front bar to hold glassware, ice, bartending equipment (ice scoop, bottle opener, cork screw, mixing cups and spoons, shot glasses, and so forth), and garnishes (lemon twist, olives, cherries, onions, celery, and so forth).

- Assign one bartender for every 50 people at either an open or cash bar.
- Check the inventory list for the event. If this is a consumption bar, record the stock you have on hand, including partially filled bottles using a "tenth count".
- Handle all bar items in a sanitary manner, especially glassware.
- Use an ice scoop, never a glass that might break in the ice.

Serving alcohol safely can be a challenge at banquets and special events, especially when there is an open or a consumption bar. Review the standards for the safe service of alcohol on page 199, and remember to ask for identification if you are unsure about a guest's age.

The Banquet

WHILE THERE IS NO SINGLE SEQUENCE that covers all aspects of every event, there is a logical flow to most events. The guests arrive, and then may have a reception of cocktail hour or they may be seated right away. The meal is served, along with appropriate beverages, followed by dessert and coffee or tea. Having all these stages flow seamlessly together is the hallmark of a well-organized event.

Banquets use several service styles: butler service for hors d'oeuvre, American or platter service for the entree, family service for side dishes, and buffet service for dessert and coffee, for example. Interactive buffet stations are essentially a type of tableside service. To be successful, personnel at a banquet or special event must master a variety of service styles. In addition, they need to know all the details of a function and its timing in order to provide the high level of professional hospitality that makes these special occasions memorable for the guest. The techniques of hand service are covered in greater detail in Chapter 4; in this chapter, we present the service styles typically associated with banquets and special events: butler, buffet, and platter (French or Russian) service.

SEATING THE PARTY

There are two types of seating at a banquet: assigned seating or general seating. The client for a buyout may choose to have assigned seating. In that case, the guests pick up a place card upon their arrival, designating their table assignment. This is usually prearranged with the management so the tables can be set accordingly.

If the host has opted for general seating, you should manage the situation as follows:

"We have three tables of six and one table for four. If the first six would follow me, please, I'll return in a moment to seat the next group of six."

This places some of the seating responsibility onto the guests and lets the guests you are not currently seating know that you will be back for them soon.

When some of the group arrives early, you must decide whether to seat them or ask them to wait in the reception or bar area. Although it is more hospitable to seat the guests upon their arrival, your guests may expect to be served immediately upon being seated. If that is not possible, it is better to ask them to wait until the rest of the group arrives.

There may be special seating issues for general seating. Often, guests will ask your help to find seats that are side-by-side. Usually, these situations can be worked out easily, especially if you have not already begun serving food. If necessary, however, you may want to ask the host of the event for assistance in finding a solution.

COMMUNICATING WITH THE KITCHEN

Constant communication is the key to providing smooth service during a banquet. Both the dining room and the kitchen should have a clear understanding of lead time necessary for both sides so that activities such as clearing, pouring wine, firing and picking up the food are in synch. The kitchen and the dining room staff will have the same information on hand from the BEO. Once the banquet begins, however, it is the job of the maître d' to stay in touch with the kitchen so they are alerted when additional food is needed on the buffet before it actually runs out, how many guests have yet to go through the line so the kitchen can prepare additional chafing dishes or platters for the buffet. For seated service with multiple courses, he or she is responsible for giving advance warning before each course that allows servers enough time to clear the previous course, replace any silverware, and pour the next wine while the kitchen finishes and plates the food. That means that foods can be served at their peak.

Allow a longer lead time before the dessert and coffee service begins, since servers must complete more steps to take to prepare the table for dessert.

The sequence follows:

1. Clear the main course plate, bread-and-butter plate, and butter or oil.

2. De-crumb the table.

3. Standing to the right of the guest, pull the dessert and coffee spoons down to the right side of the place setting using your right hand.

4. Moving to the left side of the guest, pull the dessert fork down to the left side of the place setting using your left hand.

5. Set in the sweeteners and creamers, allowing one set for every four guests.

6. Set each guest's cup and saucer (as a unit, not separately) to the right side of the guest toward the top of the spoons with the cup handle at the four o'clock position.

7. Serve the dessert course as specified in the BEO.

8. Offer hot beverages.

9. Maintain the table until the guests leave: refill water, pour more coffee, and so on.

Styles of Banquet Service

A BANQUET MAY CALL for a variety of service styles that are not typically practiced in the à la carte restaurant setting, including butler service for hors d'oeuvre and drinks, buffet service, and platter service. Other service styles including American service (see page 44) and synchronized service (see page 159) are also used. Servers should be adept at all of these styles, as well as the service of wine (Chapter 8) and a variety of hot and cold beverages (Chapter 7).

BUTLER SERVICE

Some banquets include a reception or cocktail hour before the meal. Butler service is used to serve hors d'oeuvre and drinks before the guests are seated. You may also hear this referred to a *flying service*. Servers carry trays of food or drink to the guests as they mingle. Guests help themselves from the tray, so it is important that you keep the tray well-balanced. You will also need to provide cocktail napkins on a B&B plate. Make it easier for the guest to retrieve a napkin by fanning them a bit.

Trays filled with foods are typically arranged and garnished by the kitchen staff. You should carry the tray in such a way that the guest can see the presentation. If the tray is heavy or unwieldy, you may wish to rest it on your forearm. Lighter trays are easier to manage if you grip them by the rim or hold them on the palm of your hand.

Hold the tray for the guest at a comfortable level and offer it to the guests. Make eye contact with the guest and be prepared to tell the guests what you are offering them. Offer them a napkin before they help themselves to an hors d'oeuvre if possible. Some establishments require servers to hold the cocktail napkins on a small plate in one hand while the other hand manages the tray.

Glasses of champagne or wine may be offered to the guests as they arrive and throughout the cocktail hour. Keeping the tray level as guests help themselves to a glass can be difficult. To avoid spilling or dropping anything, be sure that drinks are evenly spaced and try to turn the tray so that the guest will not have to reach over other drinks to get the one they want. Use two hands to hold the tray so that a shift in the load doesn't upset the whole tray.

Since guests will finish their drinks and hors d'oeuvre as they mingle, some servers should walk through the room with empty trays so that guests can give them their used napkins or glassware.

BUFFET SERVICE

Buffets can incorporate many different types of service. A traditional buffet can be as elaborate or as simple as the host requires. All of the menu items are arranged on the buffet, along with the necessary service pieces. Guests can then take a plate and help themselves to the items they want; this is known as self-service.

You can add servers to the buffet line to assist the guests. It will make the guests' experience more pleasant, especially if foods are difficult to get onto the plate or if there are special condiments or sauces to add. In addition, you can keep waste at a minimum if servers offer consistently sized, standard portions. They can always serve a guest more, or serve a particular piece or portion, if the guest makes a request, of course.

Servers or cooks are also occasionally stationed at interactive stations to carve meats or even prepare dishes to order. The food is plated by the server or cook, so it is important that the individual assigned to the station is adept at producing plates that are neat, clean, and attractive.

Whether or not servers are stationed on the buffet or at buffet stations, every server needs to keep the maintenance of the buffet a top priority. The buffet should always be well stocked and clean; as soon as an item is running low, the kitchen should be alerted so that a fresh item can be prepared for the line.

- Servers are responsible for pouring wine as well as cold and hot beverage service at the table, clearing, and setting coffee cups, sugars, creamers, and so on.

- During a buffet, be sure to keep the table well stocked and presentable for the guests.

- Keep the buffet table and surrounding area clean, as guests frequently drop or spill food on the table or floor.

- Sometimes a buffet cannot be replenished from behind the buffet line, which means you will have to replenish from the same side as the guests are using to serve themselves.

- When bringing in fresh food, remember that the guests have the right of way.

- Check to be sure that the correct serving tools are on the buffet so that guests are not left stranded in front a of dish with no way to serve themselves.

PLATTER SERVICE

Platter service, often referred to as French/Russian service, is an elegant service style that requires servers with considerable skill, strength, and dexterity. Trays can be heavy and hot and must be held firmly in the left hand while the food is being served with the right hand from the guest's left.

The main goal of platter service is to serve fully cooked food while it is still hot and to serve it in an elegant manner. All food is fully cooked, and then placed on silver or porcelain platters or in soup tureens by the kitchen staff. The waiter brings it to the table and serves the guests from the platter. This service style is particularly useful at banquets or wherever large groups of people must be quickly served. Platter service can be the primary style of service for all dishes on the menu, or it might be an addition to pre-plated American-style service—for example, you might serve a plated main course and then offer platters of extra helpings to the guests or pour the soup at the table.

- Set in clean plates from the guest's right; moving clockwise around the table, before bringing the platters in from the kitchen.

- Bring the platters to the dining room, present them to the head of the table, and show them to the guests before serving.

- Stand with your feet together, to the left of the guest. Rest the platter on the palm of your left hand, which you have protected from burns by padding with a clean, folded side towel.

- Bend at the waist, advancing the left foot slightly, and bring the platter close to the rim of the guest's dinner plate.

- Plate the food with a serving spoon and fork held in your right hand. Proceed counter-clockwise.

- Remove soiled plates and utensils from the guest's right with the right hand; moving clockwise around the table.

- Serve beverages from the guest's right, moving clockwise around the table.

Precise timing and organization are essential if the food is to reach the guests at its peak. The personnel in the kitchen must calculate the exact moment to platter the food so that it is presented to the guest promptly. Carving must be done in a minimal amount of time. Coordination for plating and serving throughout the meal can be achieved only if there are open and free-flowing lines of communication between the kitchen and the dining room.

While speed of service is essential, the food should still be arranged attractively and correctly. This is especially true when the dishes are accompanied by different garnishes that must blend perfectly with the principal ingredient. Traditionally, the protein is placed on the portion of the plate closest to the guest, using the appropriate utensils, and the accompaniments placed neatly above the protein. They should be arranged on the guest's plate in the same form and shape as they appear on the platter. The food should be handled as little as possible to avoid breaking and changing its appearance.

Teams of servers are sometimes used in platter service, since plattered foods or soups usually require a separate garnish, accompaniment, or sauce. The back accompaniment. The following are additional suggestions for successful platter service:

- Know the number of portions expected from each platter.

- Use a clean serving spoon and fork for each dish.

- To prevent dripping ladles, touch the bottom of the ladle to the surface of the soup in the tureen after filling the ladle. Any soup that is clinging to the bottom of the ladle will fall back into the tureen.

- Lift and place the food gracefully. Never slide it onto the guest's plate.

- Become adept at the proper use of service fork and spoon before attempting to serve the guests.

The primary disadvantage of platter service is that by the last guest, the food on the platter may look ragged and unappetizing. Another disadvantage is that guests may ask for additional portions, leaving too little for the last guest. One final disadvantage is that the entire effect will be ruined if the server spills or drips on a guest, and care should be taken not to spill or drip on the table, as well.

WINE SERVICE

It is advisable to have the host preselect the wines for a special dinner so that you can have the right wine and the right number of bottles available. Depending on the size of the group and type of celebration, you may forgo the presentation and tasting of each bottle by the host.

If the host has preselected the wines, there is no need to present the bottle to anyone before opening, but the sommelier or manager may still want to taste each bottle before it is served to avoid serving flawed wines. If the host has not preselected the wines, so he or she may need to taste each bottle before it is served.

Buyouts usually expect the wine to be served continually until the end of the event. Since partial bottles cannot be married, the best way to avoid having too many partially filled open bottles at the end of the event is to have every bottle returned to a beverage station. The partially poured wine can be used to refill glasses at any table. For smaller events, consult with the host before opening additional bottles, unless the BEO specifies differently.

If your state's liquor authority allows it, the client may be allowed to bring his or her own wines. This may happen if the event is a vintner's or wine distributor's dinner. In that case, you might charge a corkage fee of $10 to $20 per bottle to cover the costs of washing and handling the glasses and serving the wines.

When Guests Are Responsible for Beverages

In some situations, the host or leader of a group may be responsible for the food check, leaving the individual guests responsible for their own alcoholic beverages. In that case, prepare wine-by-the-glass or cocktail menus for the guests. This will not only save time for the servers but also reinforce the fact the guests are responsible for any alcoholic drinks they order.

Servers should write up checks for guests (who may ask that they be given the bill for more two or more people). Bring these checks to the table immediately after serving dessert and coffee, rather than waiting until the check has been requested, as you would during normal à la carte service. This avoids such situations as the guest forgetting about the bill as they rush from the room to visit the bathroom before boarding a bus or leaving the event early. If the participants of the group arrive using their own transportation, be aware that some guests may leave earlier than others, so be prepared to present their beverage checks before they leave.

Serve wines before the food for each course, just as you would for à la carte wine service. If there is a designated host at the table, serve that person last. Do not pour wine for an empty seat, since the seat may be filled by an underage guest or may not be filled at all.

White or sparkling wines are typically served with the first course and red wines with the main course. Some of your guests prefer red wine with the first course, however. If they ask, you can say:

"Certainly. As soon as I finish serving the white wine, I'll return with the red wine."

The same hospitality should be offered if the guest asks for more white wine rather than switching to red. In either case, remove the unused glass from the table.

DESSERT AND COFFEE SERVICE

The dining room manager/maître d' should alert the kitchen that the servers are ready to serve dessert. At this point the kitchen should be prepared to start sending out desserts. Servers should have prepared the table prepared as follows:

Coffee buffet for guests

- Plates and glassware cleared, including salt and pepper

- Table crumbed

- Coffee cups and saucers set in, if not already preset

Moving the dessert flatware into position

- ☐ Flatware set in, or if they were preset, moved into position with the dessert fork on the left and the dessert and coffee spoon on the right.

- ☐ Creamers and sweeteners set-in, if not already preset

Dessert is served first, followed by coffee. This permits all of the servers to lend a hand in delivering desserts to the table. Coffee service should begin after all the desserts have been served.

Some hosts offer a coffee station, while others may prefer that coffee and tea be poured at the table. The advantage of a coffee station is that it encourages the guests to get up from the table. The advantage of pouring at the table is that the guests are served both dessert and coffee at once.

Ask your guests if they prefer regular or decaffeinated coffee or tea. The server should proceed around the table clockwise, while another server follows with pots of regular and decaffeinated coffee.

When the banquet calls for a coffee station, extra care should be taken to set the station up properly with cups, sauces, spoons, napkins, sugar, tea packets, and so forth. Serve milk and cream from insulated containers to keep them cold. If you are providing individual milk or cream containers, keep them on ice. Sugar packets, disposable creamers, stir sticks, and the like tend to accumulate quickly. You should have a basket or container on the station for this refuse, but remember to monitor the cleanliness of the station at all times.

Espresso Carts

If the client requests it, an espresso cart may be rented to offer espresso and cappuccino. Orders can be taken by the server on a table-by-table basis or the guests can go to the espresso cart themselves. Although the word *espresso* means "fast," it can take a long time to serve a large quantity of these hot beverages. As china espresso cups are not usually available as rentals, the client should be informed in advance if paper cups have to be used.

To serve coffee at the table, set in the cups, saucers, flatware, cream, and sugar. A table of twelve will need three sugar caddies and three creamers; two is sufficient for large rounds of ten.

Your guests might feel that, once a cup and saucer has been set in, coffee should be served. If you begin pouring coffee before dessert service is complete, there might not be enough servers to run dessert plates. If you are asked for coffee before dessert is completely served, you have to decide whether you are able to pour the coffee then or if you prefer to let the guest know that you will return with the coffee as soon as dessert is served.

If the guests request a hot beverage any other time during the meal, even as they first sit down, it is hospitable to serve them. They should be served a clean cup and saucer at dessert time.

While coffee and tea are normally included in a banquet, espresso and cappuccinos may be considered an additional charge that goes to either the host of the party, to be collected along with the final bill, or to individual guests, who receive a check that is processed by the servers in the same way that alcoholic beverages might be.

Conclusion

THE SERVICE OF BANQUETS is much like professional service at other times. All of the same skills are required, but in addition to the server's normal duties, a greater awareness is required. Even more than usual, the server must be part of a smoothly coordinated team. Banquets and special events in the restaurant have the potential to be more profitable than à la carte since you have a guaranteed number of guests consuming specific foods items, but banquets are also an excellent marketing opportunity that introduces new people to the restaurant, which could result in new regular customers. Servers should be given the opportunity to work at a banquet as a way for them to develop regulars who request them each time they dine.

10

Remarkable Service Interactions

ALL THE SKILLS Described in This Book, both tangible and intangible, work together to equip servers and managers with the tools to provide remarkable service for their guests. In order for your restaurant to be successful, your staff and management need to not only master these skills but also understand the implications of their actions and how they add to the guests' experience. Without those guests, your restaurant would not exist; therefore, understanding the needs and wants of your guests is critical to your business's survival. One key component of a restaurant business is to understand your guest and create an organization that provides the expected level of service to suit their needs and wants. The critical element of success for a restaurant business is to go beyond the guest's expectations to create a loyal return customer who generates positive word of mouth to build your reputation within the industry.

Why Focus on the Guest?

AS WITH MANY INDUSTRIES, the hospitality business needs to understand its target market thoroughly in order to provide the service product required by the guest. The idea of understanding your customer is not a new concept; it has been used for years to determine products and services in various industries. What is challenging about the hospitality industry is that every guest has different expectations, different perceptions, and different requirements for their dining experience. The restaurant personnel not only have to be able to provide a certain level of service; they also have to be intuitive enough to determine what the guest actually wants in a very short period of time.

By focusing on the guest, your organization can create a service product that meets and exceeds guests' requirements and create a loyal customer base for future growth. Studying the guests' wants, needs, capabilities, and expectations in a scientific fashion is called *guestology*, a term originated by Bruce Laval of the Walt Disney Company. Once you understand what your guests want, you can create a service product that meets or exceeds those needs. Observation of guest behavior over time is a good indicator of their wants and needs. Soliciting direct feedback either through comment cards or personal discussions is also a great method for determining those guidelines. Part of this process of guest analysis is determining the key drivers and expectations of your clientele. What is it that they are looking to receive when they come to your restaurant? Excellent food? Great service? A good value for their money? Once you determine what the key drivers are, you can focus building your team and product around those core concepts in order to meet those guest expectations.

In order for your establishment to be successful at meeting guests' expectations, everyone has to be focused on the guests at all times. And while most people would say that those in direct contact with the guests—the host or hostess, the servers, or bussers—are the only ones that need to focus on the guest, it is critical for the entire organization to be focused on the guest. Not just the front-of-house staff but the kitchen staff, the management team, and the support services departments such as accounting and purchasing need to be focused on the guests' wants, needs, and expectations in order to provide the best possible service product. Creating a unified organizational culture within your restaurant leads to success.

Creating a Service-Oriented Organizational Culture

SUCCESSFUL BUSINESSES ARE UNIFIED around a solid organizational culture. Having a clear commitment to a customer service culture sets an example for all employees to maintain a high-quality customer experience.

Creating a strong service-oriented organizational culture can be a significant competitive advantage in the hospitality industry. Not only does it set the standard for guest interaction, a strong service-oriented culture can also enhance the employee's interactions with each other. Utilizing the tenets of Remarkable Service not only during interactions with guests but also with fellow coworkers helps to firmly establish a service-oriented culture. A customer-focused organizational culture can unite the kitchen and the dining room staff to provide excellent customer service.

Organizational culture is the shared philosophies, ideologies, values, assumptions, beliefs, attitudes, and norms that tie its members together. Beliefs are how people within the organization make sense of their relationships with the external world. Values are preferences for certain behaviors or certain outcomes over others. Norms are standards of behaviors that define how people are expected to act while part of the organization. All of these elements combined create the organizational culture. It is up to the leaders of the organization to be able to communicate the organizational culture. Managers are the translators of the company culture and help to teach it to all the employees. If your restaurant is focused on excellent customer service, and all of the steps of service are targeted at exceeding guests' expectations, you are teaching your employees your service-oriented culture. Rewarding behavior that provides excellent customer service also reinforces the organizational culture. Utilizing the principles of Remarkable Service inspires team performance and helps to establish effective house standards.

Using stories, legends, and heroes within an organization helps to communicate proper behaviors expected within a service-oriented culture. A great example is the Nordstrom's tire return legend, which is probably one of the best consumer relations story in recent business history. As the legend is told, a customer wanted to return two snow tires to a Nordstrom's store, which doesn't sell automotive parts, and is in fact a department-store chain that sells upscale clothing. According to company legend, the clerk accepted the tire return because that is what the customer wanted. While perhaps this actual incident might not have ever happened, the moral of the story, where the customer is always right, is what remains as a lasting impression for the culture of the company. As the story is spread throughout the company, it teaches the employees to focus on the guest and resolve problems quickly and in the guests' favor.

A critical element to creating a strong, service-oriented organizational culture is hiring employees who love to serve.

HIRING GUEST-FOCUSED EMPLOYEES

Have you ever met someone who was a "service natural?" This is someone who is so focused on pleasing others that the person goes above and beyond what is expected to provide excellent customer service. Not only is a service-natural employee attentive to the needs of the guests but also the person is also focused on anticipating what else the guest might want in order to provide it without having to be asked. These individuals are ideally suited to work in the hospitality industry. That attitude and dedication are hard to train; rather, these characteristics are ingrained in a person's personality and help them to succeed in the demanding world of customer service.

When looking for those "service naturals" to add to your team, you need to have a clear picture of the characteristics that make a successful server. Welcoming, attentive, polite, and tactful are all behavioral traits (described in Chapter 1) that a professional server must have in order to deal with people. A high level of personal concern for the customer's enjoyment can be emotionally exhausting, especially in a busy dining room with cranky customers. Serving in the dining room can be equated with an acting performance—you are always on stage in the dining room, and the guest is always watching. Keeping that image alive when your feet hurt, when you just resolved a guest complaint, after being triple sat, and in the middle of the Saturday night dinner rush is particularly challenging. These successful servers are able to connect with guests and change a regular interaction into something special and memorable. This is why many organizations try to hire employees who have these certain personality traits already, as it is easier to teach and train the mechanics of service to someone with a positive and enthusiastic attitude, rather than vice versa.

As with any employee hiring practice, the selection process is fairly straightforward:

1. Find out exactly what you are looking for.

2. Recruit a pool of good candidates.

3. Select the best candidate from that pool.

4. Bring those candidates into the organization and make them feel welcome.

Behavioral Interviews

A common method used in the hospitality industry to assess an applicant's qualifications on critical criteria is through behavioral interviews. The assumption is that past behaviors predict future performance. Behavioral-based interviews feature questions that are designed to capture past behaviors and actions. Instead of the typical interview question, "Tell me about yourself," or, "What are your strengths and weaknesses?" behavioral-based questions might include, "Give me an example of a time when a guest complained; how did you resolve it?" or, "Tell me about a time when you disagreed with your boss and describe how you handled it." The responses to the questions can help determine how the applicant would approach a similar situation in the future.

Creating a job description through a job analysis is imperative to start the process. How can you hire the best candidate if you are not aware of what job specifications and competencies are required? Recruiting candidates both internally and externally increases the chances of finding the best person for the job. Selecting candidates requires careful consideration, most often through screening of applications and interviews. Sometimes psychological tests are used to measure personality traits and behavioral predispositions, but might be cost prohibitive. One aspect of the recruitment process that should not be overlooked is following up with candidate references and performing a background check. This due diligence on the part of the employer can protect the organization and its guests.

The last step in the hiring process, that of bringing the new hire on board and into the organization, is critical to the success of that individual. *Onboarding* is a term often used to describe bringing new hires up to speed and introducing them to the culture of the organization through training and observation. How to interact with the guests and fellow coworkers, where to clock in and out, what is considered acceptable behavior, and what is taboo are all learned during the onboarding process. If the first few months of training and onboarding are successful, not only do you create a loyal employee but you also help to support the service-oriented organizational culture.

Providing excellent customer service requires the right employees with the right knowledge, skills, abilities, and attitudes. Hospitality organizations need to know what skills and attitudes to look for, where to look to recruit talented candidates, and the right way to choose from the applicants. Recruitment of new talent ties into sustaining an overall service-oriented culture and requires constant vigilance and attention. With the high level of turnover in the restaurant industry, retaining your talented employees is a constant battle and is best won through effective training and motivational techniques.

Training for Remarkable Service

Select guest-focused candidates when hiring for your team.

THE FOCUS OF ANY HOSPITALITY-TRAINING program should be to give the employees the ability to deliver service in the way the customer expects. While the tangible aspects of the dining experience, such as the flatware, glassware, food, and décor can certainly impact the guest's enjoyment, the individual delivering the service can make or break the guests' relationship with the organization. In addition to training the required job or task skills, a hospitality organization also needs to teach the server how to solve inevitable problems quickly and efficiently as well as how to interact positively with the guests. Since each guest has different expectations, the server needs to be able to respond appropriately in any given situation to create a memorable positive experience. Executing the tasks correctly is not enough, the server needs to consistently exhibit a sense of genuine caring to establish and maintain that relationship with the guest.

Not only do employees need to be taught the skills necessary to deliver remarkable service, they should also be taught the company's cultural values, beliefs, strategies, and policies. Through understanding of the culture, the employees will have the tools to respond appropriately to figure out how to fix a problem when the customer is unhappy. A manager is not always there to respond to a guest's problem immediately, the servers are the front line that interacts closely with the guest. If they do not understand the corporate values and beliefs, they cannot know what the company expects them to do. By instructing the employees on the service-oriented culture, it gives them the guidelines of how to respond to situations that supports the mission of the organization.

CREATING AN EFFECTIVE TRAINING STRATEGY

The first step to creating an effective service-training strategy is to focus on the critical skills and knowledge that the employees need to provide the expected level of service. Determining the critical skills and knowledge depends on the expectations of your guests. How do you know what your guests expect? Ask them! Ask them through customer comment surveys, utilize your regular customers' feedback, and train your employees to solicit feedback from their guests. Once you determine those critical skills that are related to your guest's satisfaction, communicate them to the rest of the organization.

In addition to finding the critical skills, the new employees need to see how they fit into the bigger picture of the organization as a whole. Learning the core values and culture of the organization will help lead the employee to do the right thing for the customer, even when faced with an unplanned problem situation. Not every guest scenario can be covered in formalized training sessions; therefore, understanding the underlying values of the organization will lead the employee in the right direction to respond in a way that supports the mission of the business.

Utilizing multiple learning approaches is necessary to reach all different employees. Each person learns differently. Some people are visual learners, some more auditory, while others are physical. By offering different methods of communicating the skills and training needed, you are more likely to be successful with your employees. The key is to determine the best method for the situation, whether it is role-playing, lectures, readings, or participatory discussions.

The final aspect of creating an effective training strategy is to commit to continuous improvement. The training and learning doesn't stop after the 90-day review. In order to remain competitive as well as empower your employees, you need to offer training opportunities throughout their careers with your organization. By offering continuous training, you can adapt more easily to changing customer preferences, challenge your employees to improve, and build loyalty to your organization.

USEFUL TRAINING METHODS FOR SERVICE DELIVERY

The most commonly used method of training is on-the-job-training where the employee learns the job by doing. The individual is placed in the work situation and the supervisor, manager, or coworker instructs the employee on how the job is done. Often referred to as shadowing, hospitality organizations use this method extensively as many of the tasks are best learned by doing. The advantages to on-the-job-training are that the employee finds out exactly what is required because they are actually doing it and the company is actually getting some productivity out of the new employees. A disadvantage includes the potential for errors due to lack of experience that may directly affect the customer and the organizations service reputation.

Classroom training, including lecture presentations, interactive case studies and team-based training, can be a cost-effective delivery method of information to new and existing employees. Not everyone listens well, however, and not everyone can learn by listening, so classroom training does have its drawbacks. Certain new-hire orientation training sessions are often conducted in a classroom setting, as it allows for a fast delivery of information in a uniform setting—for instance, presenting the company's history, organizational chart, and employee benefits are often done in a classroom setting.

Audiovisual training—using videos or DVDs or even delivered online—can be used in conjunction with a live presentation to enhance the learning material for the employees. Instantly available video is useful and practical in the traditionally high turnover environment of the hospitality industry in order to standardize the presentation of material so that everyone learns from the same source of information. They can be relatively cost-effective and can help to overcome language barriers.

Simulation or role-playing is another effective method of training that can help the employees learn by doing without the consequences of harming the relationships with real guests in real time. Practicing a task in a controlled and safe environment, such as utilizing role-playing scenarios, can build confidence and experience for all employees. Although it does take time and manpower to implement, role-playing can be an alternative to on-the-job training. Behind the bar, the bartender can practice making drinks in a prescribed period of time. In the dining room, servers can practice serving coworkers during down periods. And in the kitchen, demo plates are a common method of learning how to cook on the station. The added benefit to demo plates is that the servers can taste the dishes as a learning experience so that they are better equipped to describe the dishes to the guests.

WHAT TO TRAIN FOR REMARKABLE SERVICE

The key concepts described in this book are good starting points for an effective training program for remarkable service. Menu and beverage knowledge are important for effective sales skills. Sampling dishes, tasting beverages, and learning about key ingredients all help to provide information for servers to describe and recommend items for the guest. Sharing information through preshift meetings and message boards helps foster communication and shared knowledge. Discussing customer preferences and reservation notes helps to exceed guest expectations and create memorable experiences. All of these key pieces of information help to build a strong foundation to support a customer-oriented service environment. Learning by sharing can unify a team and help elevate the level of service for the guest.

Conducting a needs assessment is also another way to determine what training is needed. There are three levels to a needs assessment: organizational, task, and individual. *Organizational analysis* determines the skills and competencies the organization needs and whether it has the capabilities to achieve those goals with the current resources. *Task analysis* is the most significantly used in the hospitality industry, as it helps to prepare new and existing employees to perform the necessary duties and job tasks. *Individual needs assessment* is when an organization reviews the performance of employees completing tasks to determine if they are performing up to job standards.

Another method for determining training needs is through customer complaints. When customers complain about the food or the service, they are giving you the opportunity to fix the problem. But beyond the service-recovery aspect of the customer complaint, it allows the organization insight into what key attributes are not meeting the guests' expectations. This information is useful to determine what requires further training, or in some cases, revisions of the dish or service step to better serve the customer. A uniform approach to analyzing customer complaints is important to target trends and behaviors that need modification. A monthly meeting to review customer complaints, in addition to a tracking system, is imperative to help identify problem areas.

Motivating Remarkable Service

IN ORDER TO PROVIDE REMARKABLE SERVICE, servers not only need to have the service training and attitude, they also need to be highly motivated to meet the guests' expectations consistently. To *motivate* means to instill a desire within a person that encourages the person to act. The goal of any organization is to motivate its employees to act in a way that helps to promote the vision or mission of the company. If your restaurant mission is to provide excellent customer service, you need to motivate your staff to consistently, creatively, and impressively provide a level of service that meets that expectation. Understanding what motivates your employees is the key to providing that incentive for them to perform the way that you would like to achieve your organizations goals.

Theories behind motivational techniques often rely on understanding employees' needs and wants. The task of hospitality managers is to identify which needs are driving the behavior of their employees and then to offer them the combination of incentives and rewards that will satisfy or help satisfy those needs.

Once you identify the needs of your employees, you can develop a way to meet those needs. Utilizing a reward system, both financial and nonfinancial, is a method for meeting those needs. Financial rewards, such as performance bonuses (both independent and group based), merit raises, and compensation through ownership (stock options are a common financial reward for CEOs) can be effective methods in some ways to motivate individuals to perform. The best example in the restaurant industry of a financial reward is the tips received for service. Tips or gratuities, a gift or a sum of money tendered for a service performed or anticipated, is the most common monetary reward in the service industry. Ranging from 15 to 20 percent of the bill, this money often makes up the bulk of the service staffs' wages. Some organizations choose to pool tips, when all the tips are collected and divided proportionally between the service staff on duty, usually based off of a point system.

Nonfinancial rewards, such as a recognition programs to honor best-performing employees, can be extremely effective in motivating remarkable service. A nonmonetary award, such as a plaque, merchandise, or gift certificates, can create a lasting memory of the experience not only for the winning employee but also for the rest of the department. Often, organizations will feature an employee of the month award and the nominees are treated to lunch, or an end-of-year celebration to recognize and employee of the year.

Another key method to help motivate employees is to make the work environment more enjoyable. Guests expect friendly and personal service; they expect to be greeted with a smile. A happy and pleasant work setting cannot only enhance the guests' experience (and also sales), it also can improve employee retention, morale, and recruitment. The servers already have a challenging time dealing with high expectation guests, they should feel supported and appreciated for the job that they do. Little added touches to make the job more fun can help with that atmosphere. Just be careful that the fun doesn't get in the way of the organization's goals and continues to focus on job duties and customer service responsibilities.

Tip Pooling and Tip Sharing

Tip pools are common when workers such as bussers provide part of the customer service but are rarely tipped by customers. The US Department of Labor has several regulations regarding tip pools, including limiting who can receive tips from the tip pool to those employees who customarily and regularly receive tips, requiring the employer to notify its employees of any required tip pool contribution amount, and not allowing the employer to retain any of the employees' tips for any other purpose. Many states allow employers to require tip pooling. All employees subject to the pool have to chip in a portion of their tips and an employee cannot be required to pay more into the pool that is customary and reasonable.

Tip sharing (also referred to as tip outs) are a similar situation, and even more common than tip pools. The customary practice of the server distributing a portion of their tips to other staff that have helped them (bussers, bartenders, food runners, and even hosts or hostesses) is often practiced in restaurants. Typically, a server receives between 18 and 20 percent gratuity on a total check. Then, depending on the standard practice of the organization, the server might tip out from the total tips received a portion to the bussers (say 10 percent), food runners (5 percent), bartenders (5 percent of beverage sales), and perhaps the host (2 percent). So ultimately, the server might tip out between 18 and 30 percent of their tips to other support staff depending on the tip sharing arrangement. The key to a successful and harmonious wait staff is to clearly state what the expectations are regarding tip outs. In this situation, the employer can require the servers to tip share with the support service staff.

EMPOWERING YOUR EMPLOYEES

Empowerment provides an opportunity for employees to grow and develop while at the same time helping to fulfill the company's mission. BusinessDictionary.com defines empowerment as "a management practice of sharing information, rewards, and power with employees so that they can take initiative and make decisions to solve problems and improve service and performance." Giving employees the skills, resources, authority, and opportunity to provide excellent customer service and then holding them responsible and accountable for the outcome of their actions is a highly motivating process. One of the critical components of empowerment is a clear identification of the company culture, as this then tells the employees how to act in the constantly changing service environment. If the employee understands clearly what expectations the company has on the service system, they are better equipped to handle a problem when it arises in a method that helps to further the company mission. A manager is not always around to handle a problem when it occurs. An employee that recognizes the importance of customer service for their organization is more likely to respond appropriately in a service recovery situation that helps to resolve the issues quickly and effectively.

Empowerment cannot simply be decreed; you need to train your employees so that they know how to utilize their decision-making skills effectively. In order for empowerment to be successful, you need to have training, willingness from the employees, standards for measurement of their decisions, incentives, and management buy-in. Without these characteristics, you will not have an effective empowerment program. Empowerment requires knowledge of what is considered acceptable performance that can be delivered through training. The employee must be willing to perform this task and have an interest in the company and its future; otherwise, empowerment might prove risky. Utilizing standards helps the employees to measure their actions to determine what they should do and if their decisions are good or bad. Utilizing incentives and rewards to successful performance can help employees to make good decisions. Finally, an empowerment program will not work unless the management supports and trusts that the employees will be able to make their own decisions.

Leading Remarkable Service

IN THE HOSPITALITY INDUSTRY, successful leaders are able to motivate, inspire, and challenge employees. A hospitality leader creates and communicates a service-oriented culture that engages employees to make the extra effort to provide exceptional service. Not only do leaders serve as role models and examples of the organization culture to the employees, leaders also instill trust and provide guidance.

Conclusion

CREATING, DEVELOPING, AND MAINTAINING REMARKABLE SERVICE in hospitality organizations is arguably a very complex and continuously evolving process that directly impacts customer satisfaction as well as overall organizational performance, revenue, and profitability. Providing Remarkable Service is as much about taking care of the external customer as it is about taking care of the internal customer as in addition to it being the right thing to do, cultivates and fosters a culture and climate of service orientation. Regardless, without a thoughtful and thoroughly developed conceptual and managerial strategy for service delivery that encompasses all the components of a service delivery loop as discussed, customer satisfaction will surely be compromised. With the weight of hospitality organizational competitive advantage resting heavily on service delivery, owners, operators, and service managers will be most effective by focusing on and creating an atmosphere of service through their own actions as well as operational structure.

Appendix

This Appendix contains a number of resources that can help readers of this book to become more remarkable servers. The Glossary of Technical Terms defines some of the terminology that is unique to the profession. Because some of these terms sound very like one another, a second glossary, called Frequently Confused French Culinary Terms, has been included. A third listing of terms and expressions, a Glossary of Restaurant Slang Terms, is included to clarify some of the more mysterious—and sometimes amusing—aspects of our professional jargon. The Bibliography suggests a number of excellent books that can aid in the acquisition of professional knowledge.

GLOSSARY OF TECHNICAL TERMS

À LA CARTE (Fr.) A means of meal selection in which the guests compose their own meals by selecting from the menu, where each item is separately priced.

A menu of this type.

Opposite of prix fixe.

À LA RUSSE (Fr.) Russian service, traditionally performed by setting an empty plate in front of each guest from their right side, then serving the food from platters from the guests' left side. Service is provided by moving counterclockwise around the table.

À LA MINUTE (Fr.) Cooked at the moment.

À LA SERVIETTE (Fr.) Served on a fancy folded napkin on china.

AL DENTE (It.) Literally, "to the tooth," usually refers to pasta or vegetables that have not been overcooked—that is, they still maintain a bit of crispness.

AMUSE-GUEULE OR AMUSE-BOUCHE (Fr.) Either term is commonly used to refer to a small complimentary canapé or hors d'oeuvre served after the order has been taken.

APERITIF Literally, "to open," this is the first drink offered. It should be dry since it is meant to enhance the appetite rather than sweet, which would satiate the appetite. Dry fortified or aromatized wines, bitters, vermouths, or wine cocktails such as kir and kir royale are most common.

ASSIETTE (Fr.) Plate, dish.

AU PLATEAU (Fr.) Served on a platter.

BANQUET SERVICE Refers to type(s) of service used to serve parties (i.e., Russian, American, butler, buffet, French, or any combination of the above).

BRUT Very dry sparkling wine.

BUSSING Clearing off tables and dining areas.

CANAPÉ Cold hors d' oeuvre on a piece of toast, bread, or cracker.

CARTE DES METS (Fr.) À la carte menu in French.

CARTE DES VINS (Fr.) Wine list in French.

CARVING This term applies to an array of preparations on the dining room floor, replacing the following French classical terms:

Slicing charcuterie or pâtés, "couper à travers"

Slicing meat, "couper en tranches"

Portioning small game or poultry, "découpage"

Deboning and filleting fish, "desossage"

Peeling and cutting fruits, "épluchage"

CHEESE BOARD Can be any shape or material (depending on needs) but it should offer between four and eight cheeses. The cheeses offered should consist of a total of five ounces per person.

CORNICHON (Fr.) A very small sour pickle often served with pâté.

COUVERT (COVER) (Fr.) Individual setup for one guest.

CRUDITÉS (Fr.) Small cuts of fresh vegetables offered with a dip, generally served as a stationary hors d'oeuvre.

DÉBARRASSAGE (Fr.) To clear off the table.

DECANTER A wine carafe is used to separate the sediment from older wines and fortified wines. To decant: Remove the entire foil in order to see through the neck of the bottle. Place a candle on the table so the flame shines through the neck. Slowly empty the liquid contents of the bottle of wine into the decanter, leaving the sediment in the bottle. Decanting is performed at the beginning of the meal to allow the wine to get to room temperature and to "breathe."

DE-CRUMBING Cleaning the guest's table of the breadcrumbs and other debris. In all types of service this should be done at least once during the meal, usually before dessert. Use the crumber on a rolled napkin and sweep debris on to a service plate.

DECOUPAGE (Fr.) To disjoint and portion; refers to poultry and flying game served via French service.

DÉGUSTATION (Fr.) A tasting menu of wines and sometimes food, in which many dishes are offered in small portions.

DEMITASSE Literally, "half cup," a small cup used for espresso.

DEMI-SEC Literally, "half sweet"; the term refers to a sweet sparkling wine.

DEUCE (slang) A table for two.

EN PAPILLOTE (Fr.) Cooked in a parchment package.

ENTRÉE (Fr.) In the United States, it means the main course of the meal, or the protein component of a plate. In Europe, entrée refers to a separate course served before the main course.

ENTRECOTE (Fr.) "Between the ribs"; a cut of meat. Sized from petite to double. Carved like Chateaubriand when large.

ENTREMETS (Fr.) "Between courses." Simple sweet course made from fruits, puddings, mousses, pies, bavarians, tarts, simple cakes, sherbet, sorbet, ice cream, or any combination of the above.

FILET/FILLET The choice undercut of meat (such as filet mignon) or fish served off the bone.

FLAMBÉ (Fr.) Dramatic tableside preparation in which brandy or liqueur is poured over a food item, then set aflame to complete the cooking.

FLATWARE Service eating utensils; "silverware" implies it is silver rather than stainless.

FRIANDS (Fr.) A little something extra—similar to mignardises.

GAUFRETTE POTATOES (Fr.) Potatoes, thinly sliced with a lattice cut on a mandoline, then deep fried.

GRANITE (Fr.) A sweet ice with no fat or egg.

GRATIN (Fr.) A baked dish that is often topped with cheese and/or breadcrumbs, then browned under a salamander or broiler.

GRATINÉE (Fr.) To bake or broil something under a salamander or broiler until the top is browned.

GUÉRIDON (Fr.) A rolling service cart.

HOLLOWARE Soup tureens, water pitchers, coffeepots, large bowls, platters, silver trays, and so on.

HORS D'OEUVRE (Fr.) Traditionally a warm appetizer, but often includes any tidbit served before the meal, either passed butler style, at a station where the food is carved or prepared, or in a stationary display.

INTERMEZZO (It.) A light course that acts as an "intermission" between the heavier courses of a long meal. Traditionally served after the fish course. Usually a small glass of ice, sorbet, or *trou normande*. Used to cleanse the palate or ease digestion.

LAGNIAPPE (Fr.) A small complimentary treat, "a little something extra."

LINEN Or napery, any cloth used by the servers or on the tables or sidestands; napkins, tablecloths, serviettes.

LOG BOOK Calendar book kept in restaurants to store information used in predicting number of covers, and the effect on future business of weather or outside events.

MIGNARDISES (Fr.) The "sweetest of the sweets," served with coffee including; truffles, chocolates, caramels, dipped fruits and nuts, macaroons, mints, or small cookies.

MISE EN PLACE (Fr.) "To put everything in its place," a setup of required items or ingredients.

MOLLETON (Fr.) Undercloth laid on a table meant to absorb noise and spills. Otherwise known as a silence cloth.

N.V. Nonvintage, in reference to wines.

PLACE SETTING Individual setup for the guest. See couvert.

PLAT (Fr.) Dish, plate.

PLATEAU (Fr.) Platter.

PROTOCOL Set of rules concerning priorities in arriving, seating, and sequence of service during official or casual events such as state dinners or dining in a restaurant:

> **Social:** Children first, then elderly ladies, ladies, elderly gentleman, gentleman by age
>
> **Diplomatic:** By rank
>
> **Corporate:** By importance
>
> **Clergy:** By hierarchy

Usually, the guest of honor is the first and the host is the last to be seated and served. The host will taste the wine first and be served last.

RÉCHAUD (Fr.) Hot plate, food warmer; a cooking utensil used mostly for gueridon service.

REDRESSER (Fr.) To plate and garnish dishes with food taken from pans, platters, or bowls.

RESERVATION BOOK Calendar book used in restaurants to record the name, time, amount of people, special requests, and telephone number.

RÔT/ROTI (Fr.) Literally, "roasted," the main course.

SAUCE BOAT China or silver hollowware container for sauce served on the side.

SAVORIES Salty hors d'oeuvre served in lounges, pubs, and bars used to increase liquor sales; also a course near the end of a classic seventeen-course French dinner.

SERVICE PLATE A plate with a napkin folded in four on top. It is used to bring serviceware to the table. Sometimes referred to as STP (service transport plate).

SERVICE SET Set of serving fork and spoon.

SERVICE TOWEL A napkin folded in three parts along its length, draped over the left arm during service. It is used to handle clean or hot items and should be replaced if soiled.

SERVIETTE (Fr.) Napkin.

SHERBET Frozen fruit juice and sugar with milk, cream, or egg.

SILVER Silver or silver-plated flatware.

SMORGASBORD Scandinavian style buffet; also hors d'oeuvre buffet.

SOIGNÉ (Fr.) French term for service. Literally "caring" or "excellent."

SORBET (Fr.) Frozen fruit juice or tea with sugar; an ice made without fat or egg yolk. Egg white may be used in some sorbets. Used as an intermezzo after the fish course to cleanse the palate for the next course. Replaced the trou normande.

STATLER A square table with flip-up sides to make a larger, usually round table.

STEMWARE Stemmed glassware.

TABLE D'HÔTE (Fr.) Preset multicourse menu offered at a set price.

TEA CADDY Set of two pots on a small tray used for tea service. Two teabags are placed in the pot with the long spout, and it is filled with hot water. The short-spouted pot is filled with hot water so the guests can adjust the tea to their liking. The service is placed to the customer's right, with the long-spouted pot to the right and water to the left.

TROU NORMANDE (Fr.) A precurser to sorbet as the intermezzo, a traditional trou normande was a bottle of Calvados (from Normandy) encased in a small block of ice. This was meant to "burn a hole" in one's stomach to make room for the next course. A room-temperature brandy was often substituted.

UNDERLINER Additional larger plate on which plated food is served.

FREQUENTLY CONFUSED FRENCH CULINARY TERMS

SAUCES

AÏOLI Garlic mayonnaise.

AMORICAINE (Sometimes seen as "Americaine"); Lobster butter added to tomato sauce.

BÉARNAISE Hollandaise with vinegar and tarragon.

BÉCHAMEL White sauce made with milk, flavored with onions and cloves, thickened with white roux.

BEURRE BLANC White wine and butter.

BORDELAISE Demi-glace, red wine, shallots, butter, and peppercorns; garnished with marrow.

BOURGUIGNONNE Demi-glace with Burgundy, shallots, butter, and peppercorns.

HOLLANDAISE Egg yolks, peppercorns, lemon juice, vinegar, and butter.

JUS Juice from roasting.

JUS LIÉ Thickened jus to make a gravy.

MORNAY Bechamel with egg yolks, Parmesan, and Gruyère.

PERIGOURDINE Demi-glace with foie gras purée; garnished with truffles.

POIVRADE Demi-glace with pepper, mirepoix, herbs, red wine, and butter.

PROVENÇALE Shallots, garlic, white wine, tomato concassé, fines herbs, and butter.

RÉMOULADE Mayonnaise, capers, Dijon mustard, anchovies, and gherkins.

INGREDIENTS

POISSON Fish

POUSSIN Young hen

OTHER

NAPPE Tablecloth.

NAPPER To coat with a sauce.

NAPPERON Top cloth.

PATE A batter used for baking.

PÂTÉ A mixture of ground meats formed in a terrine and sliced.

GLOSSARY OF RESTAURANT SLANG TERMS

86:

1. No longer available, as in "86 veal chop"—important in communicating to the service staff.

2. No longer of any use so it should be thrown away, as in "86 it."

SUPPOSED ORIGIN(S):

1. Possibly from the depression era; soup pots held 85 cups of soup so when the pot was empty, it was called out, "86 soup."

2. Believed to be from a nautical term; the ship must be at 86 fathoms before garbage can be thrown overboard.

3. Suggested to have originated as the last stop on a Chicago train line, "86—all out."

4. The term (enthusiastically adopted by bartenders and restaurant employees) actually originated in soda-fountains during the 1920s. All of the soda jerks' codes were numeric, such as "55" for root beer, "99" for the boss, "98" for the second in command (also "pest"), and "87½" for "there's a good-looking girl out front" (Morris, Mary, and William Morris. *Morris Dictionary of Word and Phrase Origins*. 2nd ed. New York: HarperCollins, 1988).

68: The item is once again available. For example, if the veal was delivered late and was just fabricated prior to opening, the service staff would be notified, as in "68 veal chop." Usage not as common as 86.

ACE: A single diner at a table.

ALL DAY: A total count of a certain menu item by adding up all the dupes. May be in a variety of stages of preparedness.

COVER:

1. The mise en place for a single place setting.

2. A guest, as in the number of covers served.

DEUCE: A two-top, or a table for two.

DROP: To serve or present the item, as in "Drop the check on table 21."

DUPE: Abbreviation for duplicate, can be a hand-written dupe or a computer generated dupe (sometimes referred to as a *chit*).

F&B: The Food and Beverage department.

FIRE: Start preparing the next course. Can be fired by the service staff or chef/expediter, depending on house procedures; as in "Fire main course on table 16." Appetizers and desserts are generally automatically fired when ordered unless otherwise indicated by the server.

FOUR-TOP: A table for four. Similar terms are used for other-sized tables, such as "six-top," or "eight-top."

IN THE WEEDS: More multiple tasks required than can be handled; needing to be in several places at once. Also referred to as "weeded." Result of being "slammed."

ON THE FLY: Needed right away, usually as a result of an error or miscommunication, as in "One trout on the fly."

PICKUP: Announcing to kitchen line that the table is ready and flatware in place for the next course, as in, "Pickup pasta course on table 34."

REACH-IN: A free-standing refrigerator unit. If below a countertop, it may be referred to as a "low-boy."

SLAMMED: Having your entire station seated at once. This often results in slamming the kitchen as well, but can be avoided by getting the order to the kitchen as each order is taken rather than taking all the orders at once, and delivering them together.

SOS: Sauce on the side.

STIFF: To leave a restaurant without leaving a tip (see walk-outs).

STP: Silverware transport plate. The plate with folded napkin used to take clean flatware to a table.

WALK-IN:

1. The large refrigerator that you can walk into. Usually stores butter and milk products for front of house.

2. Guests without a reservation. Avoid referring to them as *walk-ins*.

WALK-OUTS: Guests who leave the restaurant without paying for their meals.

Bibliography

The bibliography includes a number of excellent books that can aid in the acquisition of professional knowledge.

BOOKS

Aresty, Esther B. *The Delectable Past: The Joys of the Table—from Rome to the Renaissance, from Queen Elizabeth I to Mrs. Beeton. The Menus, the Manners—and the Most Delectable Recipes of the Past, Masterfully Re-created for Cooking and Enjoying Today.* New York: Simon and Schuster, 1964.

Dahmer, Sondra J. *The Waiter and Waitress Training Manual*, 4th ed. Hoboken, NJ: Wiley, 1995.

Eichelberger, Ezra. *Remarkable Banquet Service*, Hoboken, NJ: Wiley, 2014.

Flower, Barbara, and Elizabeth Rosebaum. *The Roman Cookery Book: A Critical Translation of The Art of Cooking by Apicius for Use in the Study or Kitchen.* London and New York: Peter Nevill Ltd., 1958.

Ginders, James R. *A Guide to Napkin Folding.* Boston: CBI Publishers, 1980.

Griffin, Jill. *Customer Loyalty: How to Earn It, How to Keep It.* San Francisco: Jossey-Bass, 2002.

Herbst, Sharon Tyler, and Ron Herbert. *The Deluxe Food Lover's Companion*, 2nd ed. New York: Barron's, 2009.

Hetzer, Linda. *The Simple Art of Napkin Folding: 94 Fancy Folds for Every Tabletop Occasion.* New York: William Morrow Cookbooks, 2001.

Illy, Francesco, and Riccardo Illy. *The Book of Coffee.* New York, London, and Paris: Abbeville, 1992.

Jenkins, Steven. *Cheese Primer.* New York: Workman, 1996.

Ketterer, Manfred. *How to Run a Successful Catering Business.* Rochelle Park, NJ: Hayden, 1982.

King, Carol A. *Professional Dining Room Management*, 2nd ed. Hoboken, NJ: Wiley, 1988.

Kolpan, Steven, Brian Smith, and Michael Weiss. *Exploring Wine*, 3rd ed. Hoboken, NJ: Wiley, 2010.

SOMMELIER SOCIETY OF AMERICA
205 East 25th Street
New York, NY 10159
Phone: (212) 679-4190

WAITERS ASSOCIATION
1100 West Beaver Avenue
State College, PA 16801
Phone: (800) 437-7842

Index

A

accepting reservations, 114
accommodation, reservations, 118
adaptation, service, 10–11
advantages
  of accepting reservations, 114
  of American service, 45
  of banquets, 232–233
  of butler service, 42
  of English service, 43
  of menus for banquets, 235
  of no-reservation policies, 115
  of Russian service, 42
  of tableside service, 40
after-dinner beverages, 162
à la carte menus, 32
  china, 86
  standard covers for service, 97
  In time of Louis XIV, 39
a la serviette, 91
alcohol, 180. *See also* cocktails; spirits
ales, 196. *See also* beer
aligning. *See also* arranging
  covers, 94–95
  flatware, 94
allergens, identification of, 10
allergies, 68. *See also* personal safety
almond (cordials), 194
ambiance, 102–105
  flowers, 102–103
  lighting, 103–104
  music, 105
American coffee, 201–202
American service, 44–45
  banquets, 235
  full dinner covers, 97
America whiskeys, 192
ammonia, dangers of, 82
amphitryon (officer of the mouth), 25
amuse-bouche (complimentary snacks), 147
analysis
  organizational, 263
  task, 263
anise (cordials), 194
anniversaries, 132. *See also* events
anticipation of guests needs, 7–8
apéritif, 185, 195

apologies for complaints, 172–173
appearance (hygiene), 50–52
appetizers
  knives, 94
  with wine, 211
appreciated feeling (of guests), 17
aromatized wine, 195, 214
arranging. *See also* settings
  chairs/tables, 77–79
  covers, 94–95
  rooms for banquet service, 236–243
  tablecloths, 92–93
assessment of individual needs, 263
at ease feeling (of guests), 17
attentiveness, qualities of servers, 13
audiovisual training, 262
availability, reservations, 115
aviation (gin cocktail), 189

B

Bacardi cocktail (rum), 190
back waiter (commis de suite), 36
bags, checking coats and, 145–146
Baker, Jean-Claude, 168
balance
  flatware, 54
  wine, 218
banquet event order (BEO), 234–235
banquet service, 230
  arranging room and tables, 236–243
  bar service, 243–244
  booking, 233
  buffet service, 247–248
  butler service, 247
  coffee, 251–253
  communication with staff, 245–246
  decorations, 237–238
  desserts, 251–253
  dinners, 28
  menus, 235, 236
  mise en place, 238
  planning, 234–236
  platter service, 248–250
  seating the party, 245
  sequences, 244–246
  setup for buffets, 238–240
  special events, 232–233

  staffing for, 235–236
  styles, 244–253
  table settings, 240–243
  wine service, 250–251
bar service, 243–244
barware, 185
basins, 24
baskets, wine, 222–223
baths, detarnishing, 82
bay breeze (vodka cocktail), 188
Beauvilliers, A. B., 27
beef with wine, 211
beer, 195–199
  food pairings, 198–199
  serving, 197–198
  storing, 198
  types of, 196–197
behavior
  courteous, 6
  interviews, 259
  managing rude, 149, 150
  personal qualities of servers, 12–18
beverage laws, 217
beverage service, 142, 148, 176
  after-dinner, 162
  beer, 195–199
  cocktails, 180–187
  coffee and tea, 200–206
  complaints about, 169–170
  responsible, 199–200
  spirits, 187–195
  water, 178–180
birthdays, 132. *See also* events
  making special, 132
  VIP guest reservations, 125–126
bisque china, 56
bistros, 38, 47
bitters, 191
black currant (cordials), 194
black tea, 205. *See also* tea
black ties, 40
blending cocktails, 184
blood alcohol levels, 199–200
blood and sand (whiskey cocktail), 193
Bloody Mary (vodka cocktail), 188
blush wines, 212. *See also* wine service
body (wine), 218
Boke of Keruynge, The: The Book of Carving, 24

trust, 11
two-top settings, 94
types
   of beer, 196–197
   of china, 56–57
   of cocktails, 183–185
   of corks, 221
   of menus, 30–34
   of restaurants, 46–47
   of water, 178–180
   of wine, 210–214

U

underliners, 53. *See also* china
unified organizational cultures, 256
uniforms
   ease of location by, 9
   hygiene, 51
up (cocktail term), 187
updating checklists, 75–76
upselling, 141–142

V

valuables, checking, 146
veal with wine, 211
vibrations, wine storage, 215
vintners (winemakers), 211
violets (cordials), 195
VIP guest reservations, 125–126
virgin (cocktail term), 187
vocabulary, 9. *See also* communication
vodka, 181, 187–189. *See also*
   cocktails
voiture, 41
volatile activity (wine), 228

W

waiters. *See also* staff
   American service, 44
   back (commis de suite), 36
   front (demi-chef de rang),
      35–36
   head, 35
   shorthand, 152
   stations, 99–100
waiter's tool. *See* corkscrews
waiting lists, 110, 132–135
walk-ins, 135. *See also* reservations
Walt Disney Company, 256
warewashing, 53–54
washability of serviceware, 53
washing. *See also* cleanliness
   china, 56–57
   flatware, 54–55, 79
   glassware, 55–56
   hands, 52. *See also* hygiene
   serviceware, 53–54
water
   beverage service, 178–180
   bottled, 179–180
   bread and, 142, 147–148
   goblets, 94. *See also* glassware
   tap, 178–179
welcomed feeling (of guests), 17
welcoming, qualities of servers, 13
well (cocktail term), 187
whiskey, 192–193
white gloves, 40
white-tablecloth restaurants, 47
white wines, 212, 220–221
willingness, qualities of servers, 18
winemakers (vintners), 211

wine service, 10, 208
   aromatized, 195
   banquet service, 250–251
   baskets, 222–223
   buckets, 222
   coasters, 222
   corkscrews, 220
   fermentation processes, 210
   filling glasses, 229
   food pairings, 211, 216–218
   glassware, 95, 219–220
   handling rejected wines, 228
   labels, 214–215
   list presentation, 142, 148–149,
      216
   menus, 216
   mise en place for, 218–223
   opening sparkling wines, 225–228
   opening still wines, 224–225
   presentation of wine bottles, 224
   proper temperature, 220–221
   sequence of, 224–229
   storage, 215
   styles of wine, 210–214
   taking orders, 216–218
   tasting pours, 228
wine stewards (sommeliers), 35, 47,
   216
writing orders, 150–153

Y

yeast, 210. *See also* fermentation

Z

Zorks, 221